SOCIAL INFLUENCE STRATEGIES
—FOR—
ENVIRONMENTAL
BEHAVIOR CHANGE

SOCIAL INFLUENCE STRATEGIES
FOR
ENVIRONMENTAL BEHAVIOR CHANGE
SECOND EDITION

BEN TYSON

SOCIAL INFLUENCE STRATEGIES FOR ENVIRONMENTAL BEHAVIOR CHANGE
SECOND EDITION

iUniverse books may be ordered through booksellers or by contacting:

iUniverse
1663 Liberty Drive
Bloomington, IN 47403
www.iuniverse.com
1-800-Authors (1-800-288-4677)

ISBN: 978-1-5320-5631-4 (sc)
ISBN: 978-1-5320-5632-1 (e)

Print information available on the last page.

iUniverse rev. date: 08/22/2018

Authors note

This book continues to be a work in progress that evolves with my own continued learning about planning and evaluating communication campaigns for changing environmental behaviors – campaigns that involve various social influence strategies for accomplishing change at the individual, community and societal levels. Three related books that I previously published (listed below) serve as the foundation for this text. They are now out of print. There is a significant amount of new material in this book, but it should be noted that there is also a fair amount of content common to all four.

Tyson, B. (2013). *Social Influence Strategies for Environmental Behavior Change*. IUniverse Publishers, Bloomington, Indiana.

Tyson, Ben with Mercedes Hurd (2009). *Social Marketing Environmental Issues*. I-Universe Publishers, Bloomington, Indiana.

Tyson, C. B. (2003). *Strategic Environmental Communication: Communicating Strategies for Influencing Environmental Behaviors*. XanEdu Publishing; Ann Arbor, Michigan.

Contents

PREFACE

The root cause of many environmental problems is human behavior. Hence, knowing how to induce changes in environmental practices is often the key to solving many of the environmental problems we face today. Conceptualizing the issue as a behavioral problem is often not the initial tendency of individuals whose work focuses on solving environmental problems (e.g., communication specialists, educators, engineers, scientists). Communication specialists frequently attempt to heighten awareness and interest in issues through mass media. Educators often believe new knowledge and skills need to be acquired. Engineers and scientists often focus on technical solutions. Our training often dictates the way we conceptualize solutions to the problems we face. All these conceptualizations are valid and in concert can be an effective way to change environmental practices.

During the 1980s and 90s, I worked on several environmental projects in the U.S., the West Indies and southern Africa in the role of classroom teacher, extension educator, and media specialist. The stated aim of these projects was to increase awareness, interest, knowledge and/or skills. The implication was that these changes would result in better practices and that these new practices would result in a better environment; i.e., that if someone were to become more aware, interested, knowledgeable or skilled than this would affect how they behaved. The projects were all fairly successful at increasing their stated aim, but only mildly successful in bringing about permanent changes in the behaviors that were actually needed (the unstated objective). The environmental impacts that were sought were therefore only marginally achieved.

It became clear that though people may obtain requisite levels of awareness, interest, knowledge and/or skills, they still may not change their behaviors in-line with these factors. Many barriers can intervene (e.g., perceived costs may exceed benefits, opposing norms may inhibit change, confidence may be lacking, required resources may not be available). It became clear that behavior change is what was actually sought. This realization came in the 1990s at about the same time that many health communication specialists around the world were realizing high levels of success in changing behaviors associated with disease prevention and family planning. Behavior change was their stated goal and the strategy they used was termed "social marketing." The strategy involved building a foundation of awareness, interest, knowledge/skills while minimizing barriers and optimizing benefits, norms, and confidence. This realization led me to pursue doctoral study focusing on environmental social marketing. Since the mid-1990s, I have played key roles in the design, implementation and evaluation of several environmental social marketing campaigns in various countries and have found that the behavior changes that were sought were much more apt to be met using social marketing strategies rather than the educational strategies that I had been previously relied upon.

In more recent years, especially via my work in New Zealand, I have come to realize that social marketing is just one more tool in a tool box of social influence strategies to be used to affect environmental behavior change. It is apparent that many environmental problems, especially those tied to the profitability of commercial enterprises (e.g., nutrient pollution or siltation from farming, carbon loading from industry), need more than awareness, knowledge, skills and persuasive messages or social pressure to precipitate changes in behaviors. In the past decade, innovative market/incentive reinforcement strategies (e.g., carbon trading, nitrogen trading, conservation deed restrictions, and tradeoffs that lower costs by providing targeted financial incentives) have been used in conjunction with social marketing strategies to get audiences to more willingly adopt new behaviors.

In addition, in retrospect, I have come to realize that asymmetrical communication, where the onus of responsibility to plan the educational program, social marketing campaign, or market/incentive-based intervention rests with the individual/agency charged with implementing the effort, does not always lead to sustained results. Asymmetrical models may work well for acute issues that need a firm hand and a quick fix, but for long-term sustained solutions it is better to have more symmetrical communication where all stakeholders that are affected by the issue openly participate in program planning, implementation and evaluation.

The purpose of the book is to provide an applied, practical, yet theoretically grounded, reference on social influence strategies for changing environmental behaviors. The book is intended to be used as a professional reference by practitioners in governmental and nongovernmental organizations worldwide. The book is also intended to be used as a text by students of environmental science, environmental communication and environmental education.

Chapter 1 provides context for selecting when the various social influence strategies are best used. Chapter 2 discusses the basic principles and theoretical foundations of education strategies. Chapter 3 and 4 discusses the basic principles and theoretical foundations of persuasive/social marketing strategies. Chapter 5 discusses the basic principles and theoretical foundations of market/incentive reinforcement strategies. Chapter 6 discusses the basic principles and theoretical foundations of dialogic/participatory strategies. Chapter 7 provides details about the research methods used to plan campaigns for changing environmental behaviors. Chapter 8 and 9 discusses issues and methods associated with monitoring and evaluating environmental communication campaigns. Chapter 10 provides tips on how to manage a project for environmental behavior change. Chapters 11 and 12 provide case studies that illustrates the design, implementation, monitoring and evaluation of campaigns that aim to change environmental practices that employ many of the strategies discussed in this book. Sidebars are used throughout the book to illustrate issues that are discussed. The Appendices in Chapters 7 provide how-to guidance on conducting research. The Appendices in Chapter 11 provide templates for questionnaires that can be used to collect information helpful for designing, monitoring and evaluating environmental communication campaigns.

Chapter 1
Strategies for Influencing Environmental Behaviors

A Model for Determining Strategy Selection

How do advocates for the environment best fulfill their objectives when their objectives require people to change their behavior? The criteria used to select environmental behavior change strategies are unique when compared to other behavior change strategies (e.g., consumer behavior, health behavior) because environmental issues often generate high amounts of controversy. The public is often conflicted by what is in their economic versus environmental and short-term versus long-term best interest. Economic and environmental issues often seem polarized. In addition, the validity and reliability of the science underlying many environmental issues often may seem tentative at times.

Questions can be raised about the assumptions scientists make during their investigations (see associated sidebar). The rationale behind their findings can be challenged. Scientists know this and harness the controversy by using a peer review process to validate their conclusions. But the public can be confused by the complexities and ambiguities of the process and controversy that is reported in the media (see associated sidebar). Hence, it is often difficult for advocates to choose when educational, persuasive/social marketing, market/incentive, or community based dialogic/participatory strategies are most appropriate.

According to Focht (1995), environmental issues can be assessed in terms of the degree that a) the scientific community and b) the general public agree amongst themselves about the cause/effect and solutions to an issue. Focht separates environmental issues into four categories.

- High scientific and high social consensus (e.g., the need to prevent excessive nutrients from polluting a lake).
- Low scientific and low social consensus (e.g., planning for the equitable distribution of a limited water supply).
- High scientific and low social consensus (e.g., the need to manage private forest land to protect wildlife).
- Low scientific but high social consensus (e.g., the choice of paper versus plastic when choosing disposable grocery bags).

Focht (1995) posits that under conditions of high scientific and high social consensus, environmental communication can ethically mandate a reinforcement-based course of action (i.e., market/incentives strategies or laws). Under conditions of low scientific consensus and low social consensus, he suggests that dialogic/participatory communication strategies ought to be followed in which there are few preconceived outcomes (i.e., community stakeholders discuss issues until they can agree on a course of action). Under conditions of high scientific consensus but low social consensus, he believes communication could be either educational and/or persuasive to encourage action consistent with scientific knowledge. Lastly, under conditions of low scientific consensus and high social consensus, any communication that might take place would be fairly subjective and ideological and subject to questionable credibility. The first three scenarios (reinforcement, education/persuasive, dialogic/participatory) pertain to more objective/credible forms of social influence and will be addressed in this book; the later scenario (ideological) will not.

Focht's thesis is interesting and potentially helpful. Yet, a key question remains unanswered: what constitutes high and low consensus? True consensus where all parties agree is probably an unrealistic goal given the controversial nature of many environmental issues. There will always be factions of people that disagree. This raises the question: how much of the public or the scientific community must agree on an issue for there to be a clear path of action?

There is probably no definitive answer to this question. As a general rule though, it may be helpful to envision an assessment of consensus on a continuum ranging from low to high - the closer to the poles the assessment is, the more definitive the choice of communication strategy can be. But as the assessment approaches the scale mid-point, the choice of communication strategy will become less clear and the final decision will undoubtedly be based more on intuition than logic.

Questioning Science

Questions can be raised about the assumptions scientists make during their investigations. A good illustration of this was displayed in a National Public Radio broadcast entitled *The Economy and Emissions* (Baron, Siegel & Wertheimer, 1996). Three economists from the Economic Strategy Institute (conservative), the Department of Energy (moderate), and Harvard University (liberal) once debated the potential impacts of a potential treaty to prevent climate change. The trend in their responses was predictable. When asked about the effects on GDP, responses ranged from 2.5 to 3.0 percent below what it would be without the treaty (conservative), to no impact (moderate), to a gain of .69 percent (liberal). When asked about the effects on employment, responses ranged from a 1.8 million job loss, to no "net gain", to an increase of 1.2 percent. When asked about the effects on gasoline prices, responses ranged from an increase of 50 cents per gallon, to 6 to 12 cents per gallon, to about five cents. The models these economists use to make their predictions depend on the assumptions they build into them initially. For instance, regarding the issue of technological change, many studies assume companies will develop new, energy-efficient cars, appliances, and power plants at a steady rate. Other models assume the rate of innovation will accelerate.

Controversial Science

The public can be confused by the complexities and ambiguities of the scientific process and the associated controversy that is reported in popular media. An example of how scientific findings can be controversial is evident in bestselling author Michael Crichton's novel *State of Fear* (Crichton, 2005). In this novel he blends fiction with what he claims are scientific facts – "facts" he shared in congressional testimony and several public speeches (Crichton, 2003). Both Crichton's fiction and nonfiction claim that environmental advocates base their opinions on unfounded religious-like myths and that their beliefs about global warming are overemotional, unfounded and need to be better supported by objective science.

In a Hartford Courant editorial (Thorson, 2005), Professor of Geography, Dr. Robert Thorson, criticized Crichton for blurring the link between his fiction and nonfiction and doing what he considered a public disservice by minimizing the threat of global warming in his novel. In addition, a special report in Rolling Stone that same year stated that the novel has been "roundly discredited by the scientific community" and named Crichton one of the top six public "misleaders" of science in this regard (Little, 2005).

Conclusion

Focht's thesis is potentially helpful. His thoughts on using market/incentive reinforcement strategies when there is little controversy makes sense (i.e., when there is high scientific and high public consensus). Though as discussed in Chapter 5, these strategies are usually cost and/or labor intensive and may not lead to permanent behavior change. His thoughts on using dialogic/participatory communication strategies when there is considerable controversy makes sense too (i.e., when there is low scientific and low public consensus). Though as discussed in Chapter 6, dialogic/participatory strategies may take considerable time to implement.

Yet, Focht's thesis has a weakness in that it does not provide specific guidance on how to choose when educational versus persuasive strategies are called for in the face of high scientific and low social consensus. These are important and frequently used strategies by environmental advocates. Focht could strengthen his thesis by adopting what Archie, Mann and Smith (1993) said about educational strategies being suitable when issues are not immediate or acute and when the ability to think critically is the goal; and persuasive/social marketing strategies being useful when issues are believed to be more immediate and relatively quick targeted behavior change is the goal.

CHAPTER 2
EDUCATION STRATEGIES

Introduction

Focht (1995) posits that educational and persuasive strategies may be well suited when there is high scientific consensus but low social consensus surrounding environmental issues. Educational strategies play out in both formal and non-formal education settings and in general are designed to promote changes in awareness, knowledge, and skills. Formal environmental education often follows a standardized curriculum organized by an educator and presented in a classroom setting (although many educators find ways to include experiences outside of the classroom). Non-formal education includes a) extension education carried out by technical specialists and volunteers associated with Cooperative Extension Systems typically based at universities and b) learning activities at state/national parks, zoos/aquariums and other types of nature centers. It is not uncommon for formal education teachers to invite non-formal educators into their classrooms to help with student instruction.

According to Archie, Mann and Smith (1993), educational approaches equip audiences with the background needed to make informed decisions about their own choice of behavior. The goal is to build capacity and commitment to engage in problem-solving and decision-making to assure environmental quality. The audience is usually a significant portion of the population. Outcomes may include environmental sensitivity and changes in knowledge and skills. The time frame is generally long-term because of the emphasis on broad changes across an extensive social framework. A wide range of issues lend themselves to this strategy, particularly those that are not immediate or acute.

Formal Environmental Education

As stated, formal environmental education often follows a standardized curriculum organized by an educator and presented in a classroom setting. It involves the training and development of students' knowledge, skills and character in structured and certified programs that take place in schools. It is important to understand that formal education is not about changing behaviors; it is about providing information so that individuals can decide what they want to believe and how they want to act.

According to Monroe, Andrews and Biedenweg (2007), formal environmental education has two goals:

- To foster clear awareness of, and concern about, economic, social, political, and ecological interdependence in urban and rural areas.
- To provide every person with opportunities to acquire the knowledge, values, attitudes, commitment and skills needed to protect and improve the environment.

FORMAL EDUCATION STRATEGIES

According to Monroe, Day and Grieser (2000), formal environmental education teaches students "how to think" not "what to think." Thus, the goal of environmental educators is to help learners form the capacity to collect and analyze information, make good judgments, and participate fully in civic life. Monroe, Andrews and Biedenweg (2007) define the following four objectives of environmental education: convey information, build understanding, improve skills, and enable sustainable actions.

Convey Information

One objective of formal environmental education is to convey information to students. It is important that educators use an unbiased approach when teaching students. The most common methods for conveying information are through lectures, textbooks, videos and field trips. Other methods include invited presentations done by non-formal environmental educators. The outcome is for students to be able to think for themselves and manage their behaviors on their own as they see fit. The hope is that providing students with knowledge on topics will spark an interest and help them build their own understanding of the environment. It is hoped that getting students interested in caring for the environment at a young age will encourage them to continue this as they get older.

Build Understanding

A second objective of formal environmental education according to Monroe, Andrews and Biedenweg (2007) is to build better understanding of issues. This is best accomplished by facilitating interaction among students and educators. In the previous objective all the work was done by the educator. Fulfilling this second objective requires students to be an active part of the learning process. This often includes field work done by students. Monroe, Andrews and Biedenweg (2007) provide other examples of what an educator can do to collaboratively build understanding.

- Discussion
- Role play
- Simulation
- Case study
- Experiment
- Game
- Constructivist methods
- Experiential learning

Improve Skills

A third objective of formal environmental education is to improve skills. This requires an educator to provide various skill building activities. Students need to be able to ask questions if they do not fully understand how to do things. An example might be showing a young child how to separate recyclables and providing the student who recycles the most with an environmental citizenship award. Older students may be asked to engage in community service projects.

Enable Sustainable Actions

The forth objective of formal environmental education is to help students take action if they chose to. Once a student has fulfilled the previous three objectives they should be able to decide if they want to act on this knowledge/skill or not. By this time the educator has done everything they can to educate the student, show the student examples, and walk them through action steps. The final objective is for the student to choose their own long-term direction. The educator should continue to answer questions and provide guidance as needed.

Project Learning Tree – Formal Education

The American Forest Foundation has created the best known formal environmental education program in the U.S. called Project Learning Tree (PLT). It is a standardized curriculum used by educators in the classroom to teach about environmental issues. An integral part of PLT is bringing the classroom into the forest and making learning an experience. The curriculum is broken down into early childhood, elementary/middle school, and secondary school units. The program requires educators that are interested in using program materials to attend workshops and receive training in how to use them. Non-formal environmental educators are often charged with delivering this training. PLT is available in all 50 states in the United States and there are now over 500,000 educators using these resources (Connecticut Forest & Park Association, n.d.).

Early Childhood Curriculum

PLT believes that it is essential to start teaching children at a young age. Teaching methods used at this stage include learning about color and sound; e.g., learning why leaves change colors and identifying noises the animals make. PLT encourages activities to be done at home with its *Friends and Family* units. These units are also available in Spanish called *Familia y Amigos*. Project Learning Tree provides 130 different lesson plans at the Early Childhood Curriculum level.

Elementary & Middle School Curriculum

The curriculum at elementary and middle school level is provided via a K-8 *Environmental Education Activity Guide* and an *Energy and Society* study kit. Activities vary depending on grade level. Students learn about the importance of the environment and different ways they can help nurture it. The main objective of these lessons is to help students think critically so they can understand issues before making decisions.

Secondary Curriculum

PLT's secondary curriculum builds on everything that has been taught in prior grades and focuses on helping students develop the ability to make decisions on their own. PLT has created seven curriculum books at the secondary level to train students in the areas of Biodiversity, Biotechnology, Forests of the World, Places We Live, Focus on Risk, and Municipal Solid Waste.

Environmental Education in Japan

In order to help students become more aware of global environmental problems, the Ministry of Education in Japan introduced a formal environmental education curriculum called "The Period of Integrated Study." Its objective is to teach students to solve problems which they may face in the future. The program is mandatory for all primary and secondary schools. Every school is required to allocate two to three hours per week to environmental education. Teachers play the role of facilitator in the program and use local persons as guest teachers. Students are required to work outside the school to practice various problem solving methods.

A non-formal education counterpart to this formal education curriculum is called the Junior Eco Clubs. This voluntary program was initiated by the Ministry of Environment in Japan. This program also targets children at the primary and secondary levels. Its objective is to get students involved in group activities for the purpose of learning about the environment. Club activities vary but in general try to foster awareness of environmental conservation, help shape a society that has less environmental stress, and help the next generation take specific and positive actions. Student experiences are shared through a bimonthly newsletter and through national and regional exchange programs. Clubs have a minimum participation requirement of three students and a maximum of twenty. Each club has adult supporters that supervise the children's activities. Clubs are required to meet two to three hours per week and have essentially two types of activities that the children participate in – "ecological action" and "ecological training." Ecological action activities includes things like recycling and trash pickup. Ecological training activities are usually proposed by the national secretariat and are designed to connect the students with their surroundings.

Non-formal Environmental Education

Non-formal education includes a) extension education carried out by technical specialists and volunteers associated with Cooperative Extension Systems based at universities and b) learning activities at parks, zoos/ aquaria, museums, environmental organizations, and nature centers.

EXTENSION EDUCATION

The U.S. Congress created the Cooperative Extension System over a century ago to address rural development issues. Originally, the system was housed at one designated university in each state and worked in conjunction with the research function and the education (formal teaching) function of Colleges of Agriculture and Natural Resources to disseminate information to individuals, families and businesses in rural communities. The model has been adopted by many countries around the world to facilitate community development.

When the Cooperative Extension System was first developed more than 50 percent of the U.S. population lived in rural areas and 30 percent of the workforce was engaged in farming. These days, less than two percent of Americans farm for a living and only about 17 percent live in rural areas (USDA, 2011). There are currently 218 university campuses in the U.S. that support Cooperative Extension System functions and these organizations are just as likely to work in urban and suburban settings as in rural areas (Association of Public and Land-grant Universities, 2011). Today's Extension programs can be broken down into six major areas (USDA, 2011):

- 4-H Youth Development Programs cultivate important life skills in youth that build character and assist them in making appropriate life and career choices. At-risk youth participate in school retention and enrichment programs. Youth learn science, math and social skills through hands-on projects and activities.
- Agriculture Research and Educational Programs help individuals learn new ways to produce income through alternative enterprises, improved marketing strategies and management skills, and help farmers and ranchers improve productivity through resource management, controlling crop pests, soil testing, livestock production practices, and marketing.
- Leadership Development Programs for Extension volunteers is offered to help them deliver programs in gardening, environmental stewardship, health and safety, family and consumer issues, and 4-H youth development.
- Natural Resources Conservation Programs for landowners and homeowners on topics such as water quality, timber management, composting, lawn waste management, and recycling are offered to help them use natural resources wisely and protect the environment.
- Family and Consumer Science Programs help families become resilient by teaching about nutrition, food preparation skills, childcare, family communication, financial management, and health care strategies.
- Community and Economic Development Programs help local governments create viable options for economic and community development, such as improved job creation and retention, small and medium-sized business development, effective and coordinated emergency response, solid waste disposal, tourism development, workforce education, and land use planning.

The extended case study that is described in Chapter 11 of this book is a thorough example of a Cooperative Extension System project targeting an environmental issue (forest stewardship). As is typical of these types of projects, a wide array of communication channels were employed to target knowledge and skills acquisition. This project was somewhat unique in that it also attempted to incorporate persuasive behavior change, incentive-based and participatory communication strategies to some degree.

PARKS, ZOOS/AQUARIA, MUSEUMS, ENVIRONMENTAL ORGANIZATIONS, AND NATURE CENTERS

Non-formal education is defined by Kleis (1973) as an intentional and systematic educational enterprise outside of traditional schooling in which content is adapted to the unique needs of the participants (or unique situations). Its purpose is to maximize learning and minimize other elements often delegated to formal school teachers (e.g., taking roll, enforcing discipline, writing reports). Non-formal education tends to be more "learner" focused, with a greater emphasis placed on learner motivation and participation.

Non-formal educators are sometimes volunteers who simply want to share their knowledge with interested people, while others may hold paid part and full-time positions. There are two types of non-formal environmental educators. The first type is the non-formal educator who leads learning activities that help support formal education systems. Within this group, one might find parks, zoos/aquaria, museums, environmental organizations, and nature centers. These groups try to attract schools to their sites or perhaps send staff to the schools. The second type is the non-formal educator who does not try to link with a formal education program. Rather they are seeking fun, engaging and informative ideas to teach participants of all ages about the environment on their own terms. Examples may include scout leaders, Boys and Girls Clubs staff, or interpreters at parks, zoos/aquaria, museums, environmental organizations, and nature centers.

The first type of non-formal educator is concerned with bringing the environment into the classroom or the students into the environment. The challenge is to adapt learning materials to fit the school curriculum. Learners are not there by choice. The relationship with the educator has been established by their formal education system. In recent years, schools have had far less flexibility integrating non-formal environmental education programs into formal education curriculum. For non-formal education to work, it must be easily infused into standardized science, math, or language arts curricula that meet state requirements.

The second type of non-formal environmental educator requires fun, informative and engaging material to teach participants of all ages about nature. Learners are not brought to them by their school. Instead, they are there by choice. The content can be engaging without consideration of formal educational standards.

Project Learning Tree – Non-formal Education

The Project Learning Tree (PLT) program mentioned in an earlier sidebar in this chapter is an environmental education program also used by non-formal educators who work with youth through grade 12. In addition to working with their own clientele (regardless of age), non-formal educators using PLT materials are often called upon to assist formal educators in their work with their students.

Non-formal educators attend PLT workshops with the objective of acquiring practical skills and knowledge that they will use on the job. Non-formal educators engage with PLT because of their desire to promote, educate, and impart knowledge about the environment to others. They want to be taught nature-based activities, receive age-appropriate environmental education materials, and obtain tools that will facilitate their teaching of the subject.

PLT owes its success with non-formal educators in part to the numerous organizations with which it collaborates. In Connecticut, the Connecticut Forest and Park Association (CFPA) is the state designated sponsor of PLT (Ct.gov, n.d. #1). The CFPA is a non-profit, membership-based conservation organization that services Connecticut citizens (Ctwoodlands.org, n.d.). In other states, PLT is sponsored by similar environmental education organizations. The Tennessee Environmental Education Agency (TEEA) (Candace Dinwiddie, personal communication, September 21, 2012), and the Environmental Education Association of Illinois (EEAI) (Sarah Livesay, personal communication, September 22, 2012) serve as sponsors of PLT in their respective states.

The Department of Energy and Environmental Protection (DEEP) cosponsors the PLT program in Connecticut. The DEEP is a state government department responsible for environmental legislation (Ct. gov, n.d.#2). Other states utilize different state agencies to sponsor the PLT program. State forest services like The North Dakota Forest Service (NDSU) (Glenda Fauske, personal communication, September 21, 2012), the Colorado State Forest Service (CSFS) (Shawna Crocker, personal communication, September 21, 2012), and the Florida Forest Service (FFS) sponsor their respective PLT programs. The Florida PLT also partners with the local 4-H extension program to help conduct workshops (Nancy Peterson, personal communication, September 21, 2012).

At times, PLT branches have formed informal partnerships with other organizations. The Tennessee PLT has utilized the Tennessee Health Department (Candace Dinwiddie, personal communication, September 21, 2012). The Colorado PLT shares an office space with the Colorado Alliance for Education (Shawna Crocker, personal communication, September 21, 2012). The Mississippi PLT education coordinator sits on the board of directors for the Mississippi Environmental Education Alliance (Harold Anderson, personal communication, September 21, 2012).

Mystic Aquarium

The mission of Mystic Aquarium in Mystic, Connecticut is to inspire people to care for and protect the planet's oceans through education, research and exploration. The organization has a variety of non-formal educational programs for families that help build public awareness about climate change, pollution prevention, and energy conservation. They utilize exhibits and print materials such as rack cards, brochures, and signage to communicate with their audiences. The organization also utilizes social media including Twitter and Facebook. Families are reached through newsletters, family programming, special event days, field programs and during their visits to the aquarium. They try to provide opportunities for families to get directly involved in programs such as costal clean ups, population studies, and animal tagging (Mateleska, 2012).

In addition, Mystic Aquarium has an expansive program supporting school-based education including teacher training that is designed to be interactive and supply educators with numerous resources for immediate use in the classroom. The aquarium's website describes a wide array of programs that can be taught at the aquarium or brought to schools for various age groups from preschool through high school. These programs aim is to help students "build a connection with the natural world and foster understanding of how organisms, habitats, and ecosystems work. Through inquiry-based teaching and hands-on activities, these education programs encourage students to use and develop skills such as observing, hypothesizing, experimenting, and drawing conclusions" (www.mysticaquarium.org, *n.d.*).

CHAPTER 3
PERSUASIVE/SOCIAL MARKETING STRATEGIES

A Model for Designing Social Marketing Campaigns

According to Focht (1995), another strategy suited to conditions of high scientific consensus and low social consensus is persuasion/social marketing. Social marketing is a fitting label for persuasive communication strategies that promote socially-concerned environmental behaviors the same way marketers promote product-purchase behaviors. It is a research based and audience focused approach to changing the way people act. Social marketing often starts with educational objectives (e.g., awareness and knowledge of an issue) and once this foundation is laid, shifts to a focus on motivational objectives (e.g., attitude and behavior change) (Tyson, 2003).

Audiences need to perceive that the "benefits" associated with a proposed behavior exceed the "costs" if the new behavior is to be adopted. This supports Ostrom's (1990) contention that successful resource management groups perceive that the benefits of the resource cannot be discounted and costs of cooperation are low. The challenge is to identify pertinent benefits and costs so rewards can be optimized and barriers minimized.

Additional insight concerning social marketing is offered by Archie, Mann and Smith (1993). The goal they say is behavior change. The audience is generally a specific target audience that shares common values, access points, or obstacles. Social marketing strategies are good when change is needed in the short-term and are therefore well suited to issues considered acute or critical. Social marketing employs all forms of marketing/advertising techniques (e.g., interpersonal, group and mass communication channels).

Social marketing is based on the four-step strategic process diagramed below.

1) Campaign planning
   - Define issues and campaign objectives
   - Define audiences
   - Define messages
   - Define communication channels
   - Define information sources and strategic partners

2) Campaign implementation/management
3) Monitoring of campaign processes
4) Final outcome evaluation

The first three steps are iterative – that is, a campaign plan is developed, once the campaign is implemented, the effectiveness of campaign processes are monitored and problems with implementation are identified. Plans are then changed accordingly. This cyclical process continues until the campaign ends. At that point, a final evaluation is conducted to assess the extent to which planned campaign outcomes were met. Initial research findings that were used to plan the campaign serve as a benchmark to compare final evaluation data against.

Campaign Planning

DEFINING ISSUES AND CAMPAIGN OBJECTIVES

The initial challenge to campaign designers is to learn about the issues – learn what the problems are and are not, learn about similar issues in other settings, and learn about potential causes and solutions. Information gleaned from this initial research helps us define realistic campaign objectives. It is very important that campaign objectives specifically state what and how much change is expected, by whom and by when. The final evaluation assesses the degree that objectives have been met.

You have breakfast watching the morning news on television. You travel to your day's activities listening to the radio. You read a few news stories online or in a newspaper as you eat your lunch. After work you drop a book at your town library where you also pick up a copy of an informational brochure displayed at the checkout desk. When you arrive home, you go through your mail including a letter addressed to you personally inviting you to a workshop at a neighbor's property. Afterward, while checking your home email, you check out a website listed on the brochure you received earlier. Tomorrow evening you plan to attend a public meeting and video presentation at the town hall.

How has all this communication affected you? Given that the subject is the environment, perhaps you are now more *aware* of factors affecting the environmental clean-up and reuse of an old industrial site. Or perhaps you now have greater *knowledge* about the causes and effects of nonpoint source pollution affecting a local lake. Maybe you now have a higher degree of *interest* in protecting your community's natural resources. Or has your *attitude* changed regarding the importance of forest stewardship? Are you now more apt to engage in *behaviors* to protect lands from the detrimental aspects of land fragmentation?

These examples provide a sample of the audience objectives that practitioners of environmental social marketing might choose to address. The objectives of most campaigns can be characterized one of two ways. Objectives may be informational, where the aim is to raise awareness, interest and/or knowledge; or motivational, where the aim is to induce attitude and behavior change. A staged approach is often followed that starts with informational objectives and once this foundation is laid, shifts to a focus on motivational objectives. Environmental social marketing strategies specifically designed to change attitudes and behaviors (i.e., motivational objectives) are premised on the assumption that informational objectives are necessary but not sufficient to change behavior.

THE TARGET AUDIENCE

The target audience for the scenarios listed above could have been youth, landowners, volunteers, technical specialists, business owners, municipal officials, policy makers, media representatives, etc. There are many naturally occurring audience segments, clusters of individuals, groups, or organizations that can be defined by similar characteristics (e.g., geographic location, socio-economic status, profession, education level, media use). Clusters can also be defined by similar levels of awareness, knowledge, interest, attitudes or behaviors. The theories of social influence discussed in the next chapter identify specific variables that can be used to segment audience members (e.g., perceived benefits and barriers, perceived risk, norms, adopter group). Careful audience research will provide data that will allow you to define audience clusters.

From a social marketing perspective, these clusters can be thought of as potential audience segments that one could target with similar messages and channels. It is noteworthy that social marketing practitioners are much more apt to achieve their objectives when their chosen strategy is uniquely tailored to a specific audience segment. It follows that the more narrowly defined the audience segment, the more targeted a social marketing strategy can be and the more likely that strategy is to achieve its objectives. Yet fewer people are reached as the focus narrows. The challenge is to seek "least group size" defined as a large enough group so there will be a significant impact, yet a narrow enough focus so that you will realize results (Thelen, 1949). One needs to balance efficiency and effectiveness.

CAMPAIGN MESSAGES

Education and persuasion theory provides considerable guidance on formulating campaign messages. The next chapter describes how campaign planners can base messages on several psycho-social predictors of environmental behavior. The next chapter also discusses key attributes of innovations that can be important to highlight in campaign messages if they are to be adopted by an audience. In addition, the next chapter discusses the importance of messages that take into account an individual's sense-of-place and how this affects their environmental behaviors. And it discusses some adoption/diffusion approaches that provide guidance on how to frame and stage campaign messages. Three other factors worthy of consideration when formulating campaign messages are commitment, incentives and prompts (McKenzie-Mohr & Smith, 1999).

Commitment refers to the fact that once we make a stand on something we feel pressure to remain consistent with this stand. It is human nature to want to be consistent. Inconsistency is seen as undesirable. Consistency is associated with intellectual strength and is a heuristic device that minimizes the degree we need to weigh each and every issue that faces us.

The power of commitment is illustrated in an experiment described by Cialdini (2001) where subjects were first phoned and asked if they would, if needed, volunteer for an event. Other individuals did not receive the initial phone call. A few days after the phone call, everyone was phoned and asked to actually volunteer. The number that subsequently agreed to volunteer was seven times higher among those that received the initial phone and made an initial commitment. Cialdini states that when a commitment is made publicly, its strength is much stronger. Public commitment is often the key in behavioral modification programs for weight reduction, smoking cessation, and alcohol abuse. Cialdini suggests that commitments should be active, public and effortful for maximum results. Soliciting and publicizing commitments may be an effective campaign message strategy.

McKenzie-Mohr and Smith (1999) provide the following examples of using commitment to change behaviors in an environmental context:

- Ask people as they enter a grocery store to wear a button supporting the purchase of products with recycled content.
- When conducting a home energy assessment, ask the owners to participate in data gathering and when the assessment is completed ask them when they plan to install weather stripping or a programmable thermostat.
- Ask homeowners to sign a pledge to reduce water use and/or the use of lawn chemicals.
- Ask commuters to sign a pledge that they will take mass transit or carpool once or twice per week.

Prompts, perhaps the simplest form of a campaign message, refers to some sort of visual or auditory aid that reminds us to do something that we already formed an intention to do. They can be especially important in the time period immediately following the adoption of a new behavior. They help the new behavior become routine. Once routine, the prompt may no longer be needed. Recycling bins with the recycling logo printed on their sides that are strategically placed in public places can stimulate significantly greater recycling behavior. Note cards in hotel rooms that alert guests to signal when new towels are desired encourages guests to conserve and reuse. The energy star logo is a prompt to purchase energy efficient appliances. Decals affixed to light switches effectively remind people to turn lights off when leaving a room. Simple notices stenciled over storm drains remind people that these drains channel runoff to nearby rivers and therefore should not be used for discarding pollutants.

McKenzie-Mohr and Smith (1999) suggest that a prompt must be a) noticeable, b) self- explanatory, and c) made available near the behavior it is designed to impact. Prompts can be an important part of the overall campaign message strategy.

COMMUNICATION CHANNELS

One common aspect of life in the 21st century is that we are constantly bombarded with messages. Because of this, social marketers are constantly seeking ways to cut through the clutter so that they can get their messages noticed and mentally processed. To do this they use a full array of communication channels (i.e., interpersonal, group and mass communication channels).

Mass communication channels (e.g., television, radio, printed matter) can be initially used to achieve audience awareness, interest, and knowledge about the issues. Once this is achieved campaign resources can be directed to more persuasive efforts. Group communication channels (e.g., field days, demonstration tours) can be used for these purposes. Once it is determined that the audience intends to adopt the new behavior, reinforcement through interpersonal contact often becomes the method of choice. The table below describes the pro and cons of various communication channels.

Channel	Pros	Cons
Television	Reach many people. May run free PSAs. Vivid content. Cable access reaches local audience. Good for creating awareness and interest.	Expensive. Limited air time. Much clutter. Difficult to appeal to specific target audience.
Radio	Reach many people. May run free PSAs. Can target specific audiences. Good for creating awareness and interest.	Limited air time. Not vivid medium.

Print Media (newspapers, magazines)	Can provide detailed information. Can target specific audiences with specific magazines. Multiple exposure to message possible. Good for creating awareness, interest, knowledge.	Not good for less literate audiences. Reporter is gatekeeper. Little editorial control.
Print Materials (brochures, booklets)	Can provide detailed information. Good for complex subjects. Can target specific audiences with specific message content. Multiple exposure to message possible. Good for increasing knowledge.	Not good for less literate audiences. May get lost in junk-mail clutter.
Direct Mail (print, CD, video)	Can provide detailed information. Good for complex subjects. Can target specific audiences with specific message content. Multiple exposure to message possible. Can reach specific audiences with targeted mailings. Can provide detailed information in vivid format with video. Good for increasing knowledge and changing attitudes.	May get lost in junk-mail clutter. Mailing list must be recent and accurate.
Internet/ Website	Very inexpensive. Can provide detailed information in vivid format. Easy to initiate correspondence. Can simulate group discussion. Good for increasing knowledge and changing attitudes.	Not everyone has internet access. Difficult to compile mailing list.

Group Interaction (field days, tours, workshops)	Good for stimulating group cohesiveness and observability. Can provide detailed information in vivid format. Instant question/answer possible. Good for teaching skills. Good for providing reassurance. Good for increasing knowledge, changing attitudes, and stimulating behavior change.	Can only target a few people at a time. Requires time commitment by audience members. Preparation can be complex.
Interpersonal Contact (phone, face-to-face)	Instant question/answer possible. Good for providing reassurance. Good for sustaining attitude and behavior change.	Can only target one person at a time. Requires time commitment by audience members.

SOURCES AND STRATEGIC PARTNERS

Social marketing campaigns are often complex and underfunded. Because of this, organizations may need to share responsibilities for the campaign with other liked-minded groups. Alan Andreasen (1995) offers a partial list of groups that might help facilitate a campaign.

- Commercial sector distributors
- Commercial sector research agencies
- Commercial sector advertising agencies
- Governmental agencies
- Media
- Retailers
- Volunteer groups
- Funding agencies
- Other nonprofit organizations/advocacy groups
- Corporations

For example, if a campaign is launched by a university's Cooperative Extension System that addresses forest stewardship, local wildlife advocacy groups may also want to get involved (e.g., The Nature Conservancy, Audubon). State Division of Forestry specialists, private consultant foresters, and trained volunteers may be needed to help landowners translate their new knowledge and positive attitudes into a permanent changes in behavior. The news media may help highlight cases of project success. Timber corporations and other commercial enterprises may be interested in partially funding the project or providing pro bono assistance in return for public relations benefits. Retailers may play a key role in providing tools and materials required to perform the tasks being promoted.

No matter which audience the social marketer wishes to target (primary target audience or strategic partner), the strategy is often the same. They must try to figure out how to increase the positive consequences of cooperating, decrease the perceived costs and barriers, bring social pressure to bear, and make sure that they feel confident that the project will be successful (Andreasen, 1995).

Conclusion

As described, social marketing is a theory driven, research based, management strategy that can be successful at changing the behavior of target audiences. It follows the four-step strategic process diagramed in the beginning of this chapter. This chapter addressed the first stage, campaign planning in some detail. The next chapter will provide theoretical guidance on a key aspect of planning - message development.

CHAPTER 4
THEORETICAL FOUNDATIONS OF PERSUASION

Introduction

Theory is like a road map that guides us toward our goal. Without a map a person can easily become lost and never reach their destination. Theory allows us to predict the outcomes of our actions. Knowing the probable outcome of our choices ahead of time allows us to strategically plan the efforts we choose to implement. The theories presented in this chapter were chosen because of their proven usefulness in guiding environmental social marketing campaigns.

Variables Affecting Behavior Change

The intended outcome of a social marketing campaign is a change in audience behavior. Yet, various resource factors can constrain a person's intended action and many of these factors are outside the control of campaign planners. For example, employing the assistance of private forestry professionals may be necessary if the target behavior is assessing one's land and designing a long-term stewardship strategy. In addition to technical assistance, other potential resource constraints may include input supply, transportation, marketing assistance, etc.. Though social marketing practitioners spend time trying to minimize these types of resource constraints, the actual performance of behaviors by the target audience is often outside their control. According to the Theory of Reasoned Action (Ajzen & Fishbein, 1980; Fishbein & Ajzen, 1975), when behaviors require resources outside the control of the campaign planner, it may be more realistic to focus on a person's *behavior intentions.* Yet, behavior change is always the end goal.

In addition to removing resource constraints, another issue campaign planners often have to deal with initially is providing individuals with the knowledge/skills required to successfully perform the promoted behavior. Requisite knowledge/skills are necessary for successful behavior. In an environmental context, knowledge consistently accounts for a significant proportion of the explained variance in behavior intention measures (Andreasen & Tyson, 1994; Vining & Ebreo, 1990).

Removing resource constraints and possessing requisite knowledge/ skills are necessary but not sufficient conditions for behavior change. In addition, there are several social-psychological variables that can influence an individual's intention to behave in a certain way. The following diagram displays the possible relationships between behavior, behavior intention, and some key social-psychological variables thought to be predictive of environmental behaviors.

Variables Affecting Environmental Behaviors

Perceived threat to self

Anticipated consequences to self

Personal/family norms

Self-efficacy

Perceived threat to community

$\rightarrow$ Behavior intention $\rightarrow$ Behavior

Anticipated consequences
to community
$\uparrow$

Social/community norms

Knowledge, skills &
required resources

Community efficacy

Community cohesiveness/
Community interaction

As depicted in the previous diagram, motivations to engage in pro-environmental behaviors may have a personal/individual orientation and/or community orientation. An individual orientation might stress threats to one's self, the personal consequences of behavior, the power of personal/family norms and perceptions of one's own efficacy. A community orientation might stress threats to the community, the community consequences of behavior, the power of social/community norms, and perceptions of community efficacy. In addition, perceptions of high community cohesiveness and frequent interaction among community members may be important ingredients of a community orientation.

PERCEIVED THREAT

The variables, perceived severity and perceived susceptibility (of a threat to one's health), were posited in the Health Belief Model as predictors of behavior (Becker & Maiman, 1975; Janz & Becker, 1984; Rosenstock, 1974). Later, a study employing the Health Belief Model (Witte, Stokols, Itvarte, & Schneider, 1993) found severity and susceptibility variables loading on the same construct and redefined the combined variable as "perceived threat". This construct proves applicable when considering remedial behaviors in response to environmental threats -- both threats to one's self as well as threats to the larger community.

ANTICIPATED CONSEQUENCES

Anticipated consequences is a variable that crops up in numerous theories under various labels. In the education literature a variable carrying this exact label is often used to predict behavior (Cross 1981; Pryor 1990; Tough 1979). Related to predictors of health behaviors, the Health Belief Model (Becker & Maiman, 1975; Janz & Becker, 1984; Rosenstock, 1974) posits perceived benefits and barriers. In the environmental arena, anticipated consequences is similarly employed and has been defined as the perceived costs and benefits of a proposed behavior (Andreasen & Tyson, 1994; Geller, 1992; Hines, Hungerford & Tomera, 1986/87; Vining & Ebreo, 1990). When the context of the behavior requires cooperation among community members, as it does with many environmental behaviors, anticipated consequences may be perceived as the costs and benefits to the community as well as to the individual.

PERSONAL NORM

Personal Norm is a variable that is a predictor of behavior intentions in the Theory of Reasoned Action and refers to perceptions of a) what one thinks others think about a behavior and b) the personal importance of these opinions (Ajzen & Fishbein, 1980; Fishbein & Ajzen, 1975). The Theory of Reasoned Action operationalizes "others" as those individuals significant to oneself. Thus, the motivation to comply with a personal norm may be driven by the perceived benefit of agreeing with a person of personal importance.

SOCIAL NORM

Social norm refers to the most common or accepted behavior exhibited by community members (Cialdini, Reno & Kallgren, 1990; Reno, Cialdini, & Kallgren, 1993). The environmental literature indicates that social norms are often an important determinant of individual behavior. Motivation to comply with a social norm may be driven by a consensus heuristic -- the belief that what the majority does is the correct thing to do.

SELF-EFFICACY

Self-efficacy, a key construct in Social Learning Theory (Bandura, 1977, 1978, 1980), is defined as the degree to which an individual believes they can accomplish the behavior successfully. Self-efficacy is affected by perceptions of one's own knowledge, skills, degree of personal control, or difficulty of the task. According to Bandura, self-efficacy can be influenced by personal experience, vicarious learning by modeling someone else's behavior and persuasion. Ajzen and Madden (1986) in an adaptation of the Theory of Reasoned Action looked at a conceptually similar variable, perceived behavior control, and found this variable predicted behavior intention. In environmental contexts, a closely related construct, individual locus of control, has been identified as a fundamental determinant of responsible environmental behavior (Hines, Hungerford & Tomera, 1986/87; Sia, Hungerford & Tomera, 1985/86; Sivek & Hungerford, 1989/90).

COMMUNITY EFFICACY

When the context of a behavior is protecting a communally-owned resource, community efficacy may prove to be an important determinant of individual behavior. Community efficacy is defined as the degree that one believes the community can accomplish its task successfully and, similar to self-efficacy, can be affected by perceptions of the community's collective knowledge and skills, degree of control, or difficulty of the task (Bandura, 1982). Perceptions of positive community efficacy should decrease instances of noncooperation and increase intentions to behave in a cooperative manner. In environmental contexts, research has identified a closely related construct, group locus of control, as a fundamental determinant of responsible behavior (Sia, Hungerford & Tomera, 1985/86; Sivek & Hungerford, 1989/90).

COMMUNITY COHESIVENESS/COMMUNITY INTERACTION

When the theme of a campaign is conservation of a communal resource such as a water, air or wildlife, two other variables, community cohesiveness and community interaction, might be expected to affect an individual's behavioral decision. Community Cohesiveness is the extent to which the community is of one mindset with regard to a particular topic and is thought to affect the degree that individuals will sacrifice or constrain their own behaviors in the interest of the group (Brewer & Kramer, 1986; Kramer & Brewer, 1984). Members of cohesive groups tend to be more familiar and open with each other. Perceptions of strong reciprocity norms (trust that one's efforts will be matched by group members) is also an indicator of cohesive groups (Ostrom, 1990; Wiener & Doescher, 1994). Community interaction is the extent to which community members communicate with each other. It is thought to moderate the resolution of social dilemmas (Bloomquist & Ostrom, 1985; Lynn & Oldenquist, 1986; Ostrom, 1990). That is, communities in which members communicate frequently and effectively are more apt to behave cooperatively with each other.

Predictors of Land Management in the Eight Mile River watershed

The following sidebar briefly describes results of a study completed in the Eight Mile River watershed of south-central Connecticut (Tyson, 1995). Landowners with more than five acres of land were surveyed. Results were used to design a social marketing campaign promoting land management activities (see case study in Chapter 11 for a full description of this case). The attitudes and intentions of landowners were subject to a causal modeling analysis that helped identify the most important variables affecting the promoted behavior. The following diagram displays these variables. Results helped campaign designers understand the thought processes of landowners and design campaign messages accordingly.

Predictors of Land Management

Community consequences → Personal consequences → Behavior intentions → Behavior

Threat to community →

↑

Threat to self

Community Interaction →

Perceived personal consequences was the most important determinant of behavior intention. Anticipated personal consequences in turn was affected by anticipated community consequences. The fact that the consequences to the community of our behavior positively affect what we perceive as personal consequences bodes well for conservation of communal resources (i.e., what benefits the community influences what an individual feels benefits him/her).

Anticipated personal consequences was also affected by perceived threat to self, but with less potency then community consequences. The fact that the degree of personal threat attached to a situation affects the magnitude of personal consequences attributed to a remedial behavior makes intuitive sense (i.e., the greater the threat, the greater the benefit of doing something about it).

Perceived threat to self was in turn affected by both perceived threat to community and perceived community interaction. However, the influence of these relationships on behavior was comparatively less than other factors. Nonetheless, these findings do bode well for conservation of communal resources. By virtue of interacting with others, people will personalize the degree of threat they think affects the community (i.e., what threatens the community influences what an individual feels threatens him/her).

Based on the above, there is some support for the power of a community-oriented appeal. It appears that messages about perceived community consequences and community threats tend to be personalized. Yet, in a causal sequence, these variables are indirectly linked to behavior intentions. Anticipated consequences to community has the most direct and therefore greater effect on behavior intention. The relationship is mediated only by personal consequences. The correlation with behavior intention would be moderately strong. Benefits to the community should probably be emphasized in campaign messages. Perceived community threat is further back in the model. The effect on behavior intention is mediated by both personal threat and personal consequences and therefore, the correlation with behavior intention would be small. Because of this, threats to the community would warrant less emphasis in campaign messages.

Interestingly, the higher one's perception of community interaction, the greater one perceives threats to themselves. If we suppose that perceptions of community interaction are based on personal experience, then it appears that interaction with others in the community helps personalize environmental threats. This fact should be of importance to campaign planners when selecting communication channels. Interactive group activities should help personalize environmental threats (i.e., the greater the personal threat, the greater the personal benefit of doing something about it, and the more apt one is to actually do something).

Message Based Persuasion

The previous discussion described potentially important social-psychological predictors of environmental behavior/behavior intentions. Campaign messages that are patterned on these variables are apt to be of higher quality and more persuasive. Campaign planners seeking to maximize the quality of their messages need to identify the specific beliefs of their audience relative to these variables; i.e., they need to identify:

○ Which resources are perceived to be the most threatened and which of these are most important?
○ What are the positive and negative consequences of the proposed behavior?
○ What are the existing norms and who is most apt to influence these norms?
○ How confident are people that the behaviors being promoted will be adopted, why/why not?

In addition to *message quality*, it has been shown that *message discrepancy* (the discrepancy between the campaign planner's position and the audience's initial position on the issue) and the perceived *credibility of the source* of the message are important determinants of attitude change (Hamilton, Hunter, & Burgoon, 1990; Hamilton & Stewart, 1993; Hamilton & Thompson, 1994).

The receiver of a campaign message is more likely to argue against a message, and therefore less likely to change their attitudes and associated behaviors, when message discrepancy is great. This highlights the need for careful audience analysis early in the campaign planning process so that messages can be designed within an audience's latitude of neutrality/acceptance (avoiding their latitude of rejection). If the campaign is attempting to move the audience great psychological distances, then campaign designers are best to plan change in small minimally discrepant increments.

Source credibility is apt to be a function of four factors: perceived expertise, perceived trustworthiness, how likeable the source is, and how dynamic they appear (Bettinghaus & Cody, 1994). The relative importance of these four factors will depend on the nature of the topic being discussed. Complex issues demand a high level of expertise. Objective issue require an expert source. Subjective issue require a similar source. Risky issues demand trust. Emotional issues are better communicated by a likeable source. Dynamic sources do better when the issues are unfamiliar and/or controversial. Careful audience analysis early in the campaign planning process can help identify sources that are perceived to be credible. Importantly, audience analysis will also help identify which sources are *not* credible, avoiding the all too common mistake of having the wrong spokesperson.

Diffusion of Innovations

Additional theoretical guidance for designing persuasive communication campaigns can be obtained from work published by Everett Rogers (1995). Three parts to this work are relevant here -- the first provides additional ideas for message design, the second provides additional ideas for assessing target audiences, and the third contributes important ideas for sequencing the various stages of a campaign and the selection of communication channels for each stage.

ATTRIBUTES OF THE BEHAVIOR

Rogers defined five characteristics of promoted behaviors that affect the rate that they are adopted. These factors should be optimized in the early stages of a campaign when defining the new behavior (innovation) to be adopted and when designing the content of messages used to promote the behavior.

- ○ *Relative advantage* -- The economic, social, physical, and psychological costs and benefits of the proposed behavior are compared to the costs and benefits of the existing behavior. The proposed behavior must be viewed as the more profitable choice.
- ○ *Compatibility* -- The more the proposed behavior is viewed as fitting well with existing beliefs, attitudes, behaviors, and available resources, the more likely it is to be adopted.
- ○ *Complexity* -- The less complex the proposed behavior appears, the more likely it is to be adopted.

○ *Trialability* -- The more the proposed idea can be used experimentally or in a limited way initially, thus giving audience members a chance to test the innovation with minimal investment, the more likely it is to be adopted.

○ *Observability* -- The more visible and concrete the outcome of the proposed behavior is, the more likely the audience is to adopt it and the more apt they are to realize that others are engaging in the behavior, thus speeding the pace of adoption across the community.

ADOPTER GROUPS

For various reasons (e.g., available time, money, ability, or access to resources), new behaviors are adopted by individuals at different rates. Rogers (1995) describes five categories that represent the different groups that individuals might fall into based on their rate of adoption. Segmentation of an audience into these groups early in the campaign design process will help planners focus their efforts on the group that is likely to adopt early and have the most influence on the rest of the population, thus increasing the effectiveness and efficiency of their efforts. According to Rogers, over time, individuals who it was determined adopt at a slower pace and were therefore not part of the initial target audience, will model the behavior of the *Early Adopter* group.

○ *Innovators* - represent three to five percent of the population and are the first group to adopt a new behavior. This group has both the inclination and resources to adopt new ideas quickly. Innovators do not tend to adhere to social norms very closely and therefore often appear somewhat eccentric.

○ *Early Adopters* - comprise about fifteen percent of the population and follow the Innovators as the second group to adopt a new behavior. In addition to having the required resources and ability, early adopters are highly respected by peers and become role models for new ideas.

○ *Early Majority* - following the Early Adopters in terms of the pace of adoption. This group, comprising about one third of the population, prefer to ponder new ideas and observe the results of those who have gone first. They tend to have slightly less resources and/or ability and are therefore more risk adverse than earlier adopters.

O *Late Majority* - represent another third of the population and, as the name implies, adopt the promoted behavior later than previous groups. For various reasons, this group tends to be more risk adverse and/or skeptical of new ideas and will not generally adopt until social or economic pressure cause them to do so.

O *Laggards* - the remaining fifteen percent of a population, are the last group to consider adopting a promoted behavior and are often incapable of change for many socio-economic reasons.

Early Adopters tend to exhibit more education, status, and economic stability than later adopters do. Lamble (1984) states, "on the basis of personality variables, Early Adopters tend to have a higher level of empathy, ability to deal with abstractions, rationality, intelligence, achievement motivation, and aspirations, and more favorable attitudes toward change, risk, education, and science." Early Adopters are the logical audience segment to target in a communication campaign.

STAGES OF ADOPTION

A diagram displayed earlier in this chapter depicted the causal relationship between knowledge, attitudes, behavior intentions, and conservation behaviors. This model can be interpreted in a temporal sense to mean that individuals will first learn about and adopt positive attitudes about a proposed behavior prior to forming intentions to adopt the new behavior and subsequently acting on these intentions. The model suggests that the behavior change process can be broken down into distinct stages. Further support for a staged approach to behavior change can be garnered from early work by Bohlen (1955) who discussed five stages of a behavior change process (see below).

O Stage 1: Awareness – the individual becomes aware of the proposed behavior.

O Stage 2: Interest – the individual becomes interested in the proposed behavior.

○ Stage 3: Evaluation – the costs and benefits of the proposed behavior are assessed by the individual.
○ Stage 4: Trial – the proposed behavior is attempted by the individual on a limited/experimental basis.
○ Stage 5: Adoption/Rejection – the individual chooses to adopt or reject the proposed behavior.

Building on Bohlen's work, Rogers and Shoemaker (1971) reduced these five stages to four in their widely popular Diffusion of Innovation model (see below). Conceptually, in terms of temporal stages, this model closely resembles the five stage sequence.

○ Stage 1: Knowledge – the individual becomes aware and seeks knowledge concerning the proposed behavior.
○ Stage 2: Persuasion – the individual adopts/changes key attitudes reflecting that the proposed behavior is a positive activity.
○ Stage 3: Decision – the individual forms the intention to practice the proposed behavior.
○ Stage 4: Confirmation – the individual performs the behavior and either adopts it in a permanent fashion or rejects it.

Campaign planners can use these models to guide the sequencing of the various stages of a campaign. Initially campaign resources are directed to educational efforts. Mediated communication channels (e.g., television, radio, printed matter) can be used for these purposes. Once it is determined that the target audience is aware, interested, and possesses basic knowledge about the issues, campaign resources can be directed to more persuasive efforts. Mediated, as well as group communication channels (e.g., field days, demonstration tours), can be used for these purposes. Messages that discuss the consequences, risks, norms, and efficacy of the issues are presented in a motivational manner. Once it is determined that the target audience intends to act in the prescribed way, assurance that the required resources are available and reinforcement through interpersonal contact become campaign tactics.

Applying Diffusion Theory

Information used in the construction of this sidebar was adapted from Snyder, L. B. & Broderick, S. H. (1992). Communicating with Woodland Landowners. Journal of Forestry (March).

Since 1984 the Coverts Project in Connecticut has attempted to overcome motivation and adoption issues among landowners using the Diffusion of Innovations Model described by Rogers (1983). The land management project is conducted by the University of Connecticut Cooperative Extension System.

During the critical persuasion/decision stage, a potential adopter is forming definitive opinions about an innovation. Numerous diffusion studies have shown that at this stage a knowledgeable peer, one who has had positive experiences with the innovation, frequently makes a difference between whether the idea is tried or abandoned (Rogers, 1983). The presence of such an "opinion leader" who is willing to share experiences freely can reduce fear and uncertainty about the practice and encourage movement into the trial and adoption stages.

The University of Connecticut project applies the concept of opinion leadership by training volunteers to be opinion leaders in natural resource management. Their role is not only to disseminate knowledge and create awareness about natural resource management, but to close the gap between the knowledge and behavior of fellow landowners. Potential volunteers are usually nominated by natural resource professionals or existing volunteers based on their leadership ability, past community involvement, communication skills, and land management experience.

New volunteers attend an intensive three-and-a-half day training seminar. The seminar's educational messages are specifically tailored to meet the wants and needs of local woodland owners. In Connecticut this typically means emphasizing wildlife and esthetic benefits. Project sponsors invest considerable time and resources in each volunteer and provide considerable follow-up education. In exchange, volunteers are asked to share their new knowledge with other woodland owners. Specifically, participants agree to:

○ Develop and implement appropriate management practices for their own land.
○ Take advantage of opportunities to use their land as a local demonstration areas.
○ Use the library of reference materials provided by the project to answer questions from other landowners.
○ Publicize their involvement in the project and their availability as an information resource for the community.

The project was initially evaluated in 1992 and again in 1998. In 1992, significant positive differences were found between volunteer-active and inactive areas in terms of awareness of the project's existence, attitudes toward the importance of land management, and contact with natural resource professionals. Four times as many landowners who were aware of the project had management plans than those who did not, and at least one third of them developed their plans after contact with a project volunteer. In 1998, it was found that contact with project volunteers increased as people moved through the stages of adoption. People who had developed land management plans, set goals to manage their forested land, and implemented wildlife habitat improvements had the greatest contact with project volunteers. The data support the diffusion of innovation hypothesis regarding the importance of interpersonal ties in motivating people through the adoption process.

Sense of Place Theory

The theories discussed so far in this chapter were selected because of their proven practicality. A more contemporary body of theory that appears to hold promise is based on the psychological attachment a person has for their surrounding environment and how this "sense-of-place" affects their treatment of this environment. Studies of the human response to the physical environment came to light in the mid 70's with the seminal work of Yi-Fu Tuan's *Topophilia* (1974) and *Space & Place: The Perspective of Experience* (1977). Tuan coined the phrase "sense of place" and defined it as the "human need to belong to a meaningful and reasonably stable world, and [at] different levels of consciousness, from an almost organic sense of identity that is an effect of habituation ... to a more conscious awareness of the values of middle scale places such as neighborhood, city and landscape, to an intellectual appreciation of the planet earth itself as home."

Sense-of-place has been applied across the disciplines of urban planning, natural resource conservation, conservation psychology, and environmental communication. The concept has undergone a variety of reassessments, adaptations and extensions within each field based upon its applicability and appropriateness, place identity, place theory and place attachment (Bott, Cantrill and Myers, 2003; Cantrill and Senecah, 2001).

In terms of influencing environmental behaviors, sense-of-place can shape individual perceptions of place and how we act toward this environment. Sense-of-place moves beyond the supposition that place merely serves as the physical background to everyday life. Research has revealed the importance of emotional attachments to the environment in the development of identity processes, as well as the influence of environmental values in maintaining social relationships (Rogan, O'Connor and Horwitz, 2005).

Cantrill and Senecah (2001) expanded on the notion of sense-of-place to include "senses- of-selves-in-place." They defined the latter as a process by which "our perceptions of who we are given where we live... serve as potent mediators in the process of attending to or embracing conservation-oriented practices." The authors contend that "cognitive representations of the self-in-place form the major link between how people appraise communication and how they behave in the environment." In other words, people's sense of self and place tend to be directly linked to their local settings. It is through experiences in these local settings and the perceptions of local environment that influence how people view and interpret environmental issues and react to environmental communication messages. Further, sense-of-self-in-place plays a noticeable role in mediating the degree to which people adopt environmentally responsible behaviors.

Cantrill and Senecah (2001) explored cases involving regional natural-resource conflicts and tension between local stakeholders and non-local land-use advocates. One particular study addressed the State of New York's intention to implement management recommendations for the Adirondack Park. Research methods included coding of primary and archival documents, press clippings, participant observation and interviews over a nine year period.

The researchers found that the park had a long history of tension between the Adirondackers (the native people who have inhabited the park since the 1770's) and the New York State government because of the government's dependence on the annual revenue from vacationer's who use the park seasonally. Tension has been persistent between the generations of local inhabitants and the continual influx of seasonal vacationers. Understandably, the Adirondackers maintain a strong sense-of-self-in-place to the region, steeped in a long history and established culture. What the authors pointed out was how "a sense-of-self-in-place from the cultural and political past can still powerfully influence the present (194)."

Cantrill and Senecah (2001) identified the deep-seated resentments held by the native Adirondackers towards state-imposed policy which they felt catered to wealthy tourists while simultaneously marginalizing native residents. This resentment supported the authors' argument that long-term residents senses-of-selves-in-place are influenced by the residues of past relationships with humans as well as the land.

From a sociological perspective, the Adirondackers situation can be understood through Gustafson's three-pole model (Turner & Turner, 2006). Gustafson identified a) self, b) environment and c) others as the three dimensions of meaning attributed to place. *Self* involves an individual's identity and emotion. The local inhabitants of the Adirondacks maintained a strong sense of self-identity and emotion tied to their environment. The relationship between the self and the Adirondack Park environment acquired deep levels of meaning to the local inhabitants because of their long history and established culture in the region. This directly affects their environmental behaviors.

Gustafson's *environment* refers to the physical features of the place and its events and establishments (Turner & Turner 2006). Increased tourism and government-led policies changed the face of the Adirondacks for the local inhabitants. The changes in the physical environment led to increasing tension between the locals and vacationers. Finally, Gustafson's *other* refers to people's characteristics and behavior. Understandably, the self-environment relationship for vacationers differs dramatically from the self-environment relationship of the local inhabitants of the Adirondacks.

The concept of sense-of-place may be of practical importance. Environmentalists and policy makers alike are calling for societal change in terms of lifestyle, land-use, consumerism and behavior patterns. In recent decades there has been tremendous growth in participation by citizens, business groups and non-profit organizations in decisions about the environment. Understanding sense-of-place values held by a targeted audience will provide resource management and social marketing practitioner insights into how emotional bonds with a person's immediate environment affect their responses to environmental communication messages and in turn their environmentally-related behaviors.

Conclusion

The theories that have been discussed in this chapter were chosen because of their potential usefulness in guiding social marketing campaigns. Theory allows us to predict outcomes and knowing the probable outcome of our choices ahead of time allows us to strategically plan the efforts we choose to implement. Yet, conditions are uncontrolled in the "real-world" (i.e., each context is unique). The challenge is to define the context clearly and select theories to guide your decisions accordingly. Because theory application is so situationally dependent, rarely can it be applied without creative and intelligent adaptation. In addition, rarely will one theory provide all the guidance you need. The most useful guidance is achieved by applying theories in combination -- borrowing bits of wisdom from many theories.

CHAPTER 5
MARKET/INCENTIVE STRATEGIES

Introduction

As Focht (1995) states, under conditions of high scientific and high social consensus, it is ethical to mandate a required course of action. Change agents can do this by providing incentives and disincentives. A desirable behavior may be elicited and then followed with a reward (e.g., financial subsidy) or an undesirable behavior may be exhibited and followed by a punishment (e.g., legal penalty or taxation). Rewards can motivate an individual to perform the behavior repeatedly. Punishments will discourage the performance of a behavior.

McKenzie-Mohr and Smith (1999) provide several examples of using reinforcement strategies in an environmental context.

- Waste reduction – In Worchester, Massachusetts a program that required residents to purchase garbage bags (a disincentive) resulted in a 37% increase in recycling and a 45% reduction in the waste stream.
- Beverage Deposits – The introduction of bottle deposits (a disincentive) brought about a 68% reduction in litter in Oregon, 76% reduction in Vermont, and an 82% reduction in Michigan.
- Energy efficiency – Many utility companies throughout the U.S. have offered subsidized grants (an incentive) to help homeowners retrofit their homes. These changes can result in a 30-50% reduction in their energy usage.

- Transportation – Many municipalities throughout the U.S. have introduced commuter lanes that bypass traffic congestion that can only be used by multi-occupant vehicles (an incentive).

Solutions to Social Dilemmas

Reinforcement strategies are often the strategy of choice when faced with symptoms of a "social dilemma". Individuals strive to use their limited time and money in a manner that will enable them to get ahead. But sometimes this self-interest can lead to less than optimum management practices. The same principle can be applied on a larger scale. Companies and municipalities are also driven by self-interest. The deleterious practices of just a few individuals, companies or municipalities can endanger the natural resources of many. Situations like these can potentially become social dilemmas (see sidebar).

Social Dilemmas

How do we manage natural resources such as soil, water, plants, and wildlife without constraining individuals' rights to do what they choose on their own land? Individuals strive to use their limited time and money in a manner that will enable them to get ahead. This self-interest can lead to less than optimum management practices. The cumulative effects of deleterious practices by just a few individuals can endanger the natural resource base of the municipality they reside in. The cumulative effects of ill-planned growth by just a few municipalities can endanger the natural resource base of broad geographic regions.

Situations that involve multiple stakeholders, can potentially become "social dilemmas". Such dilemmas can be defined by two characteristics: a) each individual receives a higher payoff for a socially noncooperative choice than for a socially cooperative choice no matter what other individuals in society do, but b) all individuals are better off if all cooperate than if all do not (Dawes, 1980). Common reasons for noncooperation include a) the perception that the costs outweigh the benefits, b) fear of being played a "sucker" and sacrificing options and/or income by cooperating when few others actually do, and c) the belief that a critical mass of individuals is already cooperating and one can "free ride" on these efforts with little notice or effect (Weiner & Doescher, 1991).

Historically, much of the effort to resolve common property social dilemmas has involved either a) rewards or punishments to encourage or discourage behavior (i.e., governmental incentives/disincentives) or b) regulation and enforcement (i.e., laws). These measures, because they are cost/labor intensive or implemented at the expense of individual autonomy, risk being unsustainable and they tend to address symptoms of the dilemma, not the causes. Some policy makers think it would be more sustainable to formulate communication strategies that persuade individuals to voluntarily cooperate in the interest of the broader community.

Findings from a case review of successful self-governing community property management groups conducted by Elinor Ostrom (1990) found that the more successful groups tended to believe that: a) harm would come if one did not cooperate, b) benefits of the resource could not be discounted, c) personal costs of cooperation were low, d) strong norms defined proper behavior, and e) the groups were close-knit so that the efficacy of their individual and collective actions were easily observable.

Efficacy of Reinforcement Strategies

Reinforcement and regulatory strategies are frequently the choice of governmental agencies charged with protecting society against the potentially destructive actions of self-interest/social dilemmas. Though these strategies can elicit a fairly rapid change in behavior and are therefore good when problems need a quick fix, the sustainability of incentive based and regulatory strategies is questionable because they are cost and/or labor intensive.

Though Bowles (2008) states that incentives may induce long-term change by inducing more self-interested behavior even after the incentives are withdrawn, there is also evidence to suggest that reinforcement strategies do not lead to permanent behavior change; i.e., individuals are apt to revert to their original behavior once the reinforcement is removed (Bettinghaus & Cody, 1994). Bowles (2008) claims that prior to the 18th century and development of economic theories, social cooperation was achieved by appealing to a person's civic virtues; but that in today's complex global society where we are often unfamiliar with those we must interact with, civic morals are often not adequate motivation. So, the conclusion may be that incentives have their place but that consideration of the greater good is still essential to the sustainable performance of institutions and communities.

Market Based Reinforcement

An article in The Economist (2005a) suggests that a new evolving form of reinforcement may be a more efficacious route to environmental protection. The article leads with the statement that "today's environmentalism is just another special interest... where mandate, regulate, litigate has been the mantra" and goes on to say that "if environmental groups continue to reject pragmatic solutions... they will lose the battle of ideas".

The pragmatic solutions that the article refers to employ market-based incentives that may be more sustainable then other types of incentive-based strategies (e.g., subsidies) as long as the correct market forces are in place. This may include assignment of individual property rights over what have historically been unlimited public resources (e.g., a fisheries where there is an incentive for fisher-folk to better manage their patch of the ocean), tradable emissions quotas that provide companies with financial incentives to adopt clean technologies, efforts to value services such as water filtration and flood prevention to provide farmers and forest owners with incentives to practice good land stewardship, or where a water utility might charge more per liter as consumption increases therefore rewarding conservation behavior and penalizing over-consumption.

For example, there have been suggestions that users of the Panama Canal should pay surrounding landowners to reforest the watershed to control siltation and nutrient overload that threatens the ability of commerce to move through the canal. The scheme will have environmental, social and economic benefits. Another example of using market-based incentives was the decision by the City of New York to pay farmers to protect wetlands in the catchment area that supplies the city's drinking water. The wetlands filtering potential was considered a valued ecological service. The decision was significantly less expensive than building a multi-billion dollar filtration plant (see sidebar).

The challenge, according to The Economist (2005b), is to do good science so that good information can be used to set realistic prices that can lead to realistic cost:benefit analyses. Driving these initiatives is a) the realization that the environment can no longer be treated as a "free good", b) that society needs a better understanding of what the environment does for it, and c) that there is a need to accept that the marginal costs of improvement may not be worth the overall cost (e.g., the incremental cost of removing the last percentage of a pollutant may not make sense).

Market-based incentives

New York City has the largest water system in the country that draws its water from a natural, unfiltered source. This source is the upper Delaware River watershed in the Catskill Mountains approximately 120 miles to the north and west of the city. The area encompasses 2000 square miles spread across eight counties. Nearly all the land in this area is forested and privately owned. There are 500 farms and 60 towns in the area. The watershed provides 1.3 billion gallons of water per day to nine million people in the city (Appleton, 2002).

In 1989, New York City was faced with finding an affordable solution to comply with the federal Safe Drinking Water Act. Water quality was evaluated and filtration was said to be necessary for compliance. Because the estimated cost to build the necessary filtration systems was enormous ($8 billion), the city looked at alternatives. After significant research and deliberation, in lieu of constructing a filtration system, the city proposed a comprehensive, long-range watershed protection program aimed at integrating a variety of management options to protect and improve the quality of drinking water. The key to the program was to change the way many farmers practiced their trade.

To promote the use of agricultural best management practices, the New York City Department of Environmental Protection funded the voluntary Watershed Agricultural Program. The program, founded in 1992, is a voluntary partnership between the city and the farmers. The city paid both the operating cost of the program and the capital costs for pollution control measures on each farm as an incentive to get farmers to participate. Later a stipend was added to compensate farmers for their time. From 1995 to 1999, the city committed $35.2 million to support the program.

Farmers administered the program through a Watershed Agricultural Council that contracted with local farm support services and academic resources to provide needed technical assistance. The program custom designed pollution control techniques unique to each farm to maximize effectiveness and minimize cost. The techniques were integrated with the farmer's business plan and management practices (Appleton, 2002). By 1997, 287 out of 350 eligible farms in the watershed region had signed on to the program. Of these, 155 completed comprehensive plans and signed implementation agreements. The program which now includes 95 percent of all farms in the Catskills, has not only reduced agricultural pollution by close to 75 percent, but it has also earned the reputation of being one of the most successful agricultural pollution control programs in the United States.

Innovative Incentive Strategies

THE NATURE CONSERVANCY

The Nature Conservancy (TNC), the world's largest conservation organization, has pioneered several innovative incentive strategies. TNC possesses sophisticated financial expertise that has allowed it to develop unique and creative mechanism to help conserve our natural resources.

One such strategy was implemented in September of 2011 in Morro Bay, California. TNC helped the Fort Bragg Groundfish Association and the Central Coast Sustainable Groundfish Association develop a community-focused fishing agreement. The agreement "pioneered a cooperative approach between local fishery stakeholders to keep fishing communities in business, keep local seafood on our tables and help protect our marine resources" (The Nature Conservancy, 2011).

According to the Conservancy (2011) the agreement was the culmination of a six year effort to establish new fishing models that are more environmentally and economically sustainable. It involved the adoption of a fishing quota system. The Conservancy (2011) helped finalize an agreement to formalize an overfished species quota "risk pool" that helped maximize conservation and economic opportunities and retained local access to fish. Risk pool is the term used for a community-based fishing agreement.

The goal was to sustain the fishery by using improved data collection methods to monitor fish populations and promote the adoption of less damaging fishing techniques. The Conservancy wanted to help the fisherman keep better track of what they were catching while using better and safer ways to catch fish. Safer fishing meant ensuring they were not harming the areas that they fished any more than necessary. Initially, to clean the slate, TNC bought all of the fishing licenses issued for the area and purchased several of the fishermen's boats.

Skeptics initially thought that TNC was trying to shut down commercial fishing in the area. This would have been very damaging to the local communities of Monterey, Half Moon Bay and Fort Bragg. This was not the goal of the Conservancy. TNC wanted to develop a partnership that would help maintain local businesses based on a more sustainable fishing industry.

Once TNC bought the fishing licenses and boats, they then leased some back to local fisherman with the understanding that new sustainable fishing methods would be followed. TNC monitors what is caught, when it is caught and where it is caught. They rely on local fishermen to report this information using an iPad- based eCatch system provided by the Conservancy. Marketing assistance is provided to help fishermen find low volume/high dollar outlets for their catch. The program has helped maintain jobs and has provided greater stability in terms of the impact of fishing on fish populations. They say they are fishing smarter, not harder. Leslie Kaufman (2011) states that the "well-financed effort is among the most technologically advanced and coordinated [conservation efforts] in the country".

Another incentive-based conservation strategy implemented by TNC involved the Katahdun Forest in Maine. The project marked a pair of firsts for The Nature Conservancy. It was the first time a conservation group had ever financed a paper mill and it was the first use of New Market Tax credits to attract an investor to an environmental project (The Nature Conservancy, 2002).

The Great Northern Paper Company (GNPC) owned and managed forests around Mount Katahdun. The land is located in Baxter State Park and is part of the Appalachian Trail. The forests fed mills that helped make GNPC the 10th largest employer in the state.

In 2002, GNPC faced financial problems and was looking for ways to avoid bankruptcy. The easiest way to do this was to sell off the land it owned around Mount Katahdun. It was forecasted that selling this land would be catastrophic, not only to the economy and people who depended on GNPC, but to the enthusiasts who enjoyed the land for recreation, hunting and fishing.

In August of 2002 the Conservancy and the GNPC entered into an agreement to protect more than 240,000 acres of forestland around the mountain. The land around the mountain contained thousands of acres of mature forests, some of which had not been harvested in over 100 years. The goal of the project was to maintain core forest and protect wildlife corridors within the area. The basis of the agreement between the Conservancy and the GNPC was unique. The GNPC transferred 46,000 acres in the Debsconeag Lakes Wilderness area to the Conservancy, and then placed an easement on 195,000 additional acres around the mountain (The Nature Conservancy, 2002). Within that easement they guaranteed public access, recreation, sustainable forestry and perhaps most important, no further development. The Conservancy then purchased $50 million of GNPC's debt and retired $14 million of it. They refinanced the balance for less than half of the current rate, allowing the GNPC to remain in business.

The USDA Forest Service stated that by creating a working forest easement on close to 200,000 acres, the project ensured that important timberland could be sustainably managed for forest products while helping to maintain area jobs. The project brought together federal conservation and economic development funding to save trees and jobs (USDA Forest Service, 2006).

"The Katahdun Forest Project is more than an innovative agreement between the nation's largest conservation organization and the region's biggest employer," according to Kent Wommack, executive director of TNC in Maine (The Environment News Service, 2002). "The goal of this project is to provide a healthy future for these forests and long term stability for these mills. We are doing this in a way that honors GNPC's long tradition of conservation and stewardship, the community's needs, and the recreational values of Maine people".

TRADEABLE EMISSION QUOTAS

The TNC example described above illustrates how innovative incentive strategies can be employed on a local scale. On a national or international scale, cap and trade policies provide incentives for states and nations to reduce their carbon emissions in an effort to curb climate change (see sidebar). An example of a cap and trade policy on a regional scale can be seen with the innovative nitrogen trading scheme developed for the Lake Taupo catchment of New Zealand, a country which prides itself on its clean/green image and where the health of the agriculture-based economy is inherently linked to environmental conditions.

According to the *Environment New Zealand 2007* report released by the New Zealand Ministry for the Environment (2007), the health of the natural environment plays an integral role in supporting New Zealand's top two export earners: ecotourism and agriculture production. In 2007, agriculture, forestry, horticulture, and viticulture generated $16.1 billion, $3.6 billion, $2.5 billion, and $662 million respectively in export earnings. In other words, about 17 percent of New Zealand's gross domestic product (GDP) depends on the top 15 centimeters of our soil. (New Zealand Ministry for the Environment, 2007).

As the population grows, so does demand for food and therefore agricultural production increases. According to the New Zealand Ministry for the Environment, between 1996 and 2006, the national dairy herd grew by 24% (2007). To sustain these increases, greater applications of inorganic fertilizers are needed to grow feed for these livestock. Greater fertilizer applications and greater amounts of manure from increased numbers of cattle creates heightened levels of nitrogen run-off into rivers and lakes. This creates unsightly algal blooms, reduced oxygen, and a less healthy fishery.

According to Stanford ecologist Dr. Peter Vitousek, excessive nitrogen levels pollute our water bodies and weaken biodiversity (Morgan, 2008). But nitrogen regulation is difficult. First, it is virtually impossible to monitor the nitrogen runoff of individual landowners. In addition, nitrogen levels based on type of livestock and number of livestock per hectare can be calculated, but it's difficult to account for the time it takes to reach the water source, which is an important factor. Nitrogen can move very slowly through soil and can take several years to reach a waterway. This means that farms that are closer to water bodies may require more regulation because nitrogen runoff can impact the waterways faster.

One strategy to help minimize levels of nitrogen runoff is called "Nitrogen Trading". New Zealand has developed ways to estimate nitrogen losses from individual farms based on previous "peak year" production averages. Using these figures, a number of allowable credits are assigned to a farmer based on land area and average number of livestock per hectare.

The system allows farmers to trade these nitrogen credits with one another. Farmers desiring credits because they have excess runoff can purchase them from farmers who have instituted measures to decrease runoff (and therefore have excess credits available to them). This provides an incentive for famers to institute measures to curb nitrogen runoff.

However, though this system has helped maintain nitrogen levels, critics say it has done little to reduce the overall amount of nitrogen entering the watershed as the same numbers of nitrogen credits remain available in the marketplace. In order to reduce nitrogen runoff, additional incentive/reinforcement strategies may be needed.

One additional strategy created to provide further support for the nitrogen credit program in New Zealand is a public fund set up to subsidize costs associated with removing 20% of the Nitrogen runoff. This is done by buying land, taking it out of production and putting it into a public trust. Selling land to a trust helps ensure the continued use and beauty of the land so farmers are apt to see themselves contributing to environmental preservation. This has public relations benefits for farmers and positive public opinion can be a powerful reinforcement. Another strategy created to aid the nitrogen credit program subsidizes farmers who take land out of livestock production to plant woodlots. These tree farms have little nitrogen runoff and the trees sequester carbon. Famers also receive payment from government for their carbon sequestration efforts that help the country meet national emission quotas.

Carbon Cap and Trade Strategy

Carbon emissions trading (also known as cap and trade strategies) offer a major incentive to businesses to limit their CO_2 emissions, a major contributor to global warming. A financial market has developed both internationally and nationally based on a company's ability to buy and sell carbon credits. These markets trade in billions of dollars annually.

Limits and rules of this scheme vary by country depending on whether the country signed the global Kyoto Protocol which set limits on the amount of CO_2 a country can emit. Those who have signed the protocol are mandated to meet their emissions standards. The United States is not yet one of those countries.

In this scheme, a company is given a set allowance of carbon emissions each year. If the company stays under its allowance, it is allowed to sell off the difference in the form of carbon credits. They can be sold to companies that have exceeded their limits. For those companies who exceed their allowable standards, they must purchase credits from companies who have cleaned up and no longer need them. It is a win-win situation for both companies, allowing the cleaner companies a source of revenue, and the polluting companies time to figure out how to reduce their emissions.

Several companies have become industry leaders when it comes to cap and trade strategies. Bank of America and BP are among the largest in the world to pledge their commitment to carbon reduction. The long-term investment angle, according to Stillman (2008) is that significant dividends will be paid later on. Carbon credits started relatively cheap, but their value continues to rise. The drawback according to Stillman (2008) is that too many credits can flood the market and cause them to lose value. Another constraint is the enforcement of trading rules, especially for those countries that have not signed the Kyoto Protocol. Carbon cap and trade is a billion dollar business. The end result is the potential for a cleaner/safer environment.

Conclusion

As previously stated, society needs to realize that the environment can no longer be treated as a "free good" and people need to better understand what the environment does for them. As mentioned, prior to the 18th century social cooperation was achieved by appealing to a person's civic virtues but in today's complex global less personal society, social morals may not be as strong a motivating factor. One might conclude that even though consideration of the greater good is still an essential element when trying to engineer cooperative care of our environment (especially when faced by a social dilemma), reinforcement strategies have their place especially when there is high scientific and high social consensus to mandate a required course of action. Yet, as stated, though reinforcement strategies can elicit a fairly rapid change in behavior, their sustainability is questionable because they are often highly cost and/or labor intensive.

CHAPTER 6
DIALOGIC/PARTICIPATORY STRATEGIES

Introduction

Focht (1995) asserts that dialogic/participatory strategies are useful when there is low scientific and low social consensus – i.e., when no clear solution is evident and all concerned parties must participate in open discussion to arrive at an acceptable plan of action. The public often disagrees about the nature of environmental issues sometimes because their short-term economic and long-term environmental motivations conflict and sometimes because the underlying science is ambiguous. Further exacerbating the problem is the fact that advocates for industry and advocates for the environment frequently find themselves in adversarial positions.

Industry's view that they are victimized by environmental advocates is reflected in a guide once developed for industrial environmental public relations professionals (Harrison, 1992). These views are still common today. In this publication, Harrison offers the following comparison of factors affecting environmental communication by industry and environmental advocacy groups.

- *Industry favors industrial growth while environmental advocates oppose industrial growth.*
- *The public has a general mistrust of industry while the public perceives environmental advocates to have high credibility.*
- *Industry is regulated at many levels by government while environmental advocates are not regulated.*
- *Industry is not aggressive and seeks thoughtful coverage from the media while environmental advocates are aggressive and seek dramatic coverage.*

In contrast, environment advocates often feel that they are the ones victimized by industry. For example, an announcement posted on a listserv for environmental communication academics about an upcoming International Greening of Industry Networking Conference elicited the following two comments (COCE, 1997):

"Why are we posting this on our listserv? I would hope that we would not lend our efforts to help business and industry communicate their green image. I think it is relatively safe to assume that the purpose of conferences like this is to help business face environmental challenges more effectively, not develop more "sustainable practices" – or at least this is the role environmental communication would end up playing. Certainly the bridges built there are more likely to help businesses operate more efficiently, on their terms, not gain access for environmental advocates to the decision-making channels of industry."

"Let's face it, environmentalism is cluttered with ironies, and, in my presumptuous mind, any discourse that involves the threads of economics and environmentalism, woven and spun together by clout from business and industry, is not only ironic, but I have to presume that the economic thread will win out. Am I to believe that business will cut into its bottom line simply because it wants to be perceived as "sustainable" or that it's "smart business." I'm sorry but I have to be critical of such ironic discourse."

Further to this point, in a keynote speech to the Society of Environmental Journalists in 2005, Bill Moyer, a leading American Journalist stated:

"Our government and corporate elites have turned against America's environmental visionaries". They have set out to eviscerate just about every significant (environmental) gain of the past generation and while they are at it they have managed to blame the environmental movement itself for the failure of the Green Revolution". He went on to provide evidence that the [Bush] administration had staffed key environmental positions with skeptics of environmental science and that industry uses Public Relations strategies to discredit hard science findings. The result, "in July of this year (2005), ABC News reported that 66% of the people in a new survey said they don't think global warming will affect their lives... [and] 45% of Americans hold a creation-based view of the world discounting Darwin's Theory of evolution... I don't think it is a coincidence that in a nation where nearly half our people believe in creationism, much of the populace also doubts the certainty of climate change science" (Moyer, 2005).

Because controversy often surrounds environmental issues, situations where there is low scientific and low social consensus are not uncommon. In such circumstances, dialogic/participatory strategies in which all concerned parties participate in open discussion to arrive at an acceptable plan of action will be necessary.

Pseudo versus Genuine Participation

Traditional modes of public engagement include public hearings and written comment. Depoe and Delicath (2004) have found several problems associated with these methods; e.g., experts often see their role as persuader, participation sometimes occurs late in the process after key decisions have already been made, and the process often becomes adversarial, especially when experts grow defensive when their decisions are questioned. Cox (2006, pp.121-122) concurs, listing the following as critical factors negatively affecting traditional forms of public engagement:

1. Public participation typically operates on technocratic models of rationality, in which policymakers, administrative officials, and experts see their roles as educating and persuading the public of the legitimacy of their decisions.
2. Public participation often occurs too late in the decision-making process, sometimes even after decisions have already been made.

3. Public participation often follows an adversarial trajectory, especially when public participation processes are conducted in a "decide-announce-defend" mode on the part of officials.

4. Public participation often lacks adequate mechanisms and forums for informed dialogue among stakeholders.

5. Public participation often lacks adequate provisions to ensure that input gained through public participation makes a real impact on decisions and outcomes.

One instigating factor fueling a move to more genuine dialogic/participatory communication strategies has to do with the inexperience and inability of ordinary citizens to defend their environment against the interests of larger corporate or political organizations. In the past, citizens were not given the same standing or legitimacy as corporate or governmental "experts". The public was often dismissed as unqualified to speak about technical matters and accused of inappropriate behavior during regulatory forums – something Cox refers to as "indecorous voice" (Cox, 2006 pp. 288). The need for more democratic forms of inclusion and the right of affected communities to be heard has sparked interest in more genuine dialogic/participatory communication strategies (Cox, 2006).

Shirley White (1994) makes a distinction between *pseudo participation*, where people participate in providing data in surveys and listening to conclusions drawn by campaign managers, and *genuine participation*, where people work cooperatively throughout the decision making process. As she points out, in terms of how genuine the participation is, distinguishing between participative/dialogic and persuasive/educational communication strategies can be a subjective judgment. Strategically promoting ideas based on research about a target audience's desires and concerns does solicit important input from the people, even though it may be a pseudo participative approach affected by the bias inherent in questions posed by the researcher and their subjective analyses. But the "genuine" participatory communicator also operates under a set of idiosyncratic assumptions that can bias the direction and tenor of dialog with people in the community.

A lack of clear distinction between pseudo and genuine participation is also illustrated by interpretations of the classic Shannon and Weaver Information Model (1969). This model posits discrete source, message, channel and receiver factors linked in a linear fashion with recognition that the receiver provides feedback to the sender. "Successful" communication is a function of the receiver decoding the message sent through the channel in the same way that the sender originally encoded it. This is a guiding concept in much persuasive communication.

A dialogic interpretation of Shannon and Weaver's Information Model has been offered by Syed Rahim (1994). In Rahim's model the feedback mechanism implies that the role of sender and receiver continuously switches back and forth. The meaning and value of information is not fixed in discrete messages. Participants question the meaning of messages. Meaning becomes a social product, interpreted idiosyncratically by individuals at first, and then fine-tuned by all parties through dialog. Economic, social, political, and cultural variables affect messages and meaning.

As with original interpretations of the Shannon and Weaver Information Model, Diffusion Theory (discussed in Chapter 4) often tends to be seen as a linear unidirectional model in which the main preoccupation is selling ideas or products (Ascroft & Agunga, 1994). However, Rogers (1983) recognized that some types of diffusion are better described by a model in which communication is a multi-directional process in which participants share information with one another with the goal of achieving mutual understanding.

According to Robert Cox (2006), effective/genuine collaboration requires that a) all relevant stakeholders be represented and have an equal chance to talk, b) all participants have equal access to information and resources, c) that decisions be reached by consensus, and d) that the recommendations eventually developed by the collaboration are acted upon. When followed, collaboration should lead to less competitiveness and more mutual learning, alleviate feelings of alienation and powerlessness yielding feelings of greater ownership, provide a sense of responsibility and freedom from dependence on experts, and build leadership capacity in the community (Walker, 2004; White, 1982). In addition, because implementation is shared across many parties, more can be accomplished in a set amount of time.

The National Academy of Science and the National Academy of Engineering recently released a report claiming that public participation is more likely to improve rather than to undermine the quality of decisions. The report states that it is important for scientists to know public concerns when framing scientific questions so that their analyses address all relevant issues. The report recognizes that scientists are usually the best ones to analyze environmental issues but that good analysis requires information about local conditions which is best obtained from local residents (National Research Council, 2008).

Dialogic/Participatory Communication

Thankfully, dialogic/participatory communication has become an increasingly common methodology with governmental agencies, particularly with the United States Environmental Protection Agency (EPA), because it leads to greater ownership by stakeholders in decisions, which in turn leads to more sustainable results. The frustrations with traditional forms of participatory communication as discussed above, has led to new ways of achieving genuine public participation. These new strategies include: scoping meetings, focus groups, listening sessions, advisory committees, blue ribbon commissions, citizen juries, negotiated rule making, consensus building exercises, working groups, and professional facilitation (Cox, 2006). An indication of changing philosophies about public participation was President George W. Bush's executive order calling for "facilitation of cooperative conservation" which required federal agencies such as the EPA and the Departments of Interior and Agriculture to collaborate with private landowners and local governments when formulating environmental rules that impact these parties (Cox, 2006 pp.122). A more contemporary viewpoint was expressed by Miriah Russo Kelly when she was at Oregon State University (see sidebar).

Experts in the Field

Miriah Russo Kelly defines participatory communication as "the process that occurs when diverse stakeholders are called to collaborate in the process of joint decision making or for the purpose of enacting a decision" (Kelly, 2012). She noted that level of "participation" is subject to interpretation.

"Participation is perceived by some as simply allowing people to be present at public meetings" (Kelly, 2012). Alternatively, scholars like Kelly believe that true participation is achieved when the viewpoints of all parties that are impacted by the decision are considered. "In some cases it is most appropriate to have stakeholders participate in dialogue that determines how the decision making will occur," said Kelly.

Kelly's research has found the benefits of participatory communication include the opportunity for people to truly have a "say" in the process. This fosters constructive conflict, allows them to learn from others, and helps them feel empowered. Kelly believes some of the weaknesses include the amount of time it takes to develop good participatory communication and the psychological, social, organizational barriers that usually crop up when employing a more participatory approach to communicating. She is convinced that in order for this process to be successful, there are a couple requirements that must initially be met. First, it is important that there is an effective facilitator and or mediator to guide the conversation and equalize power within the group. The second requirement is the need to have a dedicated group of stakeholders who are committed to the participatory process.

There are many environmental issues that can benefit from a more participatory approach. According to Kelly, she has seen this approach work successfully in the U.S. involving fire management/prevention planning and when developing management strategies for invasive species control. One project that Kelly worked on that incorporated participatory communication was in the Lake Brunner region of New Zealand. "I worked on a project that invited landowners to join a network of other farmers/landowners who wanted to improve the water quality conditions of the region. The New Zealand Landcare Trust acted as a neutral third party who facilitated collaboration amongst state and county officials, government agencies and the local landowners. Most of the farmers in the region signed on to the project that provided them with resources and helped them improve farm practices for the purpose of water quality enhancement. Participatory communication was used throughout the project and was the main contributor to its success. The participatory approach allowed stakeholders to work together in a meaningful way, develop new ways to improve conditions, and learn about their impacts on the ecosystem."

A case study of successful collaboration in an environmental context occurred in 2000 in Haddam, Connecticut. In this particular case, a community worked together to clean up some Brownfields properties (abandoned polluted industrial sites). Their aim was to remove environmental contamination, reuse properties that had been unused for some time, and increase the tax base.

Case Study: A Rural Application of the Sustainable Brownfields Redevelopment Process

In June of 2000 the small town of Haddam, Connecticut was awarded a grant by the EPA to be used to assess possible contamination of three sites in Higganum Center and develop a plan for their reuse. The three properties were the old Higganum Fire House, a Department of Transportation maintenance facility, and the town garage. The project's goals were to assess the properties, determine if there were contaminants on the sites, estimate the cost to clean up the properties depending on the type of reuse expected, while simultaneously facilitating decisions by the public on how these locations could be reused to improve the town.

This project was part of the United States Environmental Protection Agency's (EPA) Brownfields Program. This program was developed in 1995 to "empower states, communities, and stakeholders in economic redevelopment to work together in a timely manner in order to assess, safely clean up, and sustainably reuse brownfields" (EPA website, 2012). A "brownfield" is a property whose expansion, redevelopment, or reuse may be complicated by the presence or potential presence of a hazardous substance, pollutant, or contaminant" (EPA website, 2012). According to the EPA, more than 450,000 brownfields are located in the United States. The EPA provides funding assistance to communities to help them clean up and reinvest in these properties; inevitably increasing the local tax base, encouraging job growth, while improving and protecting the environment (EPA website, 2012).

Ann Faust, the project coordinator, stated that the first task was to perform environmental assessments on the three properties. Once this was done it was determined that there were no immediate health risks, contamination did exist but it was not acute. The next step involved communicating these findings to the community and developing plans for redevelopment (Faust 2012). Four groups of stakeholders were identified. The first group was tax-paying homeowners. Any investment by the town would require their input because public approval is required to pass a town budget. The second group were local youth because the town recognized the need for recreational facilities for them. The third group of stakeholders were the business owners in town whose voice was considered integral to project success. The fourth group consisted of members of the various town committees and commissions. These individuals were considered leaders in the community who could influence friends and neighbors.

The project used the local monthly town bulletin, posters around town, the town website, and interpersonal contact to communicate with homeowners and get them to public meetings. The youth were contacted at school via the environmental club. Project staff worked with club members to show them how contaminants move in the soil and how to test for water problems. The youth and their parents were invited to public meetings. Local business owners were a challenge to communicate with because their free time is so limited. Most could not attend evening public meetings because of business responsibilities so project staff met with these people individually. Commission and committee members from the town Conservation Commission, Economic Development Commission, Planning and Zoning Commission, Board of Finance, Board of Selectman, and the Haddam Land Trust were contacted at their regularly scheduled meetings.

To get started, stakeholders' opinions were surveyed. The survey was used to determine how they wanted to see the town developed, in particular the three brownfields sites. Survey results provided discussion subjects for subsequent meetings. Meetings were held monthly for over a year. Some meetings were facilitated by a town planner/architect. Plans and designs were drafted. Results of meetings were publicized in the town bulletin. Attendance at these meetings varied, but a large core group of committed supporters surfaced. When final plans were taken to a town meeting for a public vote and the usual nay-sayers turned out claiming they had not been informed, the core group of supporters turned the tables on them and the plans were voted on affirmatively.

At the end of the project a second survey was initiated to determine if there had been any opinion changes over the life of the project. Results indicated that there had been positive changes and that the dialogic/ participatory nature of the project helped greatly in cultivating a sense of inclusion and ownership in the outcomes.

Collaborative Learning

Research by Walker, Senecah and Daniels (2006) on collaboration and consensus processes among two government agency-based planning efforts, found that stakeholders prefer active engagement, access to information and events, and clearly defined decision space. The two projects, the Allegheny National Forest management plan revision and the Columbia River regional sediment management initiative, employed Daniels and Walker's (2001) Collaborative Learning (CL) approach to stakeholder involvement.

Based on systems theory, CL attempts to promote active learning, unrestricted communication and conflict management amongst multiple parties in complex and controversial situations (Walker, et al., 2006; Daniels and Walker, 2001). The approach operates on three levels: philosophy, framework and technique (Daniels and Walker 2001). Each level attempts to improve existing situations by viewing the situations as a set of interrelated systems. Further, the approach defines improvement as "feasible change" and encourages active and mutual learning, systematic thinking, debate and shared power between stakeholders and agencies (Daniels and Walker, 2001). According to Cox (2012, pp 127), Walker's collaborative learning approach has eight attributes that distinguish it from traditional forms of public participation:

1. Collaboration is less competitive.
2. Collaboration features mutual learning and fact-finding.
3. Collaboration allows underlying value differences to be explored.
4. Collaboration resembles principled negotiation, focusing on interests rather than
5. individual positions.
6. Collaboration allocates the responsibility for implementation across many parties.
7. Conclusions are generated by participants through an interactive, iterative and reflective process.
8. Collaboration is often an ongoing process.
9. Collaboration has the potential to build individual and community capacity in such areas as conflict management, leadership, decision-making, and communications.

The Walker, Senecah and Daniels (2006) research assessed stakeholder views on civic engagement by employing Senecah's "Trinity of Voice" (Senecah, 2004). According to this collaboration and consensus-oriented approach, three interdependent elements should be present: access, standing and influence (Senecah, 2004). Access refers to stakeholders' right to openly exchange ideas and opinions. Essentially, access gives a voice to stakeholders who do not readily have a voice in conventional public involvement projects. Standing in the Trinity of Voice builds off of access and refers to evidence that stakeholder voices are not only heard but also valued, respected and honored (Senecah, 2004). Influence is a culmination of access and standing, but goes further to involve active participation in joint efforts leading to learning, the development of improvements and ultimately mutual goals (Senecah, 2004).

Schusler, Decker and Pfeffer (2003) researched "social learning" for collaborative natural resource management. Their findings echo several elements of CL and the Trinity of Voice. Open communication, diverse participation and constructive conflict were found to be associated with civic engagement and learning (Schusler, et al., 2003).

Similar to CL which emphasizes "talking with, rather than talking at," the Schusler, Decker and Pfeffer findings assert that open communication to foster learning requires dialogue as opposed to monologues (Walker, et al. 2006; Schusler, et al. 2003). Diverse participation refers to the knowledge and judgment gained from various perspectives that leads to the development of understanding informed by a breadth of viewpoints (Schusler et al. 2003). Diverse participation here reflects Walker's assertion that "deep-seated values permeate natural resource and environmental management decisions ... the complex, controversial and pluralistic development issues we face require engaging rather that avoiding the diversity of represented views (Walker, Daniels and Emborg, 2006)".

Constructive conflict first focuses on identifying common ground and proceeds to opportunities to express conflicting points of view. This process allows participants to initially concentrate on shared values and subsequently focus constructively on areas where deliberation, negotiation or conflict resolution may be needed (Schusler, et al. 2003). In both CL and constructive conflict, mutual openness and dialogue are promoted, though consensus may not be the goal.

Public Participation in Practice

Nestled in the northwestern hills of Pennsylvania, the Allegheny National Forest (ANF) boasts more than 513,000 acres of land, a 27 mile-long reservoir and hundreds of species of fish and mammals. Allegheny was designated a National Forest in 1923 and as such, it has been subject to several federal laws, including the National Forest Management Act of 1976. The act required each National Forest to have a Forest Management Plan developed with considerable public involvement.

The ANF's Forest Plan was approved in 1986, revised in 2003, and finalized in 2007. The revised forest management plan relied on the Collaborative Learning (CL) model discussed in this chapter (collaborative learning workshops, open house meetings and public hearings). The initial full-day collaborative learning workshops took place in May 2003. Goals for the workshops included learning about citizen values, concerns and interests; gathering ideas from citizens on how the ANF could be better managed; and explaining the plan revision process and the stakeholders' role in it (Walker, Senecah and Daniels, 2006). Small group discussions were utilized to bring diverse stakeholders together on a more individual level to gain mutual understanding and explore opportunities for collaboration.

Other CL workshops were held in October 2003 following the publication of the ANF's notice of intent, which described preliminary issues and information pertaining to public meetings. The October workshops specifically addressed the public's needs and concerns and focused on how public involvement initiatives could be best implemented to address such issues. Comments and feedback from stakeholders regarding the collaborative learning workshops informed subsequent rounds of meetings. The researchers found that stakeholder concerns resonated with Senecah's Trinity of Voice (Senecah, 2004): access, standing and influence.

Data obtained from the latter rounds of meetings revealed that citizens preferred forums to open houses, and favored websites and newsletters to other forms of information dissemination (Walker, Senecah and Daniels, 2006). Findings suggested that "...citizen views demonstrate that citizens can gain standing, display legitimacy, enact voice and influence decisions about public participation process[es]." The ANF research and collaborative learning workshops continued through 2006. In February 2007, the revised ANF Management Plan was officially accepted.

Conclusion

A dialogic/participatory model of communication usually requires collaboration among diverse stakeholders. The process empowers communities to work together towards shared goals and objectives. Every project is different, and every community is unique, so the process of engaging stakeholders will change depending on each situation, but the overall goals and philosophies of participatory communication remain the same. Collaboration and compromise are key.

It is easy to say that participation is important and that involving people in the decision making process is key to long-term project success. But achieving high levels of public participation in a world where there are so many competing values and demands for our time is not an easy task. It is a difficult to bring independent thinkers and opinion leaders together and believe that all dialogue will proceed smoothly (Cox, 2006). It is helpful to have skilled communication specialists to facilitate stakeholder interaction.

It should be noted that dialogic/participatory communication may not be an effective communication strategy in all contexts. Participatory strategies require a considerable time commitment and are perhaps best implemented when dealing with long-term goals, not with acute problems that need quick fixes. Participatory strategies are well suited to situations where there is low social and low scientific consensus on what to do about a problem. The effort spent by campaign managers to facilitate public involvement and participants' time spent absorbing information and engaging in discussions, must be weighed against the need for more immediate action based perhaps on the advice of experts rather than with wide public agreement.

CHAPTER 7
RESEARCH METHODS FOR CAMPAIGN PLANNING

Introduction

As depicted in Chapter 3, managing an environmental social marketing campaign generally involves four steps:

1) Campaign planning
   a. Define issues and campaign objectives
   b. Define audiences
   c. Define messages
   d. Define communication channels
   e. Define information sources/strategic partners

2) Campaign implementation/management
3) Monitoring of campaign processes
4) Final outcome evaluation

The first three steps are iterative – that is, a campaign plan is developed, once the campaign is implemented, the effectiveness of campaign processes are monitored and problems with implementation are identified. Plans are then changed accordingly. This cyclical process continues until the campaign ends. At that point, a final evaluation is conducted to assess the extent to which campaign outcomes were met. Research is the foundation for three of the four strategic management steps – only step 2, campaign implementation/management, to be dealt with in Chapter 10, is not a research function.

Step one, campaign planning, begins by defining the issues. This involves identifying the gap between the present situation and the desired situation. The research process inherent in this step is exploratory, involving either archival research (e.g., review of literature and records) and/or informal qualitative research (e.g., interviews in an unstructured setting using a few open ended questions that solicit discursive responses). The aim of this form of qualitative research is to gain a general feel for the issues. Research findings are used to define campaign objectives.

The remainder of the planning process requires research to help identify strategies pertaining to four key communication variables – audience, message, channel, and source factors. Research findings allow target audiences to be defined and persuasive communication strategies to be crafted for each group.

The sophistication of the research process inherent in this step is dependent on the degree of resources available to conduct the research. Ideally, the process begins with more ordered types of qualitative research (e.g., focus groups or interviews in a structured setting) and once a feel for how the audience perceives the issues is gained, quantitative research is conducted (e.g., surveys with larger numbers of people using closed ended questions with categorical responses). The aim of quantitative research is to generate findings from a representative sample of people that are reflective of the larger target audience population.

The following diagram depicts the range of research methods:

Archival Research	Qualitative Research	Quantitative Research
Literature review	Interviews in unstructured setting	Surveys
Review of project records	Focus groups	
	Interviews in structured setting	

Research Methods

If the correct research method is used for the right purpose and the researcher discloses relevant limitations and remains objective, then there is no reason that findings should be doubted. Yet, research is often met with skepticism. The following reasons for this should be avoided.

- People may not be trained to understand research methods and use of statistics. Their uncertainty may be masked with doubtfulness. The onus of responsibility rests with the researcher to explain the methods and findings in a manner that is clearly and comfortably understood.
- The wrong type of research is sometimes used. For instance, findings from archival and unstructured interviews are not meant to be used for assessing campaign outcomes. These methods are acceptable for assessing campaign processes, but outcome evaluations require more scientific sampling methods, larger samples, and more rigorous data collection procedures.
- Small sample sizes and/or low response rates to a survey threaten the ability to generalize findings to a larger target audience population. A small sample of people is more apt than a large sample to exhibit unique traits that are not reflective of the target audience population. The same goes if you have a low response rate.
- Questions that are biased or leading or interviewers that have not been trained to minimize influences they might exert threaten the degree that research findings truly reflect the audience's disposition.
- Research can be conducted in a biased manner and findings can be reported selectively to support the preconceived agenda of a non-objective researcher.

The following sections of this chapter describe proper use and procedures for employing various research methods for planning campaigns. The discussion begins with a description of archival exploratory methods. Qualitative methods are then described. The chapter ends with a discussion of quantitative research methods.

ARCHIVAL RESEARCH METHODS

Archival research is particularly helpful in defining issues at the beginning of the campaign planning process. Findings from exploratory archival research are used to help define issues so that realistic goals and objectives can be crafted. Archival research may include a review of an institution's historical records and in-house research reports or published literature on the subject. The initial challenge to campaign designers is to learn about the issues – learn what the problems are and are not, learn about similar issues in other settings, and learn about potential causes and solutions.

As stated, information gleaned from this research is necessary if realistic campaign objectives are to be defined. An example of this is included in the social marketing case study described in Chapter 11. Through a review of land-ownership records, it was identified that there was growing pressure from land fragmentation in a particular watershed and, contrary to past campaign strategies, smaller acreage landowners would need to be targeted.

Findings from a review of archival materials will also help researchers prepare for additional exploratory research using qualitative research methods. That is, researchers will be more apt to know what questions to ask in subsequent exploratory interviews or focus groups once they have become a bit wiser.

QUALITATIVE RESEARCH METHODS

There are three types of qualitative research methods. Each have varying degrees of rigor (demanding standards). Each method relies on open ended questions that solicit discursive response. They range from the least rigorous, interview in an unstructured setting, to moderately rigorous focus groups, to the most rigorous, interview in a structured setting. The degree of rigor will dictate the limits of each method and when each are most appropriate.

Interviews in an unstructured setting

Interviews in an unstructured setting are the least rigorous qualitative research method we will discuss and require the fewest resources. Findings are not meant to be generalized to a larger population. The method is used to gain, in a very short time, a general feel for pertinent issues and can prove useful for defining issues and monitoring campaign processes. It should be noted that interviewers should be trained to minimize any influence they might unintentionally exert on the respondent (e.g., encouraging/discouraging certain responses).

In this method, a location is selected where the type of respondent you wish to talk with is likely to be found (e.g., households in a neighborhood, grocery stores or shopping malls for general public). A convenient site for approaching potential respondents is identified at the location. The amount of time to be spent on each interview is determined and a series of questions are drafted that will span this time period. Potential respondents are intercepted and asked to assist. Their responses are recorded by the interviewer and later analyzed for trends in content. Sampling procedures or efforts to minimize response bias are generally not employed in this method (i.e., no random selection or purposeful stratification of respondent, interviewer, time of day, or site selection is employed).

Focus groups

Focus groups are a moderately rigorous qualitative research method. Though sampling procedures and efforts to minimize response bias may be employed in this method, because of the small number of subjects questioned in a focus group, findings are not meant to be generalized to a larger population.

Focus groups, as with interviews in an unstructured setting, are used to gain a feel for pertinent issues and may prove useful for defining issues. The theories discussed in Chapter 4 often underpin these issues. The method is especially good for getting information needed to fine tune questions used in subsequent surveys. The method usually yields better quality findings than interviews in an unstructured setting. There are two reasons for this. One, individuals that are invited to participate may be chosen so that they reflect the diversity found in the target population. Hence, findings may better reflect the opinions of the target population. Two, a synergy develops when a group of participants engage in discussion – comments provoke comments that might not otherwise have surfaced. This allows focus group discussion to delve deeper into an issue.

Focus groups require more resources than interviews in an unstructured setting. An appropriate venue for the event must be selected with proper ambience, food service, and recording facility. A discussion moderator, trained to minimize any influence they might unintentionally exert on the respondent (e.g., encouraging/discouraging certain responses) is needed. Someone to record responses as written text, audio, and/or videotape, will need to be present. Participants must be selected and invited, and incentives for their attendance may need to be supplied (cash stipend or gift). After the event, transcripts or tapes will need to be analyzed for trends in content. (See Appendix 1 for instruction on conducting focus groups)

Using a focus group to plan a campaign

Adapted from Creighton, J. (1999). A Strategic Communication Campaign for the Mattabesset River Watershed. University of New Haven, December, 1999

One river in Connecticut that exhibits degradation due to nonpoint source pollution is the Mattabesset River, an 18 mile river that begins in the basalt ridges of Southington, Meriden, Berlin, and Middletown and flows generally east to its confluence with the Connecticut River. The towns of Berlin, Cromwell, Middletown, New Britain, Newington, and Rocky Hill comprise over 90% of the Mattabesset River's watershed. These towns (excluding New Britain), which used to have small populations and claimed farming as their major industry, have now become much larger bedroom communities for Hartford-based companies. The Mattabesset River now suffers major problems from nonpoint source pollution due to this growth.

The Middlesex and Hartford County Soil and Water Conservation Districts (MCSWCD) have been working to build an awareness of the Mattabesset River's problems for several years. In the mid 1990's they applied for and received grant money to conduct a watershed survey of residents who live near streams in the watershed. The MCSWCD needed this information to develop a social marketing campaign addressing the problems associated with the Mattabesset River.

Before the survey questionnaire could be developed, a focus group was conducted for approximately two hours to discuss issues related to nonpoint source pollution in the Mattabesset River Watershed. The focus group allowed exploration of a) who was most affected, b) knowledge about nonpoint source pollution, c) the perceived cost/benefits of pollution remediation, and d) methods for communicating with target audiences. Findings helped guide the construction of a survey questionnaire.

The focus group consisted of nine individuals from five of the six main watershed towns. The following questions guided the focus group discussion:

- Do you know what a watershed is?
- Do you know what land comprises the Mattabesset River Watershed?
- Do you think the Mattabesset River and its tributaries are polluted?
- Do you feel any of your own or your community's assets are threatened by water pollution within the Mattabesset River Watershed?
- Do you and/or your town officials know what nonpoint source pollution is and how to prevent it?
- What benefits do you think you or your community could achieve by preventing/cleaning-up nonpoint source pollution within the Mattabesset River Watershed?
- What are some of the costs (e.g., time, effort, money) that you and your community are willing to bear to prevent/clean-up nonpoint source pollution?
- What are some of the communication channels (e.g., radio, print) that you might use to find information about nonpoint source pollution in the Mattabesset River Watershed and how to prevent it?
- What opinion leaders (e.g., town officials, experts) do you think might influence your attitudes about nonpoint source pollution prevention/cleanup in the Mattabesset River Watershed?

The following findings were obtained:

Audiences

- Industry - participants believe problems are caused by industry.
- Youth - there is a need to teach young people proper habits now to prevent problems later.
- Local government officials and residents - municipal officials will not be concerned until voters are concerned.

Knowledge

- Most people are unfamiliar with the location of the whole Mattabesset River.
- Most people do not know about the condition of the river and streams.

- Most people are only slightly familiar with the concept of nonpoint source pollution.
- Most people agree that few people know where to get information on cleaning up rivers.

Cost/Benefits

- Emotions - most people exhibit anger and fear when discussing present pollution threats to the Mattabesset River.
- Fishing – people do not fish in the river and its feeder streams due to pollution.
- Aesthetics - the view of these water bodies is unappealing.
- Property values - water pollution affects citizens' property values.
- Taxes - taxes will need to be increased to clean up polluted rivers.
- Business growth – there is a need for town governments to be business friendly.
- Water quality - municipal officials are concerned with safety of drinking water.
- Youth – these problems will affect their children.
- Wetlands - the benefits of wetlands is important.

Communication

- There is a need to use pictures in campaign messages.
- Communication channels should include schools, newspapers, local access cable, and the Internet.
- Sources of information should include local officials and friends/neighbors.

Interviews in a structured setting

Interviews in a structured setting have the potential for being a more rigorous research method than focus groups because, in addition to the use of sampling procedures and efforts to minimize response bias, it is possible to interview a larger number of subjects. Yet, because data usually consists of lengthy qualitative comments, the sample size will be limited by the researcher's capacity to handle subsequent laborious analyses of content.

Given respondents are representative of the target population, larger response numbers improve the ability to generalize findings to the target audience population. To protect the integrity of the research, it is important to have a scheme for a) randomly selecting respondents and/or stratifying respondents to reflect population demographics, b) varying the choice of interviewer, time of day, and site selection to minimize response bias, and c) training interviewers to minimize biases they themselves might interject. (See Appendix 2 for suggested interviewer training protocol)

Interviews in a structured setting, as with focus groups and interviews in an unstructured setting, are useful for defining issues. The method is also good for getting information needed to design questions used in subsequent surveys. In addition, if careful sampling and efforts to control response bias are employed, interviews in a structured setting may be used as a substitute (or complement) for quantitative methods used in campaign planning and evaluation.

Interviews in a structured setting with larger samples of subjects generally require more resources to conduct than other forms of qualitative research. The amount of resources required depends on the type of data collection method employed. Potential methods for data collection include intercepts, phone, or face-to-face.

Intercept interviews

If an intercept method of data collection is to be employed, a mechanism for selecting respondents and controlling potential response biases must be developed. As with unstructured interviews, general locations and specific sites are selected where the type of person you wish to talk to is found. The amount of time to be spent on each interview is determined and a series of questions are crafted that will span this time period. Potential respondents are intercepted and asked to assist. Their responses are recorded by the interviewer and later analyzed for trends in content.

One way to introduce some randomization into the selection of respondents is to select every n[th] person as they pass a specific data collection site. For instance, if every third person is to be approached, once an interview is completed, passer-bys are counted off and the third person to pass is approached. This minimizes selection bias that the interviewer might unconsciously interject (e.g., favor/disfavor individuals based on appearance). Another way to help ensure that your sample is representative of your target population is to stratify respondents based on known demographics of the population. To do this, the interviewer has specified quotas defined by sex, race/ethnicity, and/or age. These quotas reflect percentages found in the target population.

Aside from making sure that interviewers are trained to avoid influences that they themselves might interject, methods for controlling response biases include a) varying the selection of specific sites, b) varying individuals assigned to conduct interviews at specific sites, and c) varying the time of day that the interviews take place at each site.

Phone interviews

A mechanism for randomly selecting respondents and controlling potential response biases is also key to collecting valid data over the telephone. Yet, unlike the intercept method of data collection discussed above, it is usually necessary to have either a means of generating random telephone numbers or a master list of all telephone numbers in the population from which a random sample can be drawn.

As with other forms of qualitative research, the amount of time to be spent on each interview is determined and a series of questions are crafted that will span this time period. Potential respondents are called and asked to participate. Their responses are recorded by the interviewer and later analyzed for trends in content. Interviewers need to be trained to avoid biasing results. One caution: low response rates are common with telephone interview surveys and because of this, there are likely to be unique differences between respondents and nonrespondents -- this can greatly limit the ability to generalize findings to the target population. Nonresponse and refusal rates should be reported so that readers can assess the ability to generalize from the reported findings.

Face-to-face interviews

In-person interviews can be conducted door-to-door at randomly selected dwellings and/or in-person with randomly selected individuals. In both cases it will be necessary to have a master list of dwellings or individuals in the target population from which a random sample can be drawn. In addition, controls for response biases will need to be instituted.

Again, the amount of time to be spent on each interview is determined and a series of questions are crafted that will span this time period. Respondents are contacted and asked to participate. Their responses are recorded by the interviewer and later analyzed for trends in content. The potential for low response will probably not be as great as with telephone surveys. However, nonresponse and refusal rates should still be reported so that readers can assess the ability to generalize findings to the target population.

Use of interviews in planning a campaign

Adapted from research report *Northeast Neighborhood Pocket Park Research Project* by Ben Tyson for the Urban and Community Forestry Program, University of Connecticut Cooperative Extension System, March 1998.

As with many cities in the northeast United States, Hartford Connecticut has a considerable number of abandoned buildings and vacant lots and is grappling with the issue of what to do with them. One option is the development of "Pocket Parks". A Pocket Park is a place where people can gather to talk, play games, visit, read, and relax. They are generally landscaped with trees, shrubs, flowers and grass. Pocket Parks are not large. They might be built on the site of an abandoned single-family dwelling. Importantly, the urban forestry literature explains that attractively landscaped urban areas (to which Pocket Parks contribute) promote significantly greater interaction and cohesion among community members, reduce instances of violence, aggression and other social ills associated with high density/low income urban settings, and increase business activity.

Ideally, the reclaiming of a vacant lot and the development and maintenance of a Pocket Park should be a community initiative (as opposed to a unilateral initiative by a public agency). A heightened sense of ownership and commitment will result if Pocket Park projects are developed by groups of residents and business owners who live or work near a particular site.

In 1998 a research study was completed that included an assessment of the beliefs and attitudes of business owners toward the development of Pocket Parks in northeast Hartford. The project was sponsored by the University of Connecticut Cooperative Extension System and facilitated by ONE/CHANE, Inc., a local non-profit community development/citizen advocacy group. The four questions used in a telephone survey with members of the Hartford Enterprise Zone Business Association are listed below.

- What benefits would you/your business gain from having a Pocket Park?
- What benefits do you think people in the community would gain from having a Pocket Park?
- What do you think are the barriers to developing Pocket Parks?
- Do you think this would be a popular idea with: a) your family, b) your friends, c) your business colleagues?

To minimize response bias, interaction with survey respondents was prescriptive and each received the same introduction. Interviewee responses were recorded by hand on the questionnaire and content analyzed. The response rate to the survey was 47%; that is, 53% of the individuals were either unavailable for comment or refused to participate. A summary of the findings and recommendations for the design of a campaign are described below.

Benefits to one's business

Approximately half (47%) of respondents believed that their businesses will derive no benefit from the construction of a Pocket Park. Two primary reasons were given for this: one, their businesses do not depend on public visibility or walk-in traffic (e.g., fuel oil company, packaging company, bank) and two, a Pocket Park would not be suitable in the area where their business is located (e.g., industrial park).

Approximately one quarter (26%) of respondents believed that their business would benefit from the presence of a Pocket Park. The primary reasons given were increased visibility and more walk-in traffic. Businesses that responded in this manner included a hardware store, grocery store, auto repair garage, beauty shop, and liquor store. Four individuals (12%) stated that the existence (and recreational use) of Pocket Parks might help make clientele and/or employees more content/happier and that this would inevitably be good for business. Three respondents (9%) stated that Pocket Parks would improve the appearance of the neighborhood and this would inevitably be good for business.

Benefits to community

Most respondents (65%) thought that youth would benefit most from having Pocket Parks in the community because they are in need of safe places to spend their free time. Seven individuals (21%) think that the community as a whole would benefit because a Pocket Park could provide a needed place for people to meet, interact and recreate. Three respondents (9%) specifically mentioned the elderly as the primary beneficiaries. Five respondents (15%) believed that the development of a Pocket Park would provide a context for neighbors to work together and this could lead to a greater sense of community and better community morale. Lastly, three individuals (9%) thought that Pocket Parks were a good alternative to vacant lots because they would improve the appearance of the community.

Barriers to developing Pocket Parks

The majority of respondents (59%) thought lack of money, either from within the community or from outside sources, was a barrier to the development of Pocket Parks. Approximately one third (32%) of those who responded thought that lack of support from City of Hartford public agencies and/or other sponsors was a barrier. Four individuals (12%) thought that lack of interest/support on the part of community members would be a barrier.

Five respondents (15%) thought that park maintenance would be problematic because the city and/or the community would not be able to keep it clean. Several individuals (12%) talked about the need to keep the park safe and drug free and how difficult this might be. The same number of respondents (12%) mentioned the need for police supervision. Individuals felt that if youth activities were not structured and supervised, a park might become a breeding ground for trouble.

Normative appeal (family, friends, business colleagues)

In terms of the appeal a Pocket Park project might have across the whole community, thirteen respondents (38%) believed the idea would be well received. Five respondents (15%) believed it would not. Eight individuals (24%) felt it would be popular idea with their friends and/or family. Note: eight (24%) stated that because they did not live in the neighborhood, family appeal was not relevant. Only five respondents (15%) thought it would be popular with business colleagues. Three (9%) specifically said it would not be popular.

Recommendations

So, can the business community be counted on to support a Pocket Park project? This was the key question that the business owner survey attempted to answer. Answers to this question were inferred from responses to the interviews.

As stated above, approximately one quarter of respondents think their business would benefit in some way from a Pocket Park project. Yet about twice this number (approximately half) believe they would not derive any benefit. The other quarter choose not to respond to this question. In terms of popularity of the idea with business colleagues, only five respondents (15%) stated that they thought it would be well accepted; 9% specifically said it would not. Three quarters of the respondents did not respond to this question - perhaps because they were unsure.

Given that a) most business decisions are based on maximizing profits and that b) individual members of the business community are a good judge of how the business community as a whole will act, based on our sample, one might conservatively guess that only 15% of the business community would be initially supportive of a Pocket Park project. A more definitive and perhaps optimistic answer will depend on how nonrespondents to two key questions (approximately 25% of the sample) eventually think about the issue. If these individuals can be convinced that a critical mass of respected colleagues are supportive, one might estimate that at least 25% of the business community might eventually become involved. The behavior of the initial 15% will be fundamental in helping the idea diffuse to others members of the business community.

Self-oriented reasons for getting involved will include the increased visibility and walk-in traffic that a nearby Pocket Park might stimulate and the fact that Pocket Parks might be good for business because they would improve the appearance of the neighborhood and give clients and/ or employees a place to enjoy themselves more. Community-oriented reasons for support include the benefits of having a place for people to interact and recreate (especially for youth), improved community morale, and improved appearance of the community. Lack of support (both in terms of finances and labor) from the City of Hartford, the community, and other potential sponsors is perceived as the biggest barrier. This is followed by problems associated with park maintenance and crime prevention. Campaign messages/interventions should emphasize the benefits of developing Pocket Parks and minimize concerns about costs and barriers; and these messages should be delivered by respected colleagues (the 15% initially supportive of Pocket Parks).

QUANTITATIVE RESEARCH METHODS (SURVEYS)

Quantitative research is particularly appropriate for purposes of campaign planning. As stated in the beginning of this chapter, the sophistication of the research used to help plan a campaign's strategy is dependent on the degree of resources available to conduct the research. Ideally, the process begins with focus groups or interviews and once a feel for how the audience perceives the issues is gained, the information is used to construct a quantitative survey questionnaire. The theories discussed in Chapter 4 often underpin these issues. Quantitative research consists of surveys with large numbers of people using closed-ended questions with categorical responses. The aim of quantitative research is to generate findings from a representative sample of people that are reflective of the larger target audience population. (See Appendix 3 for how to construct questionnaires)

Quantitative surveys usually require a fair amount of resources. The amount of resources that are required depends on the type of data collection method employed. Potential methods for survey data collection include intercept, phone, face-to-face, internet, and mail. The intricacies of the first three methods have already been addressed in earlier sections of this chapter on interviewing. Methodological issues are identical regardless if the questionnaire uses open-ended qualitative questions or close-ended quantitative questions.

Internet and mail surveys are like phone and face-to-face methods of data collection in that a mechanism for randomly selecting persons to receive the questionnaire is required. It is usually necessary to have a master list of all names, addresses or emails of the population (a "sample frame") from which a random sample is to be drawn. The difference between qualitative and quantitative surveys is that the chosen sample can be much larger with a quantitative survey. This is because a quantitative questionnaire is much simpler and faster to complete and large amounts of data are more easily analyzed. Larger sample sizes mean less sampling error. Therefore, the findings from the sample can be generalized to the population with greater accuracy.

Controls for response bias with internet and mailed surveys include making sure questions are not leading. Additionally, as with telephone surveys, nonresponse can severely threaten the generalizability of findings. Nonresponse rates should always be reported so that readers can assess the ability to generalize findings to the target population. Typical methods to optimize response to mail surveys include: a) promises of anonymity, b) an initial email or postcard alert, c) a hand addressed out-going envelope with first class stamp that includes a cover letter for mailed surveys, a short attractive questionnaire, a stamped return envelope for mailed surveys, and possibly an incentive (dollar bill, raffle ticket, or emailed description of a promised reward), d) a follow-up second email or postcard alert, and e) a second emailing/mailing of the questionnaire to nonrespondents. This is what is commonly referred to as the *Dillman Technique* (Dillman, Smyth, & Christian, 2009).

SAMPLING

Sampling is generally less of an issue with qualitative exploratory research because you are not looking to generalize your findings to a larger population. As discussed earlier, qualitative research is often used for exploratory reasons following archival research. It is a way to take your archival research and localize these findings by soliciting opinions on relevant issues from a small number of people from your target population. The theories discussed in Chapter 4 often underpin these issues. Their opinions help you develop your subsequent survey questions more accurately. Participants may be quizzed in individual interviews or in focus groups and are generally chosen by convenience, not by using any probability sampling technique. They may be purposefully selected to represent subgroups within your population (e.g., representative proportions by sex, age, location). The findings from qualitative exploratory research are not meant to be generalized to your target population.

Sampling is the key to making sure your research findings can be generalized to your target population when you are doing quantitative survey research. The objective of sampling is to identify a representative subset of your population from which you want to generalize. Two key questions that must be addressed when deciding on your sampling strategy are a) who to include and b) how many to include.

If your population is small, you might consider doing a census. A census includes everyone in your target population. The advantage of doing a census is that your findings will be perfectly generalizable if everyone responds. However, this is unlikely. Those that do not respond represent a potential bias to your findings. If there are only a few nonrespondents, this presents little problem. But as your nonresponse rate grows, this may mean you are only hearing back from those that are interested in the topic and this would bias your findings. Optimizing response rates by using the *Dillman Technique* (Dillman, Smyth, & Christian, 2009) discussed earlier in this chapter is always important. Another concern with doing a census is that the "sampling frame," the list of everyone in your target population, may be flawed. For instance, a list of names, addresses or emails of all first year students at a university may invariably include some who chose not to attend school at the last minute, already dropped out, or moved from their address on record. A list of landowners taken from the Tax Assessors role in a municipality may include some who have sold their land or died. It is important to carefully assess your sampling frame for accuracy and thoroughness, and update it if necessary.

If your population is large, and therefore it is impossible to do a census of everyone, you will need to survey a smaller proportion of people. Sampling is how you identify a smaller proportion of people to survey from within the population. There are two types of sampling strategies - probability sampling and nonprobability sampling. Probability samples are representative and allow for generalizations to the target population. You can calculate the probability of a person being selected into your sample. Each person has an equal chance of being selected. Nonprobability samples are not meant to be generalized to the target population. This is the quick and convenient type of sampling used in most qualitative exploratory research.

Types of nonprobability sampling include:

- Convenience Sampling which includes people who are close at hand and easily approached.
- Convenience Quota Sampling which includes proportions of people based on sex, age, race, etc. that reflect the same proportions in the target population.

- Snowball Convenience Sampling which starts by identifying people in your population that are willing to participate and asking them to identify other potential participants. The process continues until you have everyone you need.

- Purposive Sampling using an Intercept Method of Data Collection is unique in that it is a nonprobablity sample that may yield generalizable findings. It is used when it is impossible to get a list of the population (sample frame) to select from. You start by identifying several places that a broad selection of your population will go to (e.g., grocery stores, shopping malls), you randomly select days and times to collect data, and then survey every n^{th} person that crosses your path. These randomization techniques help control for potential selection bias. You might also set quotas to sample based on the demographics of your target population. There is strong evidence that this type of sampling/data collection strategy can produce generalizable results.

As stated, in probability sampling the probability of selecting a member of the population into your sample can be calculated. A high quality sample frame is necessary. The assumption with probability sampling is that the distribution of characteristics in the population follows a normal bell shaped curve and the larger the sample, the more apt it will approximate the same distribution as the population. The smaller the sample the more likely there will be fluctuations (skewness, kurtosis) and the less likely it will approximate the same distribution as the population. This makes subsequent statistics based on the data less accurate. For instance, with a sample size of 25 the accuracy of your statistics might be as low as +/- 20%; with a sample size of 200 this might rise to +/- 7%; with a sample size of 400 it might be as good as +/- 5%; and anything over 1000 might be as accurate as +/- 2%. The required size of your sample will depend on two things: a) how accurate you need your statistics and b) the expense that you can afford because costs increase in proportion to sample size. Interestingly, the size of the population that you sample from does not affect the accuracy of your statistics. A sample of 1000 that is randomly selected from the population will have nearly the same distribution of characteristics as the whole population regardless of the size of the population.

Types of probability sampling include:

- Random Sampling in which every element of the population has an equal chance of being selected. Techniques include: drawing names from a hat, numbering people in your sample frame and using a table of random numbers to select, and random digit telephone dialing.
- Systematic Random Sampling where you take the sampling frame, pick a starting point at random, and pick every nth person depending on how many you need and how long the list is (e.g. you would choose every 10th person for a sample of 1000 if your population was 10,000).
- Stratified Random Sampling is when you set quotas to achieve in your sample based on certain characteristics in your population. Divide your sample frame into subgroups based on these characteristics and then randomly sample within these subgroups. This may be especially important when your sample size is going to be relatively small.

It needs to be noted again that nonrespondents, those selected into your sample that do not respond, threaten the ability to generalize findings to your population. Optimizing response rates by using the *Dillman Technique* (Dillman, Smyth, & Christian, 2009) is always important. Response rates always need to be reported to give the reader a feel for the external validity of your findings.

DATA ENTRY AND ANALYSIS

Qualitative Research

Data from unstructured interviews and focus groups is discursive text. This may be in the form of written notes made by the interviewer/recorder or a transcript made from an audio recording. The process of analyzing text can be laborious, though there are software programs available now that can assist with this task. Key themes are identified within the text, described, and direct quotes from respondents are inserted to illustrate concepts. The process of identifying and naming the key themes is subjective. To improve on this, more than one analyst can be used. Any disagreement between analysts is discussed and resolved. This increases the validity/objectivity of the findings.

Data from structured interviews may include both discursive text and responses to some closed-ended questions. Usually a questionnaire has been used to guide the interview and response are recorded directly on it. The process of analyzing these completed questionnaires can also be laborious, though as stated, there are software programs available now that can assist with analyzing qualitative data. Key themes are identified from responses to each question that was asked. These are described and summarized. Again, the process of identifying and naming the key themes is subjective. To improve on this, more than one analyst can be used and any disagreement resolved between analysts.

Quantitative Research

Data from quantitative research is numerical. A questionnaire is used that asks primarily closed-ended questions that solicit categorical responses (e.g., yes/no, rankings, Likert scaled items). Each category of response is assigned a numerical value. These numbers are the data that are entered into a spreadsheet for later quantitative statistical analysis. Sometimes open-ended questions are asked that require categories of responses to be later defined and assigned a numerical value. If the survey is administered via the internet, it is possible to have responses entered directly into a spreadsheet as the respondent completes the survey. There are commercial services (e.g., *SurveyMonkey, Qualitrics*) that can do this for you or you can have the IT department at your organization set up a temporary website that you can direct respondents to. If the survey is administered by mail or face-to face, then you will need to enter data into a spreadsheet manually.

Appendix 1

How to Conduct a Focus Group

Developing Questions

Focus group sessions usually last from one to two hours. In order to receive as much information as possible in that time, approximately seven to ten questions should be prepared for discussion. You will need to identify what issues need to be addressed during the discussion, develop open-ended questions congruent with these issues, and determine from which representative group the information should be gathered. You will need to determine what, if any, stimuli will be used with the series of questions and plan appropriately for how it will be presented to the participants (i.e. video, flip charts, handouts, etc.).

Selecting Participants

Focus group participants should be selected to represent the target audience of the study. Individuals may be chosen to specifically represent a broad mix based on political affiliation, gender, income, etc. If the audience is very diverse, several focus groups may be required. In general, focus group participants should be fairly homogenous so the discussion can focus deeply on a few topics. Too much audience variability will yield a broad array of opinions which may result in a lot of unproductive disagreement/argument.

A good size for a focus group is 8-10 participants. However, it should be noted that there will usually be previously confirmed participants that do not show. It is recommended that 12 be invited to each session to compensate for this. In the case that all 12 participants show up, the discussion session may be conducted with everyone or a couple of people may be thanked and excused.

After successfully identifying a pool of willing participants, you will need to contact them to relay the focus group logistics: the date, time and location of the session. Approximately one week in advance of the focus group discussion, a follow-up reminder phone call should be made or an email sent. Participants should be asked to notify the coordinator of the study if they are unable to attend to allow time to find an alternate participant.

Incentives for Participation

In addition to snacks and beverages, other incentives sometimes include a cash payment (typically no more than $50 per participant). Alternative incentives include meals, gift certificates, or small gifts.

Selecting a Time and Location

The time and location of the focus group must be sensitive to participant lifestyles. Focus groups should never be scheduled on holidays or on days of the week or times of day when participants are most likely to have a conflict. Focus group locations should be convenient and accessible to the participants. For example, a focus group with senior citizens should be scheduled during daylight hours at a near-by location. A group of urban parents should be scheduled in the early evening hours in a well-lit location with ample parking.

One option is to hold the sessions at a formal focus group discussion facility. Many marketing firms, research organizations, and universities have special facilities in which they conduct focus group discussions. Typically these venues provide a darkened observation room behind a two-way mirror, permitting clients to observe the discussions. However, this type of facility may not be necessary and would in most circumstances add to the cost of the project. Regardless of where the focus group is conducted, the discussion room should be prepared in advance and be ready for the discussion when participants arrive. One large table (preferably round) is the most effective seating configuration.

Selecting a Moderator

Good focus group moderators are able to manage group dynamics while actively listening to participants. Moderating a focus group can be a daunting task requiring someone with the ability to draw information out of participants while simultaneously coordinating who may speak and when. If it is not possible to acquire an experienced moderator, a novice with good social skills can be used but they should carefully consider the following key points.

- Focus group sessions should begin with an explanation of the purpose of the study and a description of the recording mechanisms that are being used (i.e., written, audio, video). If the focus group is held in a room with a two-way mirror, participants will need to know who is observing and their association with the study.

- The moderator's role is to coordinate the conversation. It is important that all members of the session participate as much as possible. While encouraging conversation is the goal, it is also important to stay focused on the task at hand. To maintain momentum and get closure on questions, the moderator must be wary of dominators and able to stifle their excessiveness. Dominators in any focus group can disrupt the flow of the discussion and tend to suppress viewpoints contrary to their own. One way to avoid such disruptions and ensure equitable participation is using a round-robin style of discussion; making sure that every participant has spoken before moving on to the next question or topic.

Recording and Analyzing Results

Prior to the focus group session, it must be determined what equipment is needed to record the discussions. This decision is dependent on the amount of detail needed for the analysis and final report. It is always necessary to take careful notes and a good scribe may be employed to do this. The moderator should never act as the note-taker as this would be too distracting for them. In addition to taking notes, it is often wise to audio record or video record the focus group. Having these recordings allows the researcher to go back and capture verbatim comments from participants that are useful for illustrating findings in the final report. The analysis consists of identifying key themes from the notes and recordings and summarizing the findings regarding these key themes. The scribe/note-taker often takes the lead on the analysis. The focus group moderator may assist.

Final Report

A final report should start with the objectives of the study. A description of the methods used to run the focus group should follow this (e.g., timing, location, participants). Findings for each focus group question are then provided. Findings are summarized in the order the questions were asked in the focus group sessions. It is usually helpful to illustrate these findings with quotes from participants. Summary conclusions based on the findings will complete the report.

Appendix 2

The Interviewing Process

Adapted from: Adams, J. (1958). <u>Interviewing procedures: A Manual for Survey Interviewers.</u> The University of North Carolina Press.

Interviewing can be one of the most useful research tools for developing a social marketing campaign. Skillful interviewing practices coupled with clear, concise questions can provide highly useful information. The most effective interview technique is the face-to-face method, however telephone interviewing can also be used. Face-to-face interviews will be the primary focus of the process described here. This method offers the interviewer the opportunity to clarify any misunderstandings the interviewee may have regarding the questions asked. Face-to-face interviews have an advantage over telephone interviews in that they allow the interviewer the ability to observe the respondents and gauge their general behavior during the interview. There are several considerations critical to executing an effective face-to-face interview. These are described below.

Choosing a Setting

An interview can be a failure before the first question is asked if the location is a poor choice. Interviews should not be held in public locations where they can be disrupted by the distraction of surrounding activities and noise. The interview location should be both convenient for the interviewee and private. Often it is in a person's home or office.

Unless specified, interviews should consist of only the interviewer and the interviewee. The presence of additional people during the interview can hinder the interviewee's ability to answer questions openly and honestly. To ensure that the information received is as unbiased as possible, the interviewer and interviewee should be alone.

The setting should be suitable for two and with enough space to make the interviewee feel comfortable and not "hovered" upon. Typically an interviewer will sit opposite the interviewee to gauge non-verbal reactions and to maintain a comfortable level of eye contact.

Interviewer Appearance and Demeanor

The researcher should be sensitive to the target audience, their culture, behaviors and beliefs. This will affect how the interviewer presents him/herself to respondents in terms of appearance and demeanor. First impressions can bias respondents; hence the interviewer's goal is to appear as neutral as possible. Clothing should be neither trendy nor too plain, but unclassifiable, clean and pressed. Appearing too fashion-savvy or too rumpled allows the respondent to form judgments about the interviewer's attitude, which may lead to biased responses.

In terms of demeanor, the interviewer should be courteous, pleasant and show a genuine interest in getting to know the respondent. The interviewer should have the ability to "gauge and play," a skill that allows the interviewer to determine, in a short amount of time, the type of person the respondent is and the type of person they would feel most comfortable talking to. In turn, the interviewer can then modify his or her demeanor to accommodate the respondent.

Establishing and Maintaining Rapport during the Interview Process

Generally people like to talk about matters that interest them. This willingness to share information is an important motivator but it depends heavily upon the interviewers ability to create a non-threatening atmosphere free of judgment and disapproval. The interviewer's credibility must be established from the start of the interview, typically in the introduction when the interviewer introduces themselves and states the purpose of the interview. This first step is critical when dealing with phone interviews where the interviewer can be easily mistaken for a salesperson if credibility is not first established. Credibility can be established by the following factors:

- Emphasize the reliability of the organization conducting the interviews. The interviewer should allude to their expertise and the expertise of the organization they represent.
- State the objectives of the interview and how the information will be used. Without going into too much detail, the interviewer should explain the rationale behind the interview and let the interviewee know how crucial their participation is to the findings in the study.

- Explain the interviewee selection process. Interviewees may be skeptical about why they were selected for the interview. It often helps to let the interviewee know that they were not unfairly singled out and are one of many who are being interviewed. In cases where it is necessary to expand on this, the interviewer may explain that the interviewee was selected through a randomized process or similar procedure.
- Assure the interviewee of confidentiality. In some cases respondents are not overly concerned with the confidential nature of the interview, but there are many who are and they require reassurance that the interview is confidential and their responses will be anonymous.
- Explain how the interviews are to be conducted. This helps reduce uncertainty and helps put the interviewer at ease.

The object of any interview is to receive "true" answers from the interviewees and this is facilitated by an open and nonjudgmental atmosphere. With credibility established, the interviewer should then build a rapport with the respondent by creating a permissive interview setting. Interviewers must be cognizant of their actions during the interview process, as there is the possibility that through word or gesture, the interviewer may communicate his or her own opinion about a particular question or topic. Respondents should never be made to feel as though they have given the interviewer an undesirable or wrong response. In situations where the interviewer is perceived to have an opinion on the subject, respondents have the tendency to modify their answers to what they believe the interviewer most desires. The interviewer must show no sign of disapproval or approval during the interview process. They must remain neutral and accepting when recording responses.

When the interviewer is "off script" and not using the questionnaire (e.g., during the introduction) it is very important to avoid off-putting technical jargon. As a rule, language used during the interview process should be neither highly technical nor overly simple. Rapport building will be disrupted if the interviewer is perceived to be talking "over the head" of the respondent. Conversely, the interviewer should take care not to "talk down" to the respondent or use overly simple language that might be taken offensively.

Using the Interview Questionnaire

Researchers use the questionnaire as a scientific instrument which makes it critical that the interviewer be precise in asking each question. However, it can be demeaning to respondents to feel as if they are being studied, measured or tested, which can lead to self-consciousness and biased answers. To avoid this, the interviewer must be precise in asking each question, yet use the questionnaire informally and with ease to give the impression of a natural conversation. This is usually accomplished after plenty of practice reading the questions out loud before the actual interview process begins.

Interviewers must become very familiar with the questionnaire. The questionnaire is designed to insure comparability of answers regardless of the interviewer or the respondent. It is essential that the interviewer be familiar enough with the questions in order to ask the respondents precisely what is specified on the questionnaire. Changing the language of a question will result in incomparable responses that are useless to the researcher.

The sequence of the questions on the questionnaire must not be reordered during the interview process. The questionnaire is designed with careful consideration for continuity and seamless transitions. Altering the wording or the order in which the questions are asked may cause confusion or bias responses.

Other than contingency questions, which are intended for only some respondents based on an answer to a previous question, no question on the questionnaire should be skipped. There are cases when the respondent may not understand the questions. Even in these circumstances, the interviewer is to repeat the question in the same words, and avoid paraphrasing or skipping the question all together. If a respondent truly does not understand a question after several repetitions, it is best to record the fact and move on.

Questionnaires tend to have personal questions, which may make the respondent feel uncomfortable. If a respondent has trepidations about answering a question or simply refuses to answer the question, the interviewer must handle the situation tactfully in order to maintain rapport. The interviewer should deal with questions of a sensitive nature in the same way all other questions are handled, in a matter-of-fact manner. In doing so, the question comes across very naturally in a way that assumes that the respondent should have no issue with answering it honestly. If however the respondent does show signs of hesitation, the interviewer must reassure the respondent of the confidential nature of the survey and state that all answers are to be handled as anonymous statistics. If absolutely necessary, the interviewer may proceed with the questionnaire and readdress the sensitive question at the close of the interview, during the review.

Using the Specifications/Questionnaire Instructions

Instructions for the interviewer that accompany the questionnaire are designed to provide them with specific guidelines on how to administer the instrument. The interviewer, to insure valid and useful data, must carefully follow the instructions. Instructions vary from questionnaire to questionnaire and cover topics such as when, how, and what to probe. The instructions may also include contingency questions, directions on how to record answers and, if allowed, the exact wording to be used to help a respondent understand a question more clearly.

Recording Responses

The interviewer serves as a liaison between the researcher and the interviewee. The researcher thus depends upon the interviewer to record responses exactly as given and at the exact time they are made. This exactness is essential to the recording process. If the questionnaire contains open-ended questions, those soliciting the interviewee's answers must capture the substance and meaning exactly as provided. If lengthy responses are expected, the researcher will usually have anticipated this and a recording aid will be provided to the interviewer.

The interviewer should explain any unanswered questions. This can be handled by adding comments in the margin that address the reason the respondent failed to answer a question. Additionally, margin comments should be made addressing any significant events that took place during the interview that may have had a disruptive effect on the interview. Emotional reactions, hostility, attention deficiency or any other interruption during an interview can be quite telling to the researcher when interpreting the responses.

Bringing the Interview to a Close

Before closing the interview, the questionnaire should be reviewed with the respondent to ensure accurate recording. During the review process, the interviewer may readdress any questions that may have been skipped earlier on. After reviewing the questionnaire, respondents should be thanked for their participation.

Appendix 3

Designing Questionnaires

A questionnaire is used to provide open or close-ended questions for the purpose of soliciting information that will be used as data for further analysis. Questionnaires are employed in survey research. They can be administered several ways (e.g., mail, telephone, face-to-face, internet).

Questionnaires are crafted to meet the specific information needs and research objectives of a study. Focus groups and interviews (see previous Appendices) often play a preliminary role as qualitative research tools used to uncover information that guides questionnaire construction.

Questionnaires vary in style and format depending on the type of research project being conducted and to whom the questions are being asked. However, there are several general guidelines that should be followed when constructing an effective questionnaire.

Formulating Questions

There are two formatting options available to the researcher when developing questions. These are open-ended questions and close-ended-questions. Open-ended questions are those that solicit the respondent's own answers. Close-ended questions are those that provide a selection of predetermined answers.

There are benefits and shortcomings for each type of question. Close-ended questions have the benefit of providing uniformity of responses and the data can be easily quantified and processed. The short-coming of close-ended questions rests with the researcher's ability, or lack thereof, to create answers to these types of questions that are truly exhaustive and mutually exclusive. Open-ended questions are beneficial because they provide in-depth information. The shortcoming with open-ended questions lies in the difficulty of grouping and coding the responses. The grouping/coding process is subjective and can inadvertently lead to bias.

Question Clarity

When developing questionnaire content, special attention should be paid to the wording of each question. The vocabulary should be simple and concise, avoiding technical jargon and specialized language which may be unfamiliar and confusing to the respondent. Further, questions should be as concrete and precise as possible so that the respondent can understand exactly what is being asked of them.

Contingency Questions

Questionnaires may contain questions that are relevant to one respondent but irrelevant to others. Typically, this occurs when the researcher is interested in answers to a series of questions about one particular topic. Filter and contingency questions are used to keep the questionnaire as relevant as possible for each respondent. Filter questions involve response categories that lead respondents to different sections of the questionnaire based on their answers. Contingency questions are structured for exploring a certain topic in-depth and are only intended for respondents who answered a certain way to the filter question. For example:

Do you recycle?
_____ yes _____ no (check one)
If "yes",
What items do you recycle?
_____ paper, _____ cardboard, _____ plastic, _____glass, _____metal
(check all that apply)

This example about recycling leads to another potentially problematic issue with questionnaires called normative responses. The researcher is always seeking honest responses for questions asked. Normative responses can hinder this goal by eliciting the socially responsible answer instead of the honest one. A respondent may feel uneasy replying that they never recycle because it is generally viewed as socially unacceptable behavior so they will answer "yes" even if it is untrue. The best way to avoid normative responses is by assuring respondents' anonymity and by conveying a neutral, nonjudgmental attitude.

Avoiding Double-Barreled Questions

If not developed carefully, some questions can ask for one answer to questions that could have multiple responses. For example, a question might ask respondents to agree or disagree with the following statement, "the U.S. should spend less money on military and more on environmental protection." A person could potentially agree with one part of the question (spend more on environmental issues) and disagree with the second part (spend less on military). The general rule for avoiding double-barreled questions is to pay special attention to any questions with the word "and" and check to make sure two questions are not being asked.

Avoiding Leading or Biased Questions

Leading/biased questions that should always be avoided tend to begin with "do you agree that..." or something similar. Leading and biased questions encourage respondents to answer in a particular way. Researchers should be aware and cautious of other, more subtle, wording that can have a biasing effect on responses.

Questions that include a well-known organization or person can also have a biasing effect. For example, asking if a respondent agrees or disagrees with the "Department of Environmental Protection's decision to ..." can have not only a biasing effect because of the mere mention of the respected agency, it can also trigger socially desirable answers. To avoid these types of bias, the researcher should develop questions keeping in mind the effect of the responses; i.e., will answering in a certain way cause embarrassment or a feeling of being an outcast? If so, the question should be rewritten to alleviate such reactions.

Question Format

A common mistake made in the questionnaire-construction process is too little attention spent on the actual layout of the questionnaire. Questionnaires that appear too cluttered or disorganized can result in low response rates. A great fear for inexperienced researchers is producing a questionnaire that is too long. To avoid this they mistakenly squeeze too many questions into too short a space. Questions should be spread out equally on the page with enough room for responses to be written in. Not only does this give the questionnaire a more professional look, but the space allows for fewer reading errors.

Flow of Questions

Generally, questionnaires move from general open-ended questions to specific close-ended questions. Questions should be grouped together according to the response scale used, even if the items address different issues.

Avoid Response Sets

Response sets occur when respondents begin a pattern in their answers and respond the same way to different questions regardless of their content. Response sets can be avoided by alternating the valence of item content. For example, when asking about someone's attitude toward the environment, one could question their degree of agreement with using less fossil fuel. They could follow this with a question that asks about their degree of agreement with how ineffective recycling is. Asking questions like this keeps the respondent's attention focused on the specific wording of each question and thinking about the responses available to them.

Questionnaire Instructions

Survey questionnaires should always be accompanied with some sort of cover letter stating the purpose of the study, gratitude for respondent participation and assurances of anonymity and confidentiality. The cover letter might also need to state the deadline for survey completion and provide well crafted instructions.

Specifying how the respondent should indicate their answers to questions is useful (e.g., placing a check mark in a box, circling a number). It is important that instructions be as clear and complete as possible to avoid any misunderstanding, misinterpretation or ambiguity.

In cases where open-ended responses are asked for, respondents should be given guidelines about the types of responses that are expected and whether they should be brief or more in-depth. When necessary, instructions should state when respondents are expected to elaborate on their close-ended question responses.

Pretest Questionnaires

Questionnaires should be administered to a subgroup of the target audience prior to fielding the study. This process allows the researcher the opportunity to identify potential errors in structure, wording or length of the instrument. Data from the pretest is generally not used in the final analysis. There are several key issues that should be considered during the pretest:

1. Length – approximately how long did it take the subgroup to complete the questionnaire? If the desired time limit is exceeded, the researcher may need to modify the questionnaire. If the time

limit was significantly shorter than anticipated, there may be room for additional questions.

2. Clarity – were items in the questionnaire clear and precise? Researchers should identify instances of uncertainty from the pretest group and modify the particular questions accordingly.

3. Flow – did the questionnaire have easy transitions and were respondents comfortable with the flow?

Pretest respondents should be encouraged to write down any comments they have regarding the questionnaire. Ample space should be provided for these comments, whether in the margins, or on a separate sheet provided by the researcher.

Final Steps

An edge coding system should be developed for the questionnaire. Coding is the process of converting the responses on the questionnaire into quantitative data. Edge coding identifies the columns in a spread sheet that questions are assigned to and what numeric values are assigned to which responses.

Monitoring Questionnaire Returns and Data Entry

Identification codes can be assigned to questionnaires that correspond to the list of names of persons that received the questionnaires. This gives the researcher the ability to track respondents and identify non-respondents so that they can follow-up with them. This should only be done for purposes of nonresponse followup so that guarantees of anonymity (the guarantee that responses will not connected to an individual) are not violated. The identification numbers also allows the researcher to identify which data in the spread sheet came from which questionnaire so errors in any data inputting process can be corrected if necessary.

CHAPTER 8
ISSUES WITH CAMPAIGN EVALUATION

Introduction

As resources available to support environmental campaigns have become more limited, the need for careful program evaluation has become more important. It is imperative that we use limited campaign resources in the most effective ways possible. Evaluation results can be helpful for assessing past efforts and therefore learning how to improve efforts in the future. Results that are widely shared can help others working on different campaigns learn about best practices.

Evaluation results are meant to be used. Campaign evaluation should not be viewed as just one more thing in a long list of necessary requirements from the funding agent, results of which are destined to gather dust on a shelf. This was too often the case in the past. Results are meant to identify strengths and weaknesses, inform about future options, and help in decision making.

Evaluation strategies need to be part of a campaign from the start and remain constant throughout the campaign. Thinking about how campaign outcomes will be evaluated at the end of a campaign begins at the beginning. Formative quantitative research data conducted at the start is often used as a baseline for comparing subsequent end-of-campaign evaluation research data. Carefully crafted objectives defined at the start serve to define outcomes that are to be evaluated at the end.

According to the W.K. Kellogg Evaluation Handbook (2004), you should engage in discussions with key stakeholder about the design of your evaluation strategy right from the beginning. It is vital that stakeholders feel ownership in the methods used and therefore the results that will be later obtained. Question that might initially be asked include:

- Who are the stakeholders and what will they need to know?
- What decisions will you need to make that you will need information about?

There are many barriers to overcome when conducting a campaign evaluation. According to Stacks (2011), research is often met with skepticism because stakeholders are often not trained in research methods and it is human nature to doubt what we do not know. They may think that campaigns deal with unmeasurable intangibles like beliefs and attitudes; and they may believe that poor research methods like biased questions or small samples are employed. The W.K. Kellogg Evaluation Handbook (2004) warns that those being evaluated may fear being judged or have concerns that the amount of resources being invested in the evaluation takes away from campaign implementation. It is up to the team conducting the campaign evaluation to alleviate these concerns from the very beginning.

Philosophy of Program Evaluation

As Anne Petersen, senior vice president for programs at the W.K. Kellogg Foundation, stated "Evaluation should be conducted not only to demonstrate that a project worked, but also to improve the way it works. An evaluation approach should be rigorous in its efforts to determine the worth of a program and to guide program implementation and management, as well as relevant and useful to other program practitioners" (W.K. Kellogg Evaluation Handbook (2004), pp1). Assessing impact (outcomes) and determining accountability were for many years how practitioners and sponsoring agencies perceived the purpose of evaluation. This sometimes (understandably) caused those in charge of the programs being evaluated to become defensive. People generally do not like feeling like they are being judged.

Evaluation should be much more. Evaluation is a learning tool that can help mangers do their job better. Evaluation is a tool that can shed light on midterm corrections in a campaign strategy that are necessary. Evaluation findings help not only those involved in the campaign being implemented, but also serve as a learning tool for those conducting other campaigns.

The following principles are what guide the W.K. Kellogg Foundations' approach to evaluation:

- Strengthen projects – by providing ongoing, systematic information that strengthens projects during their life cycle, and, whenever possible, outcome data to assess the extent of change.
- Use multiple approaches – multidisciplinary approaches that include a range of techniques.
- Design evaluation to address real issues – evaluation should be community-based and contextual (based on local circumstances and issues) that provide staff and stakeholders with reliable information from which to address problems and build on strengths and opportunities.
- Create a participatory process - that values multiple perspectives and involves a representation of people who care about the project.
- Allow for flexibility – projects are not discrete programs, but complex/comprehensive efforts that require approaches that are not rigid so that incremental and subtle changes can be detected over time.
- Build capacity – evaluation should be concerned not only with outcomes but also with building the knowledge and skills of those involved in the project.

Challenges to Evaluating Communication Campaigns

Over the past few decades, money for programs promoting social change has been systematically cut in drastic ways. With the realization that there is not enough money to fix everything, the focus has shifted on making sure that money is best spent where it will make a difference. This means increased pressure on developing better means of evaluating programs so that we can learn what works and what does not. There is a lot of pressure on project managers to demonstrate effectiveness.

Historically, evaluation has focused on proving rather than improving conditions. Quantitative methods that tried to establish impacts were the norm. Today there is still a strong focus on accountability (proving that a campaign worked), rather than on quality (working to develop ways to improve campaigns). The dominant evaluation paradigm is still too often the classic scientific method that uses experimental designs with treatment and control groups that look for statistically significant changes over time on targeted outcomes. These methods are designed to try to detect causal relationships between processes and outcomes. These types of evaluation designs are fine if there is a single intervention over a relatively short time period, involving a specific audience within the boundaries of a well-defined community. These designs are not well equipped to evaluate projects where there are multiple interventions, over lengthy periods of time, involving multiple audiences/stakeholders across broad geographic settings. In addition, the scientific paradigm is not well equipped to assess processes as they unfold, evolving objectives, and audiences that change at various paces – the reality of most projects. Employing the scientific paradigm can set up projects that are dynamic, complex, and comprehensive for irrational criticism and perhaps reduced funding because they appear impossible to evaluate.

This is not to say that the scientific paradigm is unimportant. Controlling outside factors that can affect the interpretation of results in a way that allows you to isolate and measure outcomes that were due to campaign interventions will always be important, but evaluation procedures also need to contribute to the body of knowledge on how to improve programs. Alternative evaluation paradigms that allow for this should also be considered.

According to the W.K. Kellogg Evaluation Handbook (2004), there are several consequences to following the scientific paradigm without regard to other paradigms. First, "the very dominance of the hypothetico-deductive paradigm, with its quantitative, experimental emphasis, appears to have cut off the great majority of its practitioners from serious consideration of any alternative evaluation research paradigm or methods" (Patton, 1997, p 270-271). Alternative paradigms that might be considered include:

- Constructivism methods – This approach is based on long-term in-depth contact with the subjects being affected by the program. It usually involves extensive qualitative descriptions and focuses on questions about processes and implementation.
- Feminist methods – This approach is especially sensitive to the inclusion of women and minorities, groups whose voices have sometimes been minimized in the past because they did not fit well with the assumption about the superiority of objective over subjective knowledge. Feminist approaches have been described

as "contextual, inclusive, experiential, involved, socially relevant, multi-methodological, complete but not necessarily replicable, open to the environment, and inclusive of emotions" (Nielson, 1990, p.6).

- Participatory methods – This approach strives to make the evaluation useful to all stakeholders, not just the evaluator or their agency. It inherently involves all stakeholders in the evaluation process from beginning to end. Results are meant to be useful and help future decision making.

- Theory-based methods – This approach tries to link outcomes to processes by relying on established theories to guide interpretations of results. These theories underlie the design of the campaign from its earliest stages of development. Theory allows evaluators to track processes and mid-term outcomes as the campaign unfolds. Theories appropriate to campaigns that seek environmental behavior change are discussed in Chapter 4.

The second consequence to following the scientific paradigm is that the results tell us little about processes - how and why programs work, who they work best for, and the circumstances that affect this. Evaluators should question the questions beings asked and strive to find out what is missing. Questions might include: Who all is affected? How? What does this mean? What have been the barriers and facilitating factors to the campaign? What lessons have been learned? What issue remain unresolved?

Third, projects that are based on "multi-source and multi-perspective community collaborations [with] goals and core activities/services constantly changing and evolving to meet the needs and priorities of a variety of community stakeholders... these initiatives are unevaluatable using the dominant natural science paradigm" (Connell, Kubisch, Schorr, and Weiss, 1995). In a climate of reduced funding and growing skepticism about the efficacy of social change programs, projects that are deemed unevaluatable may be doomed from the start.

Fourth, the scientific paradigm and its use of statistics to draw conclusions has the appearance of being objective. This perception can mask the fact that nearly all forms of evaluation are based on many value-laden assumptions about the purpose of the evaluation, whose interests are to be advanced or ignored, which respondents are to be approached, and how they will be questioned. Evaluators need to be sensitive to these potential biases and their implications. They need to challenge assumptions, foster an environment of openness and trust, and encourage stakeholders to voice their opinions and provide them with feedback.

According to Robert Hornick (2007), randomized control group evaluation designs comparing pre-campaign and post-campaign factors rarely show effects for several reasons.

He believes that the interaction of multiple campaign components over extended periods of time are complex and evolve dynamically. One-time outcome measures may not adequately capture the effects of processes on outcomes that have changed based on midterm feedback (campaign monitoring) during a lengthy campaign. In addition, many campaigns are designed to create relatively small changes that may be difficult to detect and these changes may take place within a small subset of the total audience. Evaluators need to focus on that segment of the audience that is apt to be most affected by campaign messages.

Hornick (2007) states that a pre-post design may in fact be a good evaluation design if there are few factors besides the campaign that might have influenced the outcomes. This might be the case with a short-term campaign in a narrowly defined geographic area with a specific target audience. For campaigns that take place over an extended period of time, it is important to control for outside factors that might influence the audience and to use multiple survey measures over time to assess campaign exposure.

Hornick believes it is especially important to assess exposure carefully as many campaigns fail because the audience lacks sufficient exposure to campaign messages. He states that "while it is always better to include more time points, comparison groups and mediating variables, as well as large samples, evaluators must make choices in designing an evaluation based upon what is possible given available resources" (Hornick, 2007, p 6). The issue is not if the evaluation isolates effects objectively, but whether the outcomes are truthful enough to be actionable given the limitations of the evaluation design, especially if the alternative is to have no evaluation at all. Some evaluation information is usually better than no information about how campaign processes affected outcomes as long as the potential flaws in that information are recognized.

Julia Coffman (2002) adds to the discussion of challenges that limit the ability to evaluate communication campaigns. One factor is that campaigns often seek change at multiple levels - societal level (e.g., policy), community (e.g., norms), and individual level (e.g., knowledge, attitude, behaviors).

The complexity of evaluating processes and outcomes at all these levels can be daunting. Another factor has to do with the unpredictable nature of media coverage. Often campaigns try to leverage donated media time where the timing and frequency of message dissemination can be quite variable and therefore have effects that are tough to assess. In addition, it has always been difficult to assess the number of audience members that media messages have actually reached, the frequency they have been reached, to what degree the audience has processed the messages, and the effects these messages have had. Coffman (2002), as did Hornick in 2007, recognizes the confounding influences of variables that can affect audience dispositions that are not part of the campaign and therefore can greatly complicate the ability to isolate the effects of the campaign. She states "it is difficult to isolate the effects of information campaigns on outcomes that are bombarded by many competing influences" (Coffman, 2002, p.11). In addition, she cautions that it is very difficult to secure a control group for comparison purposes when using experimental evaluation designs (w/ randomized assignment to conditions) or quasi-experimental (designs with no random assignment) and states that while these designs may not be essential, "without them it becomes difficult to say whether outcomes are the result of the campaign or would have occurred without it" (Coffman, 2002, p.12).

Conclusion

As resources to support communication campaigns affecting social change are reduced, as they have consistently been in recent decades, the importance of being able to carefully evaluate these campaigns grows. Evaluation is not just about assessing whether targeted outcomes were reached and holding people accountable for their efforts, though this is important. Evaluation is foremost is about learning from past efforts – learning how and why campaign processes worked to affect outcomes. It is important that evaluation findings be widely shared so they can help others working on different campaigns learn about best practices.

Various paradigms exist to guide evaluation efforts. The steadfast scientific approach with pre and post measures and experimental and equivalent control groups is only one paradigm. It may/may not be the best suited depending on the nature of the campaign. Campaigns that take place over lengthy time periods with multiple audiences and evolving objectives may require a different model. Context matters and various stakeholders may need to be assessed differently, perhaps more subjectively. Some evaluation information is better than no information as long as the context in which the data was collected and the objective versus subjective nature of this information is recognized.

The previous chapter (Chapter 7) discussed methods used to do formative research for planning a campaign. The next chapter (Chapter 9) will discuss monitoring and summative (evaluation) research methods. The final chapters of this book (Chapters 11 and 12) will provide cases studies that show the application of these research methods.

CHAPTER 9
RESEARCH METHODS FOR CAMPAIGN
MONITORING AND EVALUATION

Introduction

As stated in Chapter 3 and again in Chapter 7, managing an environmental social marketing campaign generally involves four steps:

1) Campaign planning
    a. Define issues and campaign objectives
    b. Define audiences
    c. Define messages
    d. Define communication channels
    e. Define information sources/strategic partners

2) Campaign implementation/management
3) Monitoring of campaign processes
4) Final outcome evaluation

The first three steps are iterative – that is, a campaign plan is developed, once the campaign is implemented, the effectiveness of campaign processes are monitored and problems with implementation are identified. Plans are then changed accordingly. This cyclical process continues until the campaign ends. At that point, a final evaluation is conducted to assess the extent to which campaign outcomes were met.

Step 3, monitoring of campaign processes, involves identifying problems associated with any of the ongoing message, channel, or source manipulations and adjusting campaign processes according to research findings. The research processes inherent in this step may involve archival research (e.g., review of project records and materials) to assess numbers of messages distributed or number of audience members reached and qualitative research (e.g., interviews in structured or unstructured settings) to assess perceptions of campaign messages and strategies.

Step 4, the final evaluation, generally has two parts – a process evaluation and an outcome evaluation. The process evaluation, a final extension of monitoring research described in Step 3, includes a summary of project archives, addresses the quality, quantity, and timing of messages and channels employed during the campaign, and draws conclusions concerning the effectiveness and efficiency of campaign implementation. The outcome evaluation assesses the degree that the campaign reached its stated objectives. The outcome evaluation is often conducted by comparing quantitative results of the pre-campaign survey described in Step 1 (see Chapter 7) with results of a post-campaign survey. Yet, if resources are limited, qualitative methods may be used to contrast pre and post-campaign audience dispositions.

Research Methods

MONITORING

Archival research findings may be used for monitoring the strengths and weaknesses of campaign processes as they unfold. This permits ongoing adjustments to be made so that campaign effectiveness can be maximized. Results of monitoring efforts may also provide information helpful for holding project partners accountable for the quality, quantity and timing of tasks they are charged with completing. A review of project records detailing what was done, how, when, and by whom will allow progress to be tracked. It is important, therefore, to keep good project records.

According to Broom and Dozier (1990), the following four variables might be useful to monitor:

- Message Content – This may help detect when content is wrong, inconsistent or insufficient. Methods for monitoring content range from intuitive judgments based on a simple subjective review of campaign materials to complex systematic coding of text using a number of coders and calculating reliability across these coders.

- Readability – This may help assess the sophistication of the language used in campaign messages. The optimum level of sophistication will range depending on the nature of the target audience. The Flesch Readability Formula (based on average word and sentence length) and the Grunig Fog Index (Broom and Dozier, 1990, pp 57-61) are two common ways to assess readability.

- Tracking – This refers to the number of messages distributed (e.g., number of brochures distributed or number of news stories generated in response to a news release). A firm may choose to contract with a company that specializes in tracking media placement. Media placement variables commonly monitored in response to a news release include column inches, amount of air time, or story location (e.g., placement on front page).

- Audience numbers – This refers to the extent that campaign messages are reaching the target audience. For mediated campaigns, five variables are commonly calculated:
  o Ratings - The percent of the total market who are watching/ listening to the program that includes your campaign message.
  o Share – The percent of the total number watching/ listening to the medium that are tuned into the specific program that includes your campaign message.
  o Cost efficiency – The total cost of placing the campaign message divided by the number of individuals who watched/ listened to it.
  o Reach - The number of individuals exposed to the message at least once in given timeframe across all media used.
  o Frequency – The average number of times an individual is exposed to a message in a given timeframe across all media used.

Social media has become a significant part of many campaigns. According to Watson and Noble (2005), monitoring the online component of a campaign includes both tracking and also identifying relevant conversations that might impact your objectives and then deciding if you want to intervene. Tracking might focus on the following variables:

- Exposure – how many people have been reached.
- Engagement – who is interacting with whom concerning the issue.
- Sentiment - what is the tone of these interactions.
- Influence – how attitudes have been affected.
- Actions – what actions has the audience taken

There are an ever-increasing number of tools available to monitor the effects of social media. A few are listed below. They are probably best used in combination to ensure that your results are valid.

- Google Alerts – a service that monitors Google web searches on specified topics.
- Google Trends – a service that monitors Google web searches on up to five topics and plots trends over a specified period of time.
- Google Analytics – a service that generates detailed statistics about visitors to websites.
- Technorati – a service that monitors and measures the scale of influence of various blogs.
- Twitter Search – a service that allows you to follow current feeds on Twitter by keywords.

FINAL EVALUATION

Process Evaluation

As stated in the beginning of the chapter, a final evaluation generally has two parts – a process evaluation and an outcome evaluation. The process evaluation part of the final evaluation is essentially a summary of project archives based on monitoring research conducted during the project. It identifies the strengths and weaknesses of the campaign strategy. When tied to program objectives and campaign outcomes, this information helps identify which processes worked best for which purposes. The process evaluation generally relies heavily on archival research methods, especially records of all the monitoring activities described above, and is sometimes supplemented with qualitative research methods such as interviews and/or focus group methods described in Chapter 7. The case study presented in Chapter 11 of this text presents an example of both archival and qualitative methods use to assess project processes.

Archival Research Assessing the Brownfields Demonstration Pilot Project, Haddam, CT.

Adapted from: Tyson, B., Faust, A., Marin, P. (2002). *A Rural Application of the Sustainable Brownfields Redevelopment Process*. Proceedings of Brownfields 2002 Conference, Charlotte, NC (Nov.).

Higganum Center, a small business center for the Town of Haddam, a small rural town (pop. 7000) in south-central Connecticut, was the setting of a Brownfields Demonstration Pilot Project awarded by the U.S. Environmental Protection Agency (EPA) that ran from fall 1999 to fall 2002. Early in the evolution of the project, after conducting extensive archival research on Brownfields projects, the Higganum Center Advisory Committee (HCAC), the local committee charged with coordinating the project, discovered that the EPA had contracted the Partnership for Sustainable Brownfields Redevelopment (PSBR) to assess the efficacy of a project model termed the Sustainable Brownfields Redevelopment Process (SBRP). The PSBR is a national multi-stakeholder non-profit organization comprised of leading organizations involved in Brownfields redevelopment in the United States.

The Partnership serves as an advisory resource for governments, community groups, corporations and developers. The Partnership is dedicated to implementing the SBRP as defined by ASTM Standard guide E 1984 – 98 developed under the jurisdiction of Subcommittee E50.03 on Global Sustainability/Pollution Prevention. The SBRP is a voluntary effort that collaboratively engages property owners, developers, government agencies, and the community in conducting corrective action, economic evaluation, and other actions to promote the long-term productive reuse of a Brownfields property.

HCAC members approached the PSBR to find out if the SBRP would be a model suitable for the Higganum project. It was and the Higganum Brownfields project ended up being one of four sites in the U.S. to pilot test the SBRP. The other sites, all urban, included Bridgeport, Connecticut; Trenton, New Jersey; and Columbia, Mississippi. The HCAC contracted with the Center for Social Research (CSR) at Central Connecticut State University (CCSU) to help evaluate the efficacy of their application of the SBRP.

The HCAC initiated implementation of the project in winter 1999/2000. The CSR collected quantitative baseline data from the three stakeholder groups in spring 2000 and final evaluation data in fall 2002. In addition, the CSR initiated an ongoing form of archival research to assess project processes. The diagram below outlines the objectives and indicators used to assess project processes and outcomes. Following this is a summary of a) project records describing publications and b) attendance records of meetings.

Objectives	Process indicators	Outcome indicators
I. Increased knowledge among stakeholders concerning environmental assessment procedures and findings	a. Number of publications b. Amount of media coverage c. Number of meetings d. Degree of attendance at meetings e. Quality of publications f. Quality of meetings g. Quality/clarity of environmental assessment reports	Pre-post survey differences in knowledge of environmental assessment issues
II. Increased input from stakeholders in process of developing village-wide development plans.	a. Survey results b. Number of meetings c. Quality of meetings d. Attendance at meetings	Pre-post survey differences in perceived input
III. High levels of confidence among stakeholders concerning the efficacy of village-wide development plans		Pre-post survey differences in perceptions of efficacy/ realism of plans

IV. Stakeholders committed to implementing development plans for Higganum Center.		Pre-post survey differences in perceptions of support for implementing plans

Summary of archival research findings:

1) Number of publications
   - 1 fact sheet
   - 1 Land Trust newsletter article
   - 8 Haddam Bulletin articles

2) Amount of media coverage
   Articles included announcements of upcoming meetings and information on environmental assessment findings, redevelopment plans for Higganum, development of youth center/veterans museum, reconstruction of the reservoir dam, new zoning regulations.
   - 15 Middletown Press articles
   - 7 Hartford Courant articles
   - 3 Hometown Journal articles
   - 1 Connecticut Business Journal article

3) Number of meetings
   - 20 two-hour Higganum Center Advisory Committee meetings
   - 2 multi-stakeholder public meetings (duration two hours each)
   - 8 homeowner stakeholder meetings (duration two hours each)
   - 13 middle school youth stakeholder meetings (duration 45 minutes each)
   - 3 business owner stakeholder meetings (duration 90 minutes each)

4) Degree of attendance at meetings
   - Higganum Center Advisory Committee : range 4-8, average = 6
   - Multi-stakeholder meetings: range 30-51, average = 40
   - Homeowner meetings: range 5-29, average = 13
   - Youth meetings: range 8-28, average = 12
   - Business owner meetings: range 11 – 6, average = 8

Outcome evaluation

An outcome evaluation assesses the degree that a campaign reached its stated objectives and is often conducted by comparing quantitative results of the pre-campaign planning survey with results of a post-campaign final evaluation survey. This is what was referred to as the "scientific approach" in Chapter 8 and as stated, may be a good evaluation design if there are few factors besides the campaign that might have influenced the outcomes. For campaigns that take place over an extended period of time it will be important to control for outside factors that might influence the audience and this may call for a different or augmented evaluation protocol.

When following the scientific method, quantitative data used to plan the campaign can be thought of as baseline data – that is, it provides a snap shot at the beginning of the project of the target audience's initial levels of awareness, knowledge, attitudes, intentions, and/or behaviors. At the end of the project another quantitative questionnaire similar to that used earlier for planning purposes is distributed and data is gathered for conducting the final evaluation. By comparing baseline levels with end-of-project levels, conclusions can be drawn about campaign effectiveness.

As discussed in Chapter 8, campaigns do not operate in a vacuum. Audience members are constantly bombarded with messages from a variety of sources, not just the campaign – and some of these messages may relate to the campaign's theme and either strengthen or weaken pursuit of campaign objectives. Results of the final evaluation need to be interpreted in this regard. Related messages and other forms of potentially relevant influence that do not emanate from the campaign should be reported so that readers can assess the degree that campaign outcomes are in fact due to campaign processes.

Two research designs are most common for final evaluation purposes. One is a simple randomized one group, pre-test/post-test design in which respondents are surveyed before and after the campaign. This can be appropriate when it is deemed there are few factors besides the campaign that might have influenced the outcomes. This may be the case with a short-term campaign. In this design, the same respondent, randomly sampled from the population for the baseline pre-test measure, can again be assessed for the final post-test measure. If this protocol is followed, individual responses at both time periods can be compared to discern changes due to the campaign. This is called a "panel" study. Alternatively, a new sample of respondents can be drawn for the post-test measure. If this protocol is followed, combined responses for the pre-test group can be compared with combined responses for the post-test group to discern changes due to the campaign. This is called a "trend" study. A panel study is a more powerful design for assessing campaign effects when there is good response to the post-test survey; but when plagued by high post-test nonresponse, a trend study may be the protocol of choice.

The second design adds a control group to the randomized one group pre-test/post-test design described above. The control group will very closely resemble the group affected by the campaign except that they are not exposed to campaign messages. As mentioned in Chapter 8, it can be very difficult to establish an equivalent control group. Nevertheless, given one can be identified, the control group receives the same pre-test and post-test surveys. Either a panel study or trend study design can be followed. The addition of the control group allows researchers, by comparing pre-test and post-test results, to define the effects of any non-campaign influences. Then by comparing changes in the group affected by the campaign with changes in the control group, actual changes due to the campaign can be isolated. If the campaign takes place over an extended period of time and changes in the audience are apt to be influenced by other factors besides the campaign, than a pretest-posttest control group design may be best.

Threats to the internal validity (i.e., the assurance that you are measuring what you intend to measure) of the one group, pre-test/post-test design include the following:

- Selection – did the random selection process work as intend to give you the same distribution in your sample as in your target population for both the pre- and post-tests?
- Mortality – did subjects you were assessing drop out between your pre- and post-test surveys (this is an issue with trend studies)?
- Instrumentation – were there biased questions or biased interviewers that affected the way subjects responded?
- Testing – were subjects sensitized by the pretest so that they could foretell how best to respond on the post-test survey?
- History – were there things that happen in the outside environment during the campaign that could have influenced subjects' knowledge, attitudes or behaviors on the post-test survey?

- Maturation – did a sufficient amount of time pass between the pre- and post-test surveys that subjects would have naturally matured in a way that would affect their post-test responses?
- Regression – did a sufficient amount of time pass between the pre- and post-test surveys that subjects who scored in the extreme would naturally regress toward the mean over time?

Comparing the group that received the campaign with a group that did not using a pretest post-test control group design allows evaluators to assess the influence of most of these internal validity threats (i,e., Mortality, Instrumentation, Testing, History, Maturation, Regression). This allows them to detect the degree that campaign outcomes are in fact due to campaign processes. The threat from Mortality can also be minimized by using a trend study rather than a panel study. One remaining threat, Selection, is always problematic but with careful randomization procedures and larger sample sizes this threat can be minimized.

There are two threats to the external validity of any evaluation design. External validity is defined as the ability to generalize results from your sample to the target population. These include Selection, as defined above, and Nonresponse. As stated, threats due to Selection can be minimized by careful randomization and larger samples. Threats due to subjects in your sample not responding can be problematic and depending on your data collection methods may be more or less of a threat. Following the *Dillman Technique* (Dillman, Smyth, & Christian, 2009) mentioned in Chapter 7 will help minimize nonresponse to surveys.

As previously stated, campaigns that take place over an extended period may call for a different evaluation protocol in which there are multiple outcome measures taken at various times. There may or may not be a control group. This design will enable researchers to account for changing campaign processes as the campaign unfolds. As stated in Chapter 8, the environment in which a campaign takes place is dynamic, it evolves based on current thinking guided by the results of careful monitoring of campaign processes. Monitoring results allow campaign managers to change their approaches to achieving their objectives as the need arises. An initial pre-test measure at Time 1 that provides you with the information necessary to design your campaign (and serves as a baseline for a subsequent outcome evaluation), can be followed by other outcome measures at Time 2, 3, 4, etc., (perhaps quarterly or biannually) to track outcomes over an extended period of time. Comparing Time 1 with Time 2, Time 2 with Time 3, etc. will allow you to assess outcomes as campaign strategies evolve (change), as they invariably should and inevitably will. Matching these various outcome evaluation results with corresponding process evaluation results assessed at the same time period will allow campaign managers to sharpen their strategies as necessary to improve odds that the campaign will eventually be successful.

Alternative Outcome Evaluation Strategies

The outcome evaluation strategy mentioned above, commonly referred to as the scientific approach, with pre and post measures and experimental and equivalent control groups is only one evaluation strategy. As stated in the previous chapter, it may/may not be the best suited depending on the nature of the campaign. The scientific approach may not be well equipped to assess processes as they unfold, evolving objectives, and audiences that change at various paces – which is the reality of many projects. Context matters and various stakeholders may need to be assessed differently, perhaps more subjectively. Alternative approaches may be better suited to tell us more about processes - how and why programs work, who they work best for, and the circumstances that affect this.

As discussed in Chapter 8, these alternative approaches may include any (or all) of the following: a) constructivism methods that involve long-term in-depth contact with the audience resulting in extensive qualitative descriptions, b) feminist methods that that are especially sensitive to the inclusion of women and minorities which also seeks to document subjective qualitative observations, and c) participatory methods that involve all stakeholders in the evaluation process from the beginning to ensure that results will be useful. These alternative approaches can be used alone, in concert with each other, or as a complement to the scientific approach. Regardless of the approach/approaches chosen, theory-based methods (also discussed in Chapter 8) will provide an underlying framework that will help link campaign outcomes to campaign processes and guide interpretations of results. Theories appropriate to campaigns that seek environmental behavior change are discussed in Chapter 4.

Planning, Implementing and Utilizing
Results of an Evaluation Program

The evaluation protocol that is chosen for a project is usually unique to that project but generally, evaluation exercises should follow certain steps if they are going to prove worthwhile. The steps described below are closely patterned on those put forth in the W.K. Kellogg Foundation Evaluation Handbook (2010). The steps may overlap and several may be worked on simultaneously.

The first step begins what the W.K. Kellogg Foundation Evaluation Handbook (2010) calls the planning phase. It involves identifying key stakeholders and establishing the evaluation team. Stakeholders can be funders, project staff, administrators, evaluators, a wide variety of audience members with divergent interests, collaborating agencies, etc.. It is best to involve as many people as possible in the design process so you get a diverse set of views. At minimum, you should get feedback from stakeholders on tentative ideas and draft materials before they are finalized.

The second step involves developing your evaluation questions. Questions to ask yourself applicable to all projects include: What do you want the project to accomplish? What are the indicators that reflect the degree that these accomplishments have been realized? What will those interested in the project want to know? What evaluation activities will be necessary? What barriers might need to be overcome? Each stakeholder will need to respond with answers to these questions. To gain consensus, stakeholders need to agree on the basic approach or philosophy that will be followed. It must be remembered that the evaluation process is as dynamic as the campaign itself and that your strategies will need to be reviewed and revised periodically.

The third step concerns budgeting for the evaluation process. Generally, a campaign evaluation exercise requires between 5% and 7% of an overall budget. Qualitative research via interviews, because it is usually labor and time intensive, is often more costly and time consuming that quantitative survey research. This needs to be factored in. The budget will also need to be reviewed and revised periodically.

The forth step involves selecting an evaluator. Evaluators can be drafted from within the organization, hired from outside the organization, or both. Their philosophy and approach to evaluation should be a critical concern.

Evaluators need to be flexible and objective. They need to be skilled in listening, negotiating, and consensus building. Their job is to help build the capacity of all stakeholders to perform their jobs well. A key question to consider is: How much do you want the evaluator engaged in the campaign versus viewing it from a distance?

The fifth step begins what the W.K. Kellogg Foundation Evaluation Handbook (2010) calls the implementation phase. It involves determining your data collection methods. Employing a combination of archival, qualitative and quantitative methods is usually best. Once you have questions, you need to decide how to answer them, what methods will be used, how the data will be analyzed, and how best to present findings so that they will be used. When choosing methods you need to consider a) what resources (i.e., money, time and talent) you have available to do the task, b) what cultural factors might come into play (i.e., language or literacy issues), c) the credibility of your measures (i.e., potential threats to both the internal validity and external validity of your research discussed earlier in this chapter). Details concerning methods for collecting archival, qualitative and quantitative data are discussed in Chapter 7.

Once your data collection methods have been decided, the sixth step involves the actual data collection process. It is important that you focus on collecting data that the stakeholders have decided is relevant for your purposes and not get sidetracked. It is important that everyone that is involved in data collection has a say in choosing the methods and developing the questions.

The seventh step involves analyzing and interpreting the data. As stated in the W.K. Kellogg Foundation Evaluation Handbook (2010), "Complex statistical analyses of a well-designed experimental investigation that does not lead to improvements are less desirable than a thorough but simple statistical analysis of existing tracking records" (p 88). An effective discussion about the types of data generated by different types of questions and the descriptive and inferential statistics suitable for these data is beyond the scope of this text. Yet, it does need to be noted that quantitative statistical evidence often has the aura of being objective and qualitative data has the aura of being subjective. This is not always the case. As mentioned above, the credibility of quantitative data is always subject to potential (and often uncontrolled) threats to both the internal validity and external validity of the research methods (e.g., small/skewed samples, non-equivalent control groups, confounding influences from outside the campaign, biased interviewers, leading questions). In addition, though qualitative findings are often useful for bring color/life to otherwise sterile statistics, this is not all they can do. Qualitative data can frequently help explain things that quantitative data cannot. Qualitative data can provide evidence for things that are hard to measure quantitatively.

The eighth step begins what the W.K. Kellogg Foundation Evaluation Handbook (2010) calls the utilization phase. This involves communicating your findings to the stakeholders. It is very important to include all stakeholders in the process of interpreting the findings. This builds ownership in the results and improves the likelihood that the results will be used. Formal reports and presentations will be necessary. We live in a busy world so it is important to keep them clear and concise. An executive summary that highlights the important points will always be necessary. More popular pieces and press releases based on the report can be written for media consumption. Press conferences can be held. Tailored presentations highlighting particularly relevant findings can be made to narrowly defined groups of stakeholders. In addition, it is important to use high quality graphics.

The ninth and last step involves making sure the findings are used. Evaluation findings are meant to be acted upon. They are not meant to just garner a cursory review and then sit on a shelf. Findings are meant to inform decisions, clarify options, identify strengths and weaknesses, and help develop ideas on how to improve the campaign. Thinking about how evaluation results will be used should be an ongoing concern all through the evaluation process. As stated, it is very important that stakeholders feel a sense of ownership in the results. This improves the likelihood that the results will be used.

Chapter 10
Project Management

Introduction

So far this book has discussed strategies for influencing environmental behaviors and the research methods used to plan, monitor and evaluate campaigns. This chapter addresses management issues involved in implementing a project. Issues are discussed in the order they happen; i.e., pre-project through post-project stages. As is the case with most things strategic, a considerable amount of effort is put into planning before the actual effort begins. The degree that implementation, monitoring and post-project evaluation stages proceed smoothly is directly related to the amount of effort initially expended in the pre-project planning stage.

Management issues are different for environmental practitioners depending if they are aligned with governmental agencies/departments, private nonprofit organizations/advocacy groups, or grassroots citizen-action groups. This chapter discusses a wide array of management issues. Not all issues are uniformly applicable. The specific application of these issues will depend on the nature of the agency/organization/group initiating the project.

Pre-project activities

PLANNING THE CAMPAIGN

Anyone attempting to initiate a grassroots campaign to clean-up and/or protect a favored natural resource will need unwavering passion for the resource and strong personal commitment to the project (Bolling, 1994).

This advice is probably applicable to any agency, organization or group initiating a campaign regardless of the environmental context. This passion and commitment helps project leaders weather the inevitable conflicts they will experience over the lengthy time period required for most successful campaigns. Additionally, the greater the motivation and strength exhibited by campaign decision-makers, the more likely that support from project partners, constituents, political allies, and other stakeholders will be sustained. This is important as the degree of success a campaign obtains is usually related positively to the number of stakeholders actively supporting the project (i.e., success in numbers). Yet Bolling (1994) cautions, passion for the resource must be tempered with the need to make rational decisions – i.e., don't let runaway emotion dictate the campaign strategy.

As stated previously in Chapter 3, managing a project strategically begins by carefully defining the issues driving the need for the campaign and the objectives that the campaign aims to achieve. Objectives may be ordered in a temporal sense. For instance, the objective early in the project may be to increase audience awareness of the project and the issues it seeks to address. Once this is achieved, the objective may shift to increasing knowledge about what is involved in performing the actions being promoted by the project. A campaign may aim to have audience members seek information/assistance from campaign partners at this stage. Once basic knowledge is imparted, campaign objectives may target positive changes in key attitudes predictive of the promoted behavior (e.g., perceptions of costs, benefits, threats, efficacy, norms). The ultimate objective would be getting audience members to perform the promoted behavior.

Once project objectives are defined, the challenge is to define target audiences. The primary target audience is the group(s) you want to see actually performing the promoted behaviors (e.g., organization members/ potential members, landowners, youth, business owners, government officials). Secondary target audiences are those groups that can help you achieve project objectives (e.g., project partners, potential suppliers, media gatekeepers, political allies). Once target audiences are defined, campaign messages are crafted for each group and spokespersons are selected and channels of delivery are determined. Defining campaign objectives, audiences, and associated messages, sources and communication channels is the drive behind the need for careful pre-campaign research.

DEVELOP PROJECT IDENTITY

Simultaneous to planning the campaign, the project will need to develop its identity. A clearly defined identity is key to increasing audience familiarity with the project. This may include: a catchy project name, clear/concise mission statement, simple/memorable logo, noteworthy signage, attractive letterhead, a basic brochure, newsletter, 1-800 phone number, a website, and a social-media presence. A vivid emotion-generating image to support the project identity that can be photographed and described creatively should be developed.

DEVELOP MANAGEMENT SYSTEMS

Once the project has started branding its identity, it will need to spend some time developing management systems. The appropriateness of the following suggestions depend on the nature of the lead agency/organization/group.

- Recruit staff – both paid and volunteer.
- Create a Board of Directors – pick those who represent key constituencies, provide expertise, lend credibility, can raise money, or help get work done.
- Establish an office - home office, shared office, or new office depending on finances.
- Establish office communications - phone, fax, email, social media.
- Choose a tax status – possibly incorporate as tax-exempt non-profit organization as this may be key for securing foundation grants.
- Construct a budget.
- Establish accounting procedures.
- Define a fund raising strategy.
- Construct a timeline showing principal project activities and staff responsibilities.

IDENTIFY AND ENLIST KEY PARTNERS AND/OR ORGANIZATION MEMBERS

As management systems develop, the organization will have greater capacity to secure assistance of project partners, volunteers, and/or build its membership. Project partners and volunteers may include organizations and individuals with complementary objectives that have a synergistic effect, potential suppliers of required information, assistance or materials, media gatekeepers whose cooperation is required to get campaign messages out, or political allies who can help remove barriers and facilitate activities.

The quality and quantity of individuals and groups supporting an effort is positively related to the amount of funds that can be leveraged and the power that can be exerted. The organization should define the role its partners/members can play and what it can offer them. Some partners/members will want to be involved, some will just believe in the cause and want a periodic update.

If the lead organization is a membership-based group, a member database will need to be constructed and a quick/timely method of contacting new members will need to be devised. The organization should develop a newsletter and use direct mail and public events to prospect for members.

Bolling (1994) suggests that special attention be paid to four groups: private landowners, business owners, the media, and politicians. Be sure to bring key landowners into the planning process early – though they may be part of the problem, they are also part of the solution. Bolling cautions that you should not appear to be restricting the individual freedoms of landowners as these concerns, aggravated by lack of information, can have very negative effects. Seek support of the business community – some say: "money makes might and might makes right". From a business-owners perspective, environmental correctness can yield economic gains via public relations profits. Cultivate relationships with media representatives and get them to experience the resources the project is trying to protect (e.g., take a hike, canoe a river). Develop a highly polished informational kit to share with the media containing fact sheets, brochures, press releases, photographs, etc. Lastly, put together a list of politicians to target and develop informational kits for them. Research a politician's history and shape campaign messages to fit their mind frame (i.e., frame issues so they will achieve political mileage and impress them with your constituent base).

Politicians as Target Audiences

Politicians, be they members of the U.S. Congress or state legislatures, can play an important role in a social marketing campaign. Politicians can be important allies or adversaries. They may be the campaign's primary target audience if the objective is to pass environmental legislation or a secondary audience if they have the ability to facilitate campaign processes (e.g., serve as a spokesperson for a campaign). Our system of democracy is built on citizen input. Environmental initiatives championed by private-sector for-profit and nonprofit organizations or grassroots citizen-action groups often become law.

Strategies for dealing directly with politicians generally have an individualized focus (i.e., unique strategies are devised for each politician targeted). Additionally, strategies that target members of a politician's constituent base are often employed to mobilize public pressure on the politician.

As stated, it is especially important to research a politician's history and shape campaign messages to fit their mind frame. Legislators tend to be very busy people, with many constituents, and limited ability to research the issues. Because of this, your approach will need to be succinct and convincing. Harrison (1992) suggests that positive and constructive messages should be used and that messages should be nontechnical and framed in a way that the legislator can use the issue to maintain/build political support at home. The initial objective is to reach broad agreement with the politician and let their staff work out the details later.

Grassroots techniques for mobilizing broad public support to influence (positively or negatively) voting on a bill before congress is an effective method of influencing environmental legislation. Grassroots techniques generally involve the formation of a Citizen Action Group with a campaign strategy for influencing legislators. As discussed in this text, a successful Citizen Action Group will select target audiences, determine message, receiver, and channel factors, define duties and create a timetable. Harrison (1992) provides the following suggestions to Citizen Action Groups:

- The final outcome in the legislative process is a hearing held before and after a bill is introduced. A Citizen Action Group

- can request an invitation to testify at these hearings. If this is granted, visit members of the hearing committee, get to know their names, get to know their views, and prepare your strategy accordingly.
- Neutralize your opposition. Let your opposition know they will be challenged. Let legislators know there is formidable opposition. Let the media know there is a knowledgeable alternative view.
- Instigate a stream of letters to legislators. Tell legislators what their home constituency expects.
- Generate favorable news coverage.

DEVELOP OUTREACH TOOLS

Based on results of initial project planning research, develop the content of campaign messages and plan the choice of communication sources/channels for each target audience for each stage of the campaign. Simultaneously, decide how these outreach tools will be produced. The sophistication of these products will depend on available finances. Outreach tools can be developed for low, moderate and high-end budgets. For instance, informational videos or websites can be developed by students studying communication/media at a local college or contracted out to a professional media production studio; publications can be designed using simple desktop publishing software at home by a volunteer or contracted to a professional graphic design firm. Message content and production designs should be pilot tested with individuals from the target audience to catch potential misinterpretation or disfavor prior to production/duplication.

Outreach tools may include: a website, social media outlets, 1-800 phone number, a variety of print materials (e.g., simple brochure, detailed instructional manual), awareness-raising video, how-to instructional video, press releases, PSAs for television and radio, etc. The project website address, social media links, and 1-800 number should be displayed prominently in most materials. It is helpful to have outreach tools produced/duplicated prior to initiation of a campaign so that roll-out of the campaign can be seamless. Distribution delays should be avoided so that scheduled sequencing of messages can be followed and effects of the campaign can be maximized.

DEVELOP A MONITORING AND EVALUATION STRATEGY

It is essential to develop a monitoring and evaluation strategy before a campaign begins. Both campaign processes (use of outreach tools) and campaign outcomes (changes in awareness, knowledge, attitudes and/or behavior) will need to be monitored as the campaign unfolds. The quality, quantity and effects of campaign processes on both primary and secondary audiences will need to be periodically assessed. Based on campaign outcome objectives, changes in initial levels of awareness, knowledge, attitudes and/or behavior will need to be monitored throughout the campaign and eventually compared to end-of-project levels to ascertain the overall effects of the campaign.

Monitoring methods usually include careful record keeping (e.g., workshop/meeting attendance, number of publications, videos or PSAs produced/distributed, record of telephone, social media and website activity), individual workshop/meeting evaluations, a clipping file of publicity generated, and summaries of informal discussion/feedback from audiences/stakeholders. Evaluation methods usually include a comparison of data collected on pre-campaign and post-campaign audience surveys.

DEVELOP A PERT CHART

PERT stands for Program Evaluation and Review Technique (Beebe and Masterson, 1994). It is an invaluable tool for managing the implementation of a campaign. A PERT chart outlines who is expected to do what by which date. It helps project managers track the myriad tasks and actors involved in the campaign. At a glance, project managers can anticipate what needs to be accomplished by when and what might be the ramifications of any delays. If necessary, the need for adjustments in scheduling tasks down-the-line can be realized early. Contingencies for delays should always be made, as delays will happen.

A PERT chart can be quite large and detailed, specifying all the tasks required of all project staff and partners from planning through final evaluation stages of the campaign. Charts can also be developed at various levels – a monthly chart can layout the major tasks required over the life of the campaign; a weekly chart can do the same on a daily basis. PERT charts are an effective tool for holding staff and partners accountable.

Establishing the Mattabesset River Watershed Association

Adapted from Creighton, J. (1999). A Strategic Communication Campaign for the Mattabesset River Watershed. University of New Haven, December, 1999

When the Mattabesset River Watershed Association (MRWA) first took shape, the first order of business was to establish its identity and develop a management structure. The organization is a grassroots effort attempting to spread environmental conservation messages about Mattabesset River across a multi-town area.

Initial meetings of the organization included interested citizens and members of Inland-Wetland and Conservation Commissions from the six main watershed towns. They agreed that the Mattabesset river watershed needed an advocacy group. The group chose the name *Mattabesset River Watershed Association* with the hope that it would draw attention to the fact that all land within the watershed affected the health of the river.

Vision and Mission Statements

An important exercise at early meetings of the Association was the creation of a vision and a mission statement. The vision statement captures the goal of the group. The mission statement is the method by which the group reaches that goal. Ideas were discussed until the group reached consensus on statements that were concise yet powerful and meaningful in their simplicity.

The *Vision* of the Mattabesset River Watershed Association is to have people within the Mattabesset watershed see it as a valued resource.

The *Mission* of the organization is to protect and preserve the waters and riparian habitat in the Mattabesset River watershed for the benefit of present and future generations.

Logo

The Association was very fortunate to have its meandering river logo provided free-of-charge by a local graphic artist. This symbol was placed on an eight foot by three foot banner which the group displays at every public function. Linking the logo with the group name and placing it on letterhead and newsletters helped the organization build its identity.

Website

The MRWA director himself built the initial website, complete with a calendar of events, pictures of recent events, a map of the watershed, and links to other similar websites. It is necessary to find responsible individuals who can communicate with others on behalf of the Association, who know the day-to-day happenings of the organization, and can see that information on the website is constantly updated. This can be difficult.

Brochure

Another main communication tool is MRWA's brochure which prominently displays the Association's name and logo. The brochure is attractive, informative and simple. It answers who the organization is, why it was formed, what it does, and why interested readers should join and support it. A map indicates the boundaries of the Mattabesset River watershed. Black printing on any color of paper allows for easy printing.

Newsletter

Members don't receive a lot in return for their membership dues other than the regular newsletter. Succinctly named "Mattabesset Matters", the organization keeps members abreast of recent activities with the quarterly newsletter. Common word processing software allows for easy layout on a home computer.

Tax status

Any organization expecting to collect money from others must declare a tax status through incorporation with the Internal Revenue Service. At one of the early meetings of the organization, an individual from "Rivers Alliance of Connecticut", a mentoring group that helps new watershed groups establish themselves, explained various options available under the U.S. tax code. MRWA chose the nonprofit designation of 501(c)(3) which allows the group to collect dues and donations and raise funds as long as funds are spent only in support of the organization. The designation as 501(c)(3) allows individuals who donate money to the group to itemize that donation on their own individual tax return. The designation as a 501(c)(3) does not allow MRWA to lobby politicians.

Bylaws and a Board of Directors

To incorporate under the 501(c)(3) status, a group must have bylaws which dictate how directors of the organization are appointed and how officers of that board are determined. A common practice, which was followed by MRWA, is to duplicate the bylaws of a similar nonprofit group, amend the wording to fit the desires of the new group, and approve the new set as the bylaws of the new group. MRWA patterned their bylaws on the existing bylaws of another small watershed group.

Individuals who had attended the startup meetings became the first board of directors. The bylaws dictate that each town within the watershed should be represented by a director, but that other interested volunteers not from those towns can become "at large" directors.

Budget

MRWA has not had large sums of money to budget. Expenses consist of photocopies, supplies, and refreshments for meetings, river cleanups, and other events. A rule of thumb is that membership dues should account for 75% of an organization's income. MRWA's goal is to increase its budget via increased membership.

Staff

Through a small watershed assistance grant provided by the State of Connecticut, MRWA was able to hire its first employee on a part time basis in the summer of 2002. Prior to this, volunteers organized all events. Volunteers will no doubt continue to shoulder the bulk of the work.

Office location

MRWA operates out of the homes of its Director and volunteers. Meetings are held in public meeting rooms of town halls or libraries. It is hoped that with paid staff, MRWA can invest time and resources into fundraising and membership drives (including events such as canoe trips and river clean-up days). With a larger budget, MRWA could then rent an office location.

Basic Communications (email, phone, website)

The lack of a central office has not meant a lack of communications between volunteers and the public. Volunteers communicate with each other through their own email addresses. The phone number on the brochure is the home phone number of the Director. The website provides basic information for newcomers about the organization.

Implementing and Monitoring the Project

Given that sufficient time and effort was allocated to the pre-project planning activities described above, implementation of the campaign should begin smoothly. Yet, changes in the initial campaign plan (i.e., changes in outreach tools, partners involved, target audiences, pace, scheduling or staff responsibilities) will undoubtedly need to be made based on monitoring results as the campaign unfolds. Campaign management is a cyclical process of planning, implementation, and assessment.

Evaluating the Communication Campaign

The initial survey conducted to collect information necessary for planning the campaign also provides benchmark data to evaluate project outcomes. The challenge at the end of the campaign is to ascertain the degree that project outcome objectives were met for each target audience and what campaign processes were most/least effective (i.e., to assess whether targeted changes in initial levels of awareness, knowledge, attitudes and/or behavior were realized and what outreach tools worked best).

An overall assessment of campaign processes can be assembled from documented monitoring results. Outcomes can be assessed by conducting a post-campaign survey and comparing pre-campaign findings with post-campaign findings. Basic campaign effects can be determined by assessing pre-post changes in awareness of campaign identity and interest in campaign objectives. Intermediate campaign effects can be determined by assessing pre-post changes in knowledge and key beliefs associated with campaign messages. Advanced campaign effects can be determined by assessing pre-post changes in attitudes, intentions and behaviors/practices associated with campaign objectives.

CHAPTER 11
CASE STUDY: THE EIGHT MILE
RIVER WATERSHED PROJECT

Information used in the construction of this chapter is adapted from: three research reports completed by the author for the University of Connecticut Cooperative Extension System Forestry Program (2000): 1) The Eight Mile River Watershed Resource Planning and Outreach Project – A Model for the Connecticut River Ecosystem, 2) The Eight Mile River Watershed Resource Planning and Outreach Project Process Evaluation Report, and 3) The Eight Mile River Watershed Resource Planning and Outreach Project Outcome Evaluation Report.

The chapter provides a case study that illustrates the design, implementation and evaluation of a program for environmental behavior change that uses most of the social influence theories, strategies, research methods, and management principles discussed in this book.

Introduction

The Eight Mile River Watershed Project conducted by the University of Connecticut Cooperative Extension System is a good example of a campaign that blended educational, persuasive, reinforcement, and participatory strategies. The campaign addressed forest conservation issues in the Connecticut River "Tidelands Region" of south-central Connecticut. This is an area of Connecticut recognized as a wetlands system of international importance by the Ramsar Convention (Tyson & Worthley, 2001). The campaign dealt with both acute and nonacute problems. Though there was a lot of varied public opinion surrounding the issues, there was considerable agreement among project technical advisors concerning the required changes and the science supporting these interventions. Hence, according to Focht (1995), because the campaign has low social and high scientific consensus, education and social marketing strategies would be appropriate. The general objectives of the campaign were for landowners with five or more acres to:

1) Become knowledgeable about the importance of their land management practices in the context of the long-term health of the watershed.
2) Become knowledgeable about resource inventory and stewardship planning and the benefits of those activities.
3) Show positive pre- to post-campaign changes in attitudes that influence stewardship behavior.
4) Assess conditions and compile an inventory of forest resources.
5) Formulate specific stewardship goals and develop forest stewardship plans.

Funding for the project was provided by the U. S Forest Service Stewardship Incentive Program (SIP). In addition to funds provided for the education/communication aspects of the campaign, cost-share monies were available to help offset what landowners paid for improvements to their properties. These cost-share monies were an important incentive (reinforcement strategy), especially for the larger landowners, as some of the practices being promoted were costly (e.g., comprehensive assessment and planning, selective forest cuts, wetlands protection measures).

Research was initially conducted to define the primary target audience, messages for this audience, and their preferred communication channels and sources of information. Those who showed strong inclination to protect land from development and develop forest stewardship plans were chosen as the primary target audience (35% of the population).

Findings showed that this group, compared to other segments, believed strongly that watershed resources were indeed at risk. They thought that rivers and streams, trees and plants, and production of forest products were at greatest risk; and they perceived that the top three benefits of forest stewardship planning were preserving natural beauty, insuring that heirs will be able to enjoy the land, and keeping drinking water safe.

These factors became the content of campaign messages that were passed through mass communication channels for achieving educational objectives and through personalized channels for achieving motivational objectives. Audio-visual channels were selected for conveying emotions associated with risk and written channels were selected for conveying detailed information. The primary sources of information were state and university specialists who the target audience perceived were the most credible.

An evaluation of project processes and outcomes was conducted at the end of the five year project. This assessment identified which messages and channels worked best and the extent to which project objectives were achieved. The project turned out to be moderately successful in increasing landowner knowledge of watershed issues and resource evaluation and stewardship planning strategies. The success the project had in increasing knowledge was due mostly to field demonstrations and tours. The personal contact that landowners had with professional foresters at these events was key to teaching about complex tasks. The project was particularly successful in changing attitudes associated with the impact forest stewardship had on the community. This was an important factor because forest stewardship is inherently about caring for resources that extend beyond individual property boundaries. In the end, the number of completed resource inventories and stewardship plans increased significantly during the project. Nearly half the landowners that were surveyed reported completing some form of assessment and plan during the time of project.

The Eight Mile River Watershed

The Connecticut River is the largest river in the northeast U.S. with no city at its mouth. It has suffered no major dredging or filling, and its system of salt, brackish and freshwater marshes remains remarkably pristine. The 480 square mile "Tidelands Region" (the tidal portion of the river and its watershed) is home to at least 43 rare or endangered species, including several which are globally rare. The national significance of the Connecticut River ecosystem is reflected in several designations. In 1991 the Silvio O. Conte U.S. National Fish and Wildlife Refuge was established. The refuge is comprised of over seven million acres that encompass the Connecticut River and its tributaries from the Canadian border to the Long Island Sound. In 1993 the Nature Conservancy (TNC) named the Tidelands region of the river as one of the 40 "Last Great Places" in the Western Hemisphere. This enables the area to be included in a $300 million program that seeks to protect fragile habitat while promoting compatible human activity. In 1994, 12,000 acres in the Tidelands Region of the river was designated a "wetlands of international importance", a designation established by international treaty and supported by the U.S. Fish and Wildlife Service. In 1998, the federal government named the Connecticut River an American Heritage River.

The lower Connecticut River is divided into seventeen subwatersheds - tidal marsh systems and forested uplands linked by drainage patterns. The Eight Mile River watershed is one of these seventeen. It drains into the beautiful, historic and ecologically diverse Hamburg Cove. The watershed's combination of rare and endangered species, high quality fish, wetland and waterfowl habitats, and other ecological features resulted in its designation as a "special focus area" in the Conte Refuge final action plan.

Since 1995, the three principal towns in the watershed (East Haddam, Salem and Lyme) have collaborated with the University of Connecticut Cooperative Extension System (CES), the Silvio O. Conte U.S. National Fish and Wildlife Refuge, TNC-Connecticut, and other partners on a comprehensive watershed project. The goal is to balance conservation and growth in the watershed by identifying, protecting and enhancing its priority natural resources, and encouraging land uses and land use patterns protective of those resources. While the watershed is steadily suburbanizing, approximately two-thirds of its land area remains in parcels of fifty acres or more, and over three-quarters of its land area is forested. Over 80% of that forest belongs to non-industrial private (NIPF) owners.

The Eight Mile River Watershed Project had two components:

1. The compilation of a detailed three-part inventory and analysis of natural resources within the watershed (forest resources, water resources and human/cultural resources) that provides local planners and decision makers with the data they need to make effective, high quality plans of conservation and development that will guide future growth in their towns.

2. A comprehensive education/communication campaign on forest stewardship targeted to private land owners who control the majority of land and water resources in the watershed.

Planning the Communication Campaign

The Eight Mile River Watershed Project campaign was based on a set of key strategic principles. The objectives of most public communication campaigns can be characterized two ways. Objectives may be *informational*, where the aim is to raise awareness and/or knowledge, or they may be *motivational*, where the aim is to induce attitude and/or behavior change. Often a staged approach is followed that begins with informational objectives and, once this foundation is laid, shifts its focus to motivational objectives. The Eight Mile River Project was staged in such a manner. Planning the process involved defining several key issues:

- Define objectives
- Define audiences
- Define messages
- Define communication channels
- Define information sources

DEFINE OBJECTIVES

Data from the Connecticut River Estuary Regional Planning Agency and the Connecticut Department of Economic Development paint a clear picture of slow, steady, and primarily residential population growth in the Tidelands Region. The population grew 27% between 1980 and 2010. This growth pattern is both incremental and fairly predictable. Over time, it results in significant conversion of forested habitats to other uses, as well as widespread and essentially random fragmentation of the land base. The negative impacts of such land-use trends on resource biodiversity and productivity are well known.

Markets for local high quality timber products are strong, but marginal or lacking for lower quality products such as pulpwood and fuelwood. Further, studies suggest that less than one Connecticut timber harvest in eight have any professional forestry input or oversight. Over the past several decades, these factors have lead to a loss of economic and habitat productivity, sometimes accompanied by unnecessary degradation of wetland and riparian habitats.

The Eight Mile River Watershed Project campaign was launched in response to these issues. Its goals were to increase awareness and knowledge of these resource-related problems, as well as the need for good forest stewardship within the watershed. Once these informational objectives were realized the focus would shift to motivational objectives by promoting the adoption of specific stewardship behaviors. Because, more than 80% of the forest belongs to nonindustrial private forest (NIPF) owners, they became the logical priority audience.

More specifically, the specific objectives of the campaign were to get NIPF owners to...

1) Become familiar with the broader Eight Mile River Watershed Project and its goals.
2) Become knowledgeable about the importance of their land and behavior in the context of long-term health of the watershed.
3) Become knowledgeable about resource inventory and stewardship planning, the benefits of those activities, and cost-share monies available to help offset the costs of implementing those activities.
4) Show positive pre- to post-campaign changes in attitudes that are key predictors of stewardship behavior (anticipated personal and community consequences, perceived threats to self and community, family and community norms, self efficacy, collective efficacy, and perceived community interaction) (see Tyson, et. al., 1998).
5) Seek information about forest stewardship planning.
6) Obtain professional assistance for forest stewardship planning.
7) Assess conditions and/or compile an inventory of forest resources.
8) Formulate specific forest stewardship goals.
9) Develop forest stewardship plans.

Define Audiences

Efforts aimed at a broad and amorphous group like NIPF owners can hope to achieve informational objectives at best. Narrower, prioritized target audience definition allows for the sharper focus necessary to achieve motivational objectives. The more focused the campaign, the more communication strategies and behavioral messages can be custom tailored to a specific audience segment. Doing this effectively requires campaign planners to learn as much as possible about the characteristics of a potential target audience.

Research helps campaign planners identify important source, message and channel factors. Yet, how does one choose the right research questions? The answer lies in communication theory. *Information processing models* provide important guidelines about the stages people go through when they process messages, assess source credibility and message quality, and ultimately accept or reject the message. *Expectancy value models* tell us something about the determinants of attitudes and behaviors - important information when designing message content. *Adoption/diffusion models* provide important guidelines about the stages of a campaign and selection of communication channels.

In the Eight Mile River Watershed Project, Tax Assessor maps and taxpayer lists were used to create a database of all 686 landowners who owned five or more acres of land in the watershed. A mail survey of this population was then conducted. A search of the theoretical literature led us to construct questions about:

- Whether NIPF owners perceived that there were currently threats to the watershed's environment (Witte, Stokols, Itvarte, & Scheider, 1993).
- The potential costs and benefits of stewardship planning (Andreasen & Tyson, 1994).
- Threats to the efficacy of performing stewardship behavior (Bandura, 1982).
- The opinions of family and friends relative to forest stewardship (Ajzen & Fishbein, 1980).
- The degree of interaction among NIPF owners in the watershed (Ostrom, 1990).
- Favored sources and channels of conservation related information (Tyson, Hamilton, & Snyder, 1996; Rogers, 1995).

These variables are thought to be important determinants of conservation behavior and therefore have great potential as campaign message factors. A focus group session with a small group of landowners was then conducted to discuss these issues and to gauge their feelings and knowledge levels concerning resource protection and planning. The baseline Eight Mile River watershed landowner assessment questionnaire was then finalized.

The questionnaire was mailed with a cover letter and return envelope to all 686 landowners. A lottery prize of $100 was offered as an incentive for returning the questionnaire. Phone calls were made to landowners shortly after the mailing to encourage participation in the study. One hundred ninety four landowners (28.3%) completed the questionnaire -- a fair response considering its very long length and single mailing. Because low response can skew findings, phone calls were made to 50 nonrespondents to check for potential response bias. No significant mean differences were discovered between respondents and nonrespondents for 15 demographic, attitudinal and behavioral variables.

The analysis began by segmenting respondents into four groups differentiated by their land ownership and stewardship planning intentions:

- Sellers (13%) - those that intend to sell their land on the open market in the near future.

- Non-intenders (27%) - those who plan to pass their land on to family, but show little inclination toward forest stewardship planning.

- Intenders (35%) - those who show strong inclination to protect land from development and/or develop forest stewardship plans within the next five years.

- Planners (26%) - those who profess to have already taken measures to protect land from development and/or develop forest stewardship plans.

The Intenders group was chosen as the primary target audience. This group already possessed the desired values, beliefs and intentions. They would require no hard-sell convincing, just added knowledge/skills, direction, and perhaps a little motivation and reinforcement. With limited campaign resources, they promised to be the most cost-effective target.

Non-intenders became a secondary audience. They have some appreciation of land stewardship evidenced by their desire to keep their land intact for the next generation, and therefore might be receptive to messages regarding forest stewardship. Based on Diffusion Theory (Rogers, 1995), it was felt that if Intenders could be persuaded to adopt the stewardship behaviors being promoted, they might serve as a model and exert influence on Non-intenders. Planners professed to have already adopted what was being promoted, and Sellers were seen as a group that would most likely drain campaign resources with little positive effect.

DEFINE MESSAGES

With priorities/objectives established and the target audience identified, the next step was to utilize what had been learned about them from the survey. This would help formulate ideas for message content. Findings showed that Intenders, compared to other segments, believed strongly that watershed resources were indeed at risk. They thought that rivers and streams, trees and plants, and production of forest products were (respectively) at greatest risk. This was followed by soils, drinking water, and wildlife. Intenders perceived that the top three benefits to be gained from forest stewardship planning were (in priority order) preserving natural beauty, insuring that heirs will be able to enjoy the land, and keeping drinking water safe. Not surprising, the most important cost considerations were time, money, and effort (in priority order). However, when compared with Non-intenders and Sellers, Intenders perceived the costs of doing a stewardship plan to be relatively modest.

What family and friends thought about forest stewardship was very important to Intenders. Finally, the data showed that the more Intenders perceived that community members interacted with each other, the more they favored and personalized the need for stewardship planning.

DEFINE COMMUNICATION CHANNELS

According to Diffusion Theory (Rogers, 1995), mass channels are good for achieving informational objectives and personalized channels are good for achieving motivational objectives. Audio-visual channels are good for conveying emotion and are therefore good for creating and maintaining interest. Written channels are good for conveying detailed information that may require repeated reference. These factors were kept in mind when designing the communication campaign strategy.

Analyses showed that Intenders' favored mass communication channels were newspapers and TV. The more popular papers, stations, and viewing times were identified. We also discovered that dialogic/participatory channels that promote community interaction, such as neighborhood meetings or group field workshops, would help personalize the need for conservation planning. As a communication strategy, newspapers and TV could be used to inform and participatory group activities could be used to motivate. In addition, project planners decided to use direct mail videotapes (a unique channel at that time having both mass and personal attributes) to build knowledge and maintain interest. Booklets, distributed through the mail and at group activities, would carry the detailed information required for actual behavior.

DEFINE INFORMATION SOURCES

According to Information Processing Theory (Tyson, Hamilton & Snyder, 1996), positive attitude change is a function of high source credibility, high argument quality and low message discrepancy (the difference between the promoter's position and the receiver's initial position). These factors should always be kept in mind when designing a communication campaign strategy.

In the Eight Mile River watershed, analyses showed that the most credible sources of information in the minds of the Intenders were Cooperative Extension System personnel, Department of Environmental Protection foresters, and specialists from The Nature Conservancy. Interestingly, members of these groups comprise much of the project's steering committee. Intenders considered local landowners and town conservation officials to be significantly less credible. This was a noteworthy finding as it was the original intention of project planners to send campaign messages through local opinion leaders as much as possible and downplay their own involvement -- the exact opposite of what research results indicated was the best strategy.

Implementing the Communication Campaign

The project was implemented in a series of stages (re. Diffusion Theory – Rogers, 1995). Each stage overlapped the one that came before it. The first stage involved pre-campaign preparatory activities in which mediated messages and instructional materials were prepared. Once preparations were completed, early informational objectives of the project dealing with awareness and knowledge guided the second stage.

As the project matured and landowners became more knowledgeable, motivational objectives targeting attitude change were addressed in the third stage. Translating attitudes into behavior became the objective in the final (fourth) stage of the project. Message strategies and channel selection was uniquely designed to support the specific nature of each informational/ motivational stage.

It should be noted that some audience members will be quick to move through the stages; i.e., gain knowledge and motivation and translate this into behavior in a much quicker manner relative to other landowners. However, the majority of landowners will adopt new behaviors at a more moderate pace. A third group of landowners will be slow to adopt. Hence, there is need to run campaign activities associated with several stages of adoption concurrently. This will allow landowners to progress at their own pace. It should also be noted that landowners may move forward as well as backward in the adoption process – i.e., learning and forgetting, reminding themselves, trying, stopping, and trying again. This provides additional justification for running activities associated with several stages of the campaign concurrently.

STAGE 1: PRE-CAMPAIGN ACTIVITIES

Pre-campaign preparatory activities can be separated into the four categories described below.

1) Develop campaign identity – this included project name, staff, office, and 1-800 phone number. This was completed during first month of the campaign.
2) Identify and enlist key partners – in the case of the Eight Mile River project this included town managers, town conservation commission members, state service foresters, private consulting foresters, volunteer master stewards, local landowner opinion leaders, and key member of local land trusts. This was initially completed during months 1 to 3 of the campaign and then became an ongoing effort.
3) Developing outreach tools - there were five aspects to this task in the Eight Mile River project. Campaign messages were based on results of the landowner survey. Messages were tailored for an Intender target audience.

a) Create print materials
- An informational brochure on the goals and objectives of the Eight Mile River watershed project was completed/distributed during months 1-3 of the project.
- A forest stewardship brochure w/ return postcard requesting personal contact by a project staff member and accompanying refrigerator magnet showing the 1-800 number was used for informational purposes. This was completed/distributed during months 6 to 9 of the project.
- A detailed publication in handbook format (titled "Consider the Source") describing actual stewardship tasks that could be completed was used for motivational purposes. This was completed/distributed during months 12 –15 of the project.

b) Create a ten-minute informational video for direct mailing to landowners.
- A ten-minute informational video about forest stewardship in the Eight Mile River watershed was developed that defined the watershed community and explained the importance of stewardship planning. Copies were made and distributed to 194 landowners who requested it. This was completed/distributed during months 1 to 3 of the project.

c) Generate press releases and cultivate media/journalist contacts.
- Several press releases, announcement of project activities, and feature articles were published about the project in various local/regional newspapers and organization newsletters. This was completed during months 1 to 6 of the campaign and as an ongoing effort.

d) Create PSAs for television and radio depicting the key benefits of the forest stewardship practices being promoted; include the website address and 1-800 number.
- A thirty second video PSA was developed and distributed to five local television stations. This was completed/distributed during months 1 to 6 of the project.

e) Develop a promotional website with an option to engage in a discussion forum.
   - Because of technical and staffing difficulties, the website that was initially developed for the project was quickly rendered inoperable. This may have been forgivable several years ago when the project was initiated, but today the power a website offers in terms of instruction and influence is crucial. This should have been completed during months 1 to 6 of a project.

f) Create a detailed instructional "how-to" video on forest stewardship planning
   - Because of funding limitations, this instructional video was not developed as part of the Eight Mile River project. Yet, because of the complexity of the practices being promoted, it is highly suggested that projects modeling these efforts complete this task. This proposed video would have helped landowners overcome doubts/inhibitions (boost self-efficacy) and helped them translate their knowledge and interest into action. This should have been completed during months 12 –15 of a project.

STAGE 2: INFORMATIONAL OBJECTIVES

Objective: landowners should become aware/knowledgeable of what is meant by the "Eight Mile River Watershed" and become familiar with the identity of the Eight Mile River Watershed Forest Stewardship Project.

Campaign Messages: Messages were based on results of the landowner survey and were tailored to an Intender target audience. These messages were designed to: a) define "watershed" and stress landowners' roles in the watershed system/community, b) promote watershed identity, c) highlight the perceived benefits of forest stewardship activities and the key concerns that landowners have, d) explain about cost-share incentives, and e) create project name recognition.

Communication Channels:

1) The direct mailing of the ten-minute informational video to the 194 landowners who requested it when responding to the survey was completed/distributed during month 3 of the project.

2) Using the mailing list compiled for the landowner survey (landowners with five or more acres in the watershed), invitations were mailed for an initial orientation meeting. A copy of the Eight Mile River Watershed Project brochure was included with the invitation. All project partners were in attendance at the event. A list of attendees was developed from the event and follow-up efforts were conducted with any attendees who requested information. This was completed during month 6 of the project.

3) Newspaper press releases, features articles, TV/radio news coverage, PSAs, newsletter articles, etc. were developed/ distributed. This was completed during months 3 to 9 of the project and as an ongoing effort.

4) A public event with press coverage in which the town managers of the three towns that comprise the watershed signed an "Eight Mile River Watershed Conservation Compact" was engineered and promoted. Several newspaper articles were spawned by this event increasing public awareness of the project. The compact committed the town mangers (in a public yet non-legal/non-binding fashion) to protect and enhance the watershed's natural resources to ensure the long-term social, economic and environmental health and vitality of the communities in the watershed.

5) The 1-800 number were promoted on all correspondence, publications, broadcasts as an ongoing effort through the life of the project.

6) Project staff responded to requests made by landowners via the 1-800 number. This was completed as an ongoing effort throughout the life of the project.

7) The website and chatroom/discussion group activity was to have been maintained/monitored. Project staff were to have prompted issues and answered questions raised by the discussion group. Requests by landowners for additional assistance would have been followed-up. This should have been completed as an ongoing effort throughout the life of the project.

8) A direct mailing to state service foresters and private consulting foresters working in the watershed seeking their ideas and support for the project was completed during month 6 of the project.

9) A direct mailing to volunteer master stewards was completed (these are individuals selected and trained under the auspices

of another University of Connecticut Cooperative Extension Service project dealing with natural resource conservation/forest stewardship). This mailing sought ideas and support for the project and requested that they serve as potential mentors to interested landowners in the watershed. This was completed during month 6 of the project.

10) The direct mailing of the stewardship brochure, with return postcard and refrigerator magnet, to all landowners with five or more acres in the watershed, was completed. Copies of clippings of recent newspaper coverage were included. Personal phone contact with landowners who returned the postcards was conducted. This was completed during month 9 of the project.

STAGE 3: ATTITUDE CHANGE/MOTIVATION

Objective: landowners should develop concern for risks associated with the watershed's environmental health, positive perceptions concerning individual and community oriented benefits of stewardship planning, confidence in their ability to do stewardship planning, and the belief that many other landowners are engaging in these activities. These beliefs should translate into an overall positive attitude towards stewardship planning that should directly influence landowners' motivations to engage in stewardship planning.

Messages: Messages are based on results of the landowner survey and are tailored to an Intender target audience. Messages should mention a) key threats to the watershed's environmental health and explain how stewardship planning will help alleviate these threats, b) highlight favored benefits of stewardship planning and try to alleviate concerns about the perceived costs, c) explain/depict what is involved in stewardship planning and attempt boost landowners confidence in their own ability to carry out these tasks, d) explain about cost-share incentives, and e) impress on landowners that many landowners in the watershed are engaging in these activities.

Communication Channels:

1) A series of participatory field-days were conducted on the properties of volunteer master stewards in or near the watershed. Invitations were mailed to all landowners with five or more acres

in the watershed. Activities during these field days consisted of guided tours by landowners, project staff, and invited specialists (e.g., state service foresters and private consulting foresters) to view and discuss the layout of trails and scenic vistas, wildlife ecology and habitat improvement, timber stand improvement, stream and water quality protection practices, and stewardship assessment and planning activities. Considerable time was allotted for participants to engage in dialog amongst themselves and with experts. The names and addresses of landowners who attended these events were added to the list of landowners who requested and received the video earlier in the project – this list comprised the actual "Intender" audience segment. Field-days were initiated in month 12 of the project and continued each year as an ongoing effort.

2) A detailed publication in handbook format (entitled "Consider the Source") describing actual stewardship tasks that could be completed was mailed to the Intender audience (the 194 landowners who requested and received the video earlier in the project plus the landowners who attended project field-days). This was completed during month 15 of the project and as an ongoing effort as new landowners exhibit interest and motivation.

3) Contact with state service foresters, private consulting foresters, and volunteer master stewards was continued to encourage support for the project.

4) The 1-800 number continued to be maintained, monitored, and promoted on all correspondence, publications, and broadcasts.

5) Newspaper features/articles, TV/radio news coverage and PSAs, newsletter articles, etc. continued to be developed/distributed.

6) The following activities were planned but went uncompleted:

7) A direct mailing to all landowners with five or more acres in the watershed should have been completed that included the names, postal addresses, email addresses, and phone numbers of volunteer master stewards. Landowners should have been encouraged to contact these volunteers for advice/ assistance. Printed testimonials by these volunteers should have been included with the mailing. This should have been completed during month 15 of the project and accompanied the "Consider the Source" handbook when it was mailed.

8) Personal phone calls to key landowners should have been made by project staff to encourage their participation in the project. Landowners to be called could have been be prioritized by the amount of acreage they own and/or by the importance or sensitive nature of their landholdings. If landowner survey data is geographically coded and associated parcel data is digitized so that human dimension data can be layered with natural resource data, biographical sketches could then be developed for each landowner in sensitive areas. These biographical sketches could help project staff develop highly personalized persuasive messages. (for an example of this see: Tyson, Worthley & Danley, 2004). This should have been completed during month 15 of the project.

9) Individual "Eight Mile River Watershed Conservation Compacts" should have been initiated in which landowners signed a formal (yet non-legal/non-binding) agreement to actively practice forest stewardship for the sake of their land and the watershed community. These landowners would receive a "Personalized Eight Mile River Watershed Conservation Kit" including a series of detailed GIS maps of their property and the watershed. Because of staffing limitations, the individual compact and personalized conservation kit ideas were not developed as part of the Eight Mile River project. Yet, because it is important that landowners feel a part of the watershed community and given the tendency of people to procrastinate unless formally/publicly committed, it is highly suggested that projects modeling these efforts complete this task. This should have been completed during month 15 of the project and as an ongoing effort as new landowners exhibit interest and motivation.

STAGE 4: SEEK ASSISTANCE/BEHAVIOR CHANGE

Objective: landowners should seek assistance from project staff, state service foresters, private consulting foresters, and/or volunteer master stewards concerning forest inventory/assessment and stewardship plan activities and engage in these activities.

Messages: There are three principal messages at this stage: a) landowners should contact project staff, state service foresters, private consulting foresters, and/or volunteer master stewards via mail, phone, or email and request personal assistance; b) in-depth detailed information should be provided concerning the tasks that are involved in forest inventory/assessment and stewardship planning activities and cost share incentive opportunities; and c) stories of successful stewardship activities by peer landowners in the watershed should be shared.

Channels:

1) Project staff, state service foresters, private consulting foresters, and/or volunteer master stewards who were contacted by interested landowners visited them at the site of their land holdings and assisted them with their forest inventory/assessment and stewardship planning activities. This was completed during month 18 of the project and as an ongoing effort as new landowners exhibited interest and motivation.

2) Field-days were continued and successful landowner efforts were showcased.

3) The "Consider the Source" handbook and the names/contact numbers for volunteer master stewards was mailed to new/ additional members of the "Intender" audience segment that were identified by attendance at project field-days.

4) Contact with state service foresters, private consulting foresters, and volunteer master stewards continued to be encouraged.

5) The 1-800 number continued to be maintained, monitored, and promoted on all correspondence, publications, and broadcasts.

6) Newspaper features/articles, TV/radio news coverage and PSAs, newsletter articles, etc. continued to be developed/distributed.

The following activities were planned but uncompleted:

7) Personal phone calls to key landowners (prioritized by the amount of acreage they own and/or by the sensitive nature of their landholdings) should have been made by project staff to encourage their participation in the project.

8) A detailed "how-to" video on forest stewardship planning should have been mailed to the "Intender" audience segment. This should have been completed during month 18 of a project and as an ongoing effort as new landowners exhibit interest and motivation.

Evaluating the Communication Campaign

When evaluating a communication campaign, two aspects of the project will need to be assessed – the processes and the outcomes. A process evaluation assesses the effectiveness of the planning and implementation stages of the project. An outcome evaluation assesses audience impact; i.e., the degree that the project reached its stated objectives.

PROCESS EVALUATION

Individuals surveyed as part of the Eight Mile River Watershed Project included:

Project staff
1) UConn Forest Stewardship Project Director
2) UConn NEMO Project Manager
3) UConn Forest Stewardship Project Coordinator
4) UConn GIS specialist
5) Eight Mile River Watershed Project Coordinator

Project cooperators
1) First Selectmen for East Haddam
2) First Selectmen for Salem
3) Salem Land Trust director
4) Lyme Land Trust director
5) East Haddam Trust
6) Department of Environmental Protection Service Forester I
7) Department of Environmental Protection Service Forester II
8) Private consultant forester I
9) Private consultant forester II
10) Private consultant forester III
11) Private consultant forester IV
12) Volunteer master steward (Coverts volunteer) I
13) Volunteer master steward (Coverts volunteer) II

Landowners
1) Large acreage forest landowners
2) Moderate acreage forest landowners
3) Small acreage forest landowners

Qualitative Assessment of Project Planning and Implementation

The qualitative assessment of project planning and implementation efforts involved a survey of project staff, volunteer master stewards, state and private foresters, town officials, key members of local land trusts, and a few forest landowners. A copy of the survey questionnaire can be found in Appendix 1. The questionnaire was either self-administered or administered via a personal interview. A content analysis of the responses was conducted to identify common perceptions (themes) across the respondents. Results of this analysis are described below using questions from the survey instrument as a framework to order findings.

1) Project involvement

Approximately two thirds of the project staff that were surveyed had been with the project since its inception in 1995; the other third joined the project approximately half way through its five-year tenure. It should be noted that the first half of the project was administered by the UConn Forest Stewardship Project director from an office at considerable distance from the project site. The administration of the second half of the project was assisted by two coordinators from a local office. This allowed for much closer personal oversight of project activities.

The two volunteer master stewards that were surveyed became involved during the second half of the project. Involvement by land trust members was variable – two of the three individuals that were surveyed felt they were never really involved; one stated that he was involved since the beginning of the project because of his role representing the town of Salem on the project advisory committee. Of the two First Selectmen surveyed, one felt somewhat involved in the project, especially since the public signing of the *Conservation Compact*, the other felt he had very little involvement.

Two of the four private consultant foresters that were surveyed did not feel they were ever really involved in the project; the other two felt their involvement was peripheral at best (i.e., they only attended one demonstration field tour). The two state foresters that were surveyed felt they had been involved since project inception. All three of the forest landowners became involved in the last two years of the project.

It would appear that the involvement of key project partners was quite variable. Few were active in the early stages of the project. More became involved as the project progressed. Their increased involvement in the latter stages of the project may have contributed to the subsequent increase in landowner involvement. Several key partners stated they never felt very involved with the project.

Involvement by volunteer master stewards in the beginning of the project (as vectors of detailed information about forest stewardship practices) would have been helpful; as would a greater sense of involvement by land trust members and town officials (as vectors of general information/publicity about the project). Technical assistance by state and consultant foresters was crucial to project success and the low level of involvement by consultant foresters was no doubt a constraint.

2) Project responsibility

For the most part, project staff, state and consultant foresters, and volunteer master stewards identified themselves as playing the roles that they were meant to – respectively, coordinate the project, help landowners evaluate their property/develop stewardship plans, provide answers to questions asked by landowners. Unfortunately, town officials and land trust members did not have a clear perception of their role in the project (i.e., helping to engineer public support/publicity, and keeping the project in the public agenda). The large and moderate acreage landowners that were surveyed each hosted a field demonstration tour exhibiting their stewardship practices; the small acreage landowner developed a stewardship plan but did not host a tour.

3) Goals of the project

All of the individuals that were surveyed properly identified the overarching goal of the project (i.e., to educate landowners about forest stewardship). Importantly, project staff, state and consultant foresters, and the landowners surveyed defined project goals in more specific behavioral terms (i.e., to get landowners to plan for good forest stewardship). Land Trust members, town officials, and volunteer master stewards tended to think more in terms of general impacts (i.e., to protect water quality and preserve healthy open space). A clearer focus on the behavioral goals of the project by members of these three groups may have been more beneficial.

4) Evaluation of project objectives

Objective 1: Landowners will become familiar with the forest stewardship component of the Eight Mile River Watershed Project

> ➤ How successful do you think the forest stewardship component of the project has been in achieving the objective?

About half of the individuals surveyed (half of the project staff, both town officials, both volunteer master stewards, and all landowners) felt the campaign was successful in establishing familiarity with the project. The other half of those surveyed (half of the project staff, land trust members, and state and consultant foresters) either felt it was only marginally successful or were unsure. Given that project familiarity is crucial to subsequent involvement in other project activities and necessary for fulfilling higher level objectives (e.g., knowledge, attitude, and behavior change), this ambiguity in the perception of project staff and partners is concerning.

> ➤ What do you think have been the strengths of the forest stewardship component of the project regarding the objective?

The project staff, land trust members, state and consultant foresters, and landowners that were surveyed all felt that the printed matter that was mailed to landowners and the demonstration field tours for landowners were the major strengths of the project. Town officials and volunteer master stewards spoke in more general terms (i.e., increasing landowners' levels of awareness).

> ➤ What do you think have been the weaknesses of the forest stewardship component of the project regarding the objective?

Responses to this question were wide ranging. The project staff that were surveyed felt that weaknesses of the project included: lack of highly visible success stories, lack of publicity, little activity by volunteer master stewards, and the fact that there were few state and consultant foresters to assist landowners in developing (all too) expensive/resource intensive plans. One landowner specifically mentioned the lack of project publicity.

State foresters felt they were too few in number. Private consultant foresters felt they were never asked to be involved in the project and that greater demand from landowners would be needed to increase their involvement. Volunteer master stewards and land trust members agreed that not enough landowners were involved. Town officials felt that long-term consistent contact with landowners is what was necessary. Related to this, land trust members felt that there were large gaps in the campaign in terms of consistent contact between project staff and landowners.

> What would you advise someone in another watershed to do differently regarding the objective?

Responses to this question were closely related to concerns already expressed. Project staff that were surveyed felt that more help from local volunteer master stewards, more publicity, and less focus on formal written plans is what is needed. State and consultant foresters and landowners agree that more publicity was required. All parties that were surveyed stated that additional forums for educating landowners are warranted. Specifically, additional demonstration field tours and a project newsletter were mentioned.

Objective 2: Landowners will know what is involved in conducting a forest inventory/assessment and stewardship plan

> How successful do you think the forest stewardship component of the project has been in achieving the objective?

Of all the parties surveyed, only half of the project staff felt unconditionally that the project was successful in increasing landowner knowledge of what is involved in forest inventory/assessment and stewardship plan. The other half of the project staff and the state foresters felt the project was successful in this regard, but only for those few landowners that attended the demonstration field tours. The landowners that were surveyed felt the project met their needs successfully. All other parties that were surveyed either did not know (because of their low involvement in the project) or felt the project was unsuccessful in this regard.

> What do you think have been the strengths of the forest stewardship component of the project regarding the objective?

Project staff felt that the direct mail video, mailed printed matter, and the demonstration field tours were the major strengths of the project in regard to this objective. Town officials, state foresters, and volunteer master stewards all agreed that mailed publications were key strengths. The private consultant foresters felt a major strength was that the project's effort to link landowners with state and consultant foresters. Landowners confirmed these observation. They felt that a) the mail-in card requesting personal assistance that accompanied one of the brochure mailings and b) walking their property with a professional forester were the two most effective communication channels.

> What do you think have been the weaknesses of the forest stewardship component of the project regarding the objective?

Again, responses to the question about project weaknesses were wide ranging. Project staff that were surveyed felt that weaknesses of the project included: an inability to stimulate landowners, little activity by volunteer master stewards, and the fact that there were few professional foresters to assist landowners in developing (all too) expensive/resource intensive plans.

Private consultant foresters felt they needed to be more involved because interpersonal contact with them is how landowners truly learn what is involved in conducting a forest inventory/assessment and stewardship plan. State foresters felt there was a need for additional cost-share monies to provide incentives for landowner involvement. Town officials felt landowners were too busy to read much of the materials provided and questioned the long-term commitment of the project to the watershed. Landowners felt that people need to be more informed about the complexities involved in practicing forest stewardship.

> What would you advise someone in another watershed to do differently regarding the objective?

Project staff felt that the video and project publications need more frequent play and wider distribution, and that there should be less focus on formal written plans. Town officials feel there needs to be a long-term commitment to cost-sharing. They also feel that a quarterly project newsletter would help promote the project. Private consultant foresters feel that a greater number of success stories need to be more widely publicized. Landowners feel that people initially need to be better taught what questions they need answer to.

Objective 3: Landowners will seek information about forest stewardship planning

> How successful do you think the forest stewardship component of the project has been in achieving the objective?

Most respondents felt that the project was successful to at least a fair degree regarding this objective. State foresters believe the project has been successful in getting landowners to seek information *before* they potentially make poor decisions. Private consultant foresters believe several landowners may have been motivated by project literature to contact them. Landowners felt the project helped fulfill their information needs. The volunteer master stewards, key vectors of project information, did not feel that project was successful in this regard.

> What do you think have been the strengths of the forest stewardship component of the project regarding the objective?

Most respondents felt that the direct mail video, mailed printed matter, and the demonstration field tours were the major strengths of the project regarding this objective. The state and consultant foresters and the volunteer master stewards felt that connecting landowners with other landowners in the presence of professional foresters effectively reinforced printed messages. Landowners again confirmed these observations – they felt that a) the mail-in card requesting personal assistance that accompanied one of the brochure mailings and b) walking their property with a professional forester were the most effective communication channels.

> ➤ What do you think have been the weaknesses of the forest stewardship component of the project regarding the objective?

Project staff felt that weakness included: the need to reach a larger audience, the fact that the website was never fully developed, the fact that there were too few foresters to assist landowners, and that formal stewardship plans were too expensive/resource intensive to compile. Consultant foresters felt they needed to be more involved in the project from the beginning. State foresters and volunteer master stewards felt the project needed greater publicity. Land Trust members felt that printed materials need wider and constant distribution.

> ➤ What would you advise someone in another watershed to do differently regarding the objective?

Advice to other watersheds was closely patterned on solving many of the weaknesses described above. Project staff feel there is a need to reach larger audiences with messages that promote more informal types of stewardship planning; i.e., messages that do not strictly focus on formal written stewardship plans. More landowner-to-landowner educational events and the need for more project publicity were suggested by several respondents. Private consultant foresters suggested that they should be involved more actively. Landowners stressed the importance of the mail-in card that people can use to indicate a desire for assistance.

Objective 4: Landowners will show positive pre-survey to post-survey changes in key beliefs/attitudes regarding forest stewardship (anticipated personal and community consequences, perceived threats to self and community, family and community norms, self efficacy, collective efficacy, and perceived community interaction)

> ➤ How successful do you think the forest stewardship component of the project has been in achieving the objective?

Four respondents felt that the project succeeded in this objective (two project staff, one state forester, and one volunteer master steward). Most other respondents were simply unsure of project results in this regard.

> What do you think have been the strengths of the forest stewardship component of the project regarding the objective?

Project staff, state foresters, and all three landowners felt that because of information disseminated by the project, people now understand their connection to land much better. Most respondents were unsure regarding the answer to this question.

> What do you think have been the weaknesses of the forest stewardship component of the project regarding the objective?

Project staff felt that weakness included: the need for more interpersonal contact with landowners and, again, the fact that there were too few foresters to assist landowners and that formal stewardship plans were too expensive to compile. Once more, private consultant foresters stated that they needed to be more involved in the project. Landowners felt the pre- and post- survey questionnaires used to assess changes in beliefs/attitudes were too long. Most respondents did not offer a response to this question.

> What would you advise someone in another watershed to do differently regarding the objective?

Project staff suggested there is a need for greater project publicity and that messages should not focus strictly on formal written stewardship plans. Private consultant foresters suggested that more interpersonal contact with foresters is necessary. Town officials suggested that planning/zoning changes should complement project efforts.

Objective 5: Landowners will obtain professional assistance for stewardship planning

> How successful do you think the forest stewardship component of the project has been in achieving the objective?

Many of the project staff, Land Trust members, state foresters, and landowners that were interviewed felt the project was successful in helping landowners who requested assistance get the assistance they asked for. Yet, most agreed that few had asked for this assistance. Private consultant foresters and volunteer master stewards felt that even if assistance had not yet been requested, many landowners at least know that assistance is available and how to obtain it.

> What do you think have been the strengths of the forest stewardship component of the project regarding the objective?

Many respondents that were interviewed felt that interpersonal contact between landowners, project staff, and forestry professionals at public meetings and field demonstration tours were strengths in this regard. State and private consultant foresters and landowners felt the referral system linking landowners and professional foresters was a key component of the project. Land Trust members and landowners mentioned the high quality of forestry professionals available to assist.

> What do you think have been the weaknesses of the forest stewardship component of the project regarding the objective?

Most respondents agreed that more interpersonal contact between landowners, project staff, and forestry professionals is needed. Project staff stated that there is a need to work with groups of smaller acreage landowners (5-20 acre owners). Several respondents feel there are too few professional foresters that can actually assist. They also expressed the need to clearly illustrate the value of professional assistance, especially with small acreage landowners. Land Trust members felt that formal stewardship plans are too expensive and resource intensive for many landowners.

> What would you advise someone in another watershed to do differently regarding the objective?

As might be expected, based on project weaknesses expressed so far, project staff cited the need to work with groups of smaller acreage landowners, the need to publicize the project more using local media, Land Trust and garden club members and town officials, and the need to reduce the focus on formal written stewardship plans. State foresters suggested promoting the consequences of *not* getting professional help.

Objective 6: Landowners will assess conditions of forestland and/or compile a written inventory of forest resources

> How successful do you think the forest stewardship component of the project has been in achieving the objective?

Most respondents chose not to respond to this question indicating either lack of knowledge concerning the objective or the fact that they felt their comments to previous questions adequately covered their response to this question. Project staff who did respond to the question stated that only those enrolled in the federally funded Stewardship Incentive Program (SIP) had their resources professionally evaluated. They also stated that they thought some landowners had assessed the condition of their forestland in a more informal fashion. The landowners that responded to this survey had compiled a formal inventory of resources. Volunteer master stewards believe the concept is just catching on.

> What do you think have been the strengths of the forest stewardship component of the project regarding the objective?

Responses were fairly predictable. Project staff and state foresters mentioned publications, interpersonal contact with landowners, and the mechanism for referring landowners to forestry professionals. Consultant foresters and landowners mentioned the structured nature of the program.

> What do you think have been the weaknesses of the forest stewardship component of the project regarding the objective?

Project staff felt that the formal inventory process is too expensive/ resource intensive, and therefore, too few landowners requested assistance. Related to this, Land Trust members think the process is only for wealthier landowners. Most of the respondents feel the project needs to have more interpersonal contact with a greater number of landowners.

> What would you advise someone in another watershed to do differently regarding the objective?

Project staff suggest that some sort of structured planning process should be kept in place, but that the project should not focus only on the need for *formal* professional resource inventories. Land Trust members suggest that a mechanism for working with underfunded landowners should be developed. Many respondents suggest that more interpersonal assistance is necessary. Private consultant foresters feel there is a need to streamline the process.

Objective 7: Landowners will formulate specific stewardship goals

➢ How successful do you think the forest stewardship component of the project has been in achieving the objective?

Several respondents (project staff, state/consultant foresters, and volunteer master stewards) feel that large landowners are usually the only ones to develop formally stated goals. Several of these landowners developed goals for their properties. Other (smaller acreage) landowners are unsure what they might do and why.

➢ What do you think have been the strengths of the forest stewardship component of the project regarding the objective?

Those who responded to this question agreed that project literature, field events, and interpersonal contact with forestry professionals were key components of the project. Landowners felt that discussion during field events and with professional foresters was key.

➢ What do you think have been the weaknesses of the forest stewardship component of the project regarding the objective?

Land Trust members and private consultant foresters felt that too few landowners were reached by the project. Project staff felt more interpersonal contact with landowners was needed but that there were too few professional foresters available to do this. Landowners felt that more varied subjects needed to be addressed at field events.

➢ What would you advise someone in another watershed to do differently regarding the objective?

Project staff and landowners feel there is a need to have more professional contact with landowners on their own properties and that the project should promote alternatives to formally written plans. Private consultant foresters and landowners agree that landowners should be presented with a variety of management options.

Objective 8: Landowners will develop forest stewardship plans

> How successful do you think the forest stewardship component of the project has been in achieving the objective?

Project staff and private consultant foresters believe that only a few landowners developed formal written stewardship plans. The landowners responding to this survey were three of these individuals. Project staff believe that several landowners probably have less formal plans developed. Volunteer master stewards believe the concept is just catching on.

> What do you think have been the strengths of the forest stewardship component of the project regarding the objective?

Those respondents who answered this question (project staff, state and consultant foresters) believe strengths lie in the project's structured nature. Landowners mentioned contact with forestry professionals as key strength.

> What do you think have been the weaknesses of the forest stewardship component of the project regarding the objective?

Comments to this question were wide ranging. Project staff again stated that there were too few professional foresters to adequately assist landowners. Volunteer master stewards and project staff agreed that the process of developing formal stewardship plans was too expensive/resource intensive. Project staff felt a variety of planning options are needed. Town officials felt the project was run by competent and passionate technical specialists who needed to adopt a more empathetic perspective about landowners' needs/capabilities. Land Trust members felt that many landowners were either not getting the message or were getting it too sporadically. State foresters felt that evaluation based on total acreage under formal stewardship plans conflicted with what was actually needed by landowners in this watershed. Consultant foresters and landowners felt that procedures were too complicated and required too large a commitment from landowners.

> What would you advise someone in another watershed to do differently regarding the objective?

Several respondents suggested the need to reach larger numbers of landowners with more visible success stories and the need for more landowner forums and interpersonal contact. Project staff and private consultant foresters suggested the need for a more flexible/informal definition of a stewardship plan. In addition, consultant foresters felt there was a need to streamline the process. They also felt they could have provided greater assistance if they had been asked to help disseminate project messages.

EVALUATION OF COMMUNICATION CHANNELS USED IN PROJECT

1. Publications produced/distributed

> How successful do you think the method has been?

For the most part, respondents felt that project publications were well done and well received. It should be noted that two private consultant foresters and one Land Trust member never received the mailings.

> What do you think have been the strengths of the method?

Respondents agree that mailing materials was an effective way to target the right audience. They also agree that the publications were of high quality, concise, and easy to read.

> What do you think have been the weaknesses of the method?

Several respondents raised the question that, given the large amount of direct mail that clutter our mailboxes, to what degree do landowners really read the materials sent them? These respondents feel that many landowners probably did not read the materials and were therefore missed by the project. Several respondents stated that the material seemed too general, containing little detailed information describing specific tasks landowners should actually do.

> What would you advise someone in another watershed to do differently?

Suggestions included making publication more focused/brief, personalizing them with local examples, and distributing them more widely and frequently.

2. Field days and workshops held

> How successful do you think the method has been?

Nearly all respondents agreed that these events were successful, involved credible speakers, and drew a fair number of people. Town officials did not attend any of the events.

> What do you think have been the strengths of the method?

All respondents agree that the strengths of this method lie in the fact that local examples were presented and discussed by highly credible peer and expert sources.

> What do you think have been the weaknesses of the method?

Most respondents agreed that to be effective, demonstration field tours can only accommodate a limited number of people. Scheduling is difficult and events need to be offered on other than Saturday mornings. Several respondents mentioned the need for attracting more and different types of landowners and the need to adopt a less technical approach.

> What would you advise someone in another watershed to do differently?

Suggestions included having more events at various times (perhaps half-day tours followed by half-day short courses), the need for more publicity (perhaps using telephone follow-up to mailed invitations), the need to more fully describe the objectives of the events, and the need to do follow-up with participants after the event.

3. Newspaper, radio, TV feature stories/articles placed

➤ How successful do you think the method has been?

About half the respondents were unaware of this type of project publicity. Those that were aware felt it was best with local newspapers. Yet overall they felt it was only marginally successful.

➤ What do you think have been the strengths of the method?

Though the project did not benefit from a full-length feature article, several respondents stated that they felt this type of publicity would have been effective.

➤ What do you think have been the weaknesses of the method?

Respondents to this question generally agreed that media coverage was too scattered and infrequent, especially in the Hartford Courant.

➤ What would you advise someone in another watershed to do differently?

Respondents to this question agreed that it is important to cultivate and maintain media contacts at various media outlets.

4. PSAs aired/printed

Most respondents were unaware of the existence of the project PSAs. Those few that were aware felt it was ineffective and not worth the investment it took to produce and distribute.

5. Videos produced/distributed

➤ How successful do you think the method has been?

About half the respondents felt the direct mail video developed/distributed in the beginning of the project was effective, especially in establishing awareness and interest in the project. The other half of respondents had not viewed or did not remember it.

➢ What do you think have been the strengths of the method?

Those that did remember viewing the video felt that because it was mailed to them directly, it was well targeted. They felt it was effective because it was personal, entertaining, attractive and easy to use.

➢ What do you think have been the weaknesses of the method?

Respondents' felt it needed to be of higher quality, distributed more widely, and shown more frequently.

➢ What would you advise someone in another watershed to do differently?

As stated, respondents felt that the video needed to be distributed more widely and shown more frequently, and that an instructional counterpart video needed to be produced detailing technical aspects of implementing forest stewardship plans.

6. Use of the website

Most respondents were unaware of the project website. This is understandable given that it was developed during the second half of the project and for much of that time, for technical reasons, it was inoperable. Several respondents agree that it could have become an important communication tool, especially if it had a chatroom/bulletin-board function. Several other respondents stated that they did not feel it was an appropriate tool in this watershed because the advanced age of the average landowner meant they were less technologically inclined.

Quantitative assessment of the communication/ education tools and events

1. Newspaper and newsletter stories/announcements published

For the first four years of the project, prior to the final project evaluation, the following general interest publications appeared: five newspaper articles (Hartford, Middletown Press, New London Day), two newspaper announcements (Pictorial Gazette, New London Day), one Coverts Project newsletter article, two Eight Mile River Watershed newsletter articles, and two short magazine articles (CT Woodlands, Nature's Window).

2. Special events conducted

Approximately two years into the project, Selectmen from the three towns in the watershed signed a "Conservation Compact" committing the town to preserving the watershed's natural resources. Newspaper coverage of the event was printed in the Hartford Courant, New London Day, Middletown Press, and the Pictorial Gazette.

3. PSAs aired

Two 30-second PSAs were produced, and copies were distributed to six different TV stations in the state. Channel 26 out of New London aired them several times. Airplay at other outlets is unknown.

4. Brochures/pamphlets produced/distributed

Two publications were produced exclusively for the project: a general-information 15-page 7x11 inch brochure and a more detailed 15-page 8.5x11 inch motivational brochure. In addition, two brochures from the federally funded SIP program were used to complement project stewardship activity. One of these included a return post-card requesting personal assistance. The mailing of this brochure also included a refrigerator magnet depicting the project's 1-800 number. In addition to random distribution at special events and to walk-in visitors, each project publication was distributed by mail to approximately 700 landowners. The two SIP publications were distributed to all landowners who had registered their property for tax reduction in a state program for landowners with ten or more acres of land in the watershed (PL 490 list).

5.   Video produced/viewed.

A 10-minute introductory video was produced and mailed directly to the 194 landowners that responded to the initial project planning survey questionnaire.

6.   Field days held/attended

-   Year 1: project "kick-off" meetings in East Haddam and Salem (approximately 130 people).
-   Year 2: Taylor property tour (approximately 25 people).
-   Year 2: Hammond Mill Preserve tour (approximately 25 people).
-   Year 3: Larson property tour (approximately 25 people).
-   Year 4: Goodwin property tour (approximately 25 people).
-   Year 4: Bodman property tour (approximately 25 people).

7.   Phone calls to the 1-800 number/number of follow-up responses.

Approximately 25 inquiries were received from landowners in the watershed calling the project's toll free number.

8.   Website chatroom traffic and email follow-up to requests.

The website was inoperable for most of the project.

9.   Cooperating volunteer master stewards contacted by landowners.

Four inquiries by landowners to the project coordinator were referred to volunteer master stewards (trained "Coverts Volunteers"). Members of the public also had the opportunity to contact Coverts Cooperators during field meetings and workshops. Out of approximately 25 audience members at any particular field event, four to six were current or former Coverts Volunteers. The degree that Coverts Volunteers publicized their role in the project and attracted inquiries is unknown. One Coverts volunteer, reached quite a few landowners with a newsletter he produces for the East Haddam Land Trust.

10. Cooperating state service foresters contacted by landowners.

There were two state service foresters working in the watershed during the time of the project. Between the two, it is estimated that they acted on thirty requests for assistance from people in the watershed.

11. Cooperating private consultant foresters contacted by landowners.

It is estimated that there were eight private consulting foresters working with people in this watershed during the time of the project. Some assisted landowners with SIP Stewardship Plans; others worked with landowners in different capacities. Two of the foresters are employees of the same firm. It is estimated that most of the private consultant foresters have more than one client in the area.

CONCLUSION – PROCESS EVALUATION

It would appear that the involvement of key project partners was quite variable. Few were active in the early stages of the project. More became involved as the project progressed. This increase in involvement in the latter stages of the project may have influenced landowner participation, which also increased during this time. Several key partners stated they never felt involved with the project.

Involvement by volunteer master stewards in the beginning of the project as vectors of detailed information about forest stewardship practices would have been helpful; as would a greater sense of involvement by land trust members and town officials as vectors of general information/ publicity about the project. Personal technical assistance by state and private consultant foresters was crucial to project success and the low level of involvement by consultant foresters was no doubt a constraint.

For the most part, project staff, state and consultant foresters, and volunteer master stewards identified themselves as playing the roles they were meant to in the project – respectively, coordinate the project, help landowners evaluate their property/develop stewardship plans, provide answers to questions asked by landowners. Unfortunately, town officials and land trust members did not have a clear perception of their role in the project (i.e., helping to engineer public support/publicity, keeping the project on the public agenda).

All of the individuals that were surveyed properly identified the overarching goal of the project (i.e., to educate landowners about forest stewardship). Importantly, project staff, state and consultant foresters, and landowners defined project goals in more specific behavioral terms (i.e., to get landowners to plan for good forest stewardship). Land Trust members, town officials, and volunteer master stewards tended to think more in terms of broad impacts (i.e., to protect water quality and preserve healthy open space). Perhaps a clearer focus on the behavioral goals of the project by members of these three groups would have been more beneficial.

The conclusion about whether the project was successful in establishing project familiarity is ambiguous. Given that project familiarity is crucial to fulfilling subsequent higher-level project objectives (e.g., knowledge, attitude, and behavior change), it is disconcerting that about half of the respondents felt the project was only marginally successful in establishing familiarity among watershed forest landowners. This may have been caused by lack of project publicity, little activity by volunteer master stewards, and the fact that there were few state and consultant foresters to assist landowner. The publications mailed directly to landowners and the demonstration field tours were considered the most successful channels of information for establishing project familiarity. More consistent and frequent contact between project staff and landowners in the form of demonstration field tours and the development of a project newsletter were two key suggestions.

The success the project had in increasing knowledge about forest resource inventory and stewardship planning tasks probably resides mostly in those landowners who attended the demonstration field tours. The publications that were mailed to these landowners prior to their attendance were no doubt helpful in getting them there. The contact they had with professional foresters at these events and subsequently on their own properties was probably the most important communication channel in this regard. Because interpersonal contact was so important, lack of assistance by volunteer master stewards and professional foresters was a key constraint.

Many of the conclusions stated above are also relevant when assessing the success the project had in getting landowners to seek information about forest stewardship. The publications that were mailed to landowners prior to their attendance at demonstration field tours were most effective in this regard. The contact that landowners had with professional foresters at these events and subsequently on their own properties was a key source of information. The mail-in card requesting personal assistance that accompanied one of the mailings was cited as a particularly effective communication tool. Greater publicity for the project would probably have generated more information-seeking behavior on the part of landowners. And more personal contact by private consultant foresters and volunteer master stewards would be key follow-up activities to this publicity.

The project was successful in helping landowners who requested assistance get the assistance they asked for. Many landowners now know that assistance is available and how to obtain it. Interpersonal contact between landowners and forestry professionals at project events and the referral system linking landowners and professional foresters on landowner properties was a key component of the project.

Only a small number of landowners had their resources professionally evaluated. Other landowners assessed the condition of their forestland informally. Publications, interpersonal contact with landowners, and the mechanism for referring landowners to forestry professionals were identified as key communication channels in this regard. The structured nature of the program is seen as strength by many. But the project should not focus solely on formal, professionally conducted, resource inventories. A mechanism for working with underfunded landowners or landowners less motivated to develop formal resource inventories should be devised.

Larger landowners are more inclined to develop formally stated stewardship goals. Many other landowners are probably actively thinking about what they might do and why. Discussion during field events and with professional foresters is key to helping landowners develop their goals. Alternatives to formal written plans are needed. Landowners should be presented with a variety of management options.

Only a few landowners developed formal written stewardship plans; though several landowners probably have less substantial plans developed. The concept may just be catching on. Contact with forestry professionals is key to stewardship planning. It is felt that there are too few professional foresters to adequately assist landowners and that developing formal stewardship plans is too expensive. Some procedures and regulations are viewed as too complicated and require a big commitment from landowners. A more flexible definition of a stewardship plan is needed.

Mailing publications was an effective way to target the right audience with the right information. Though project publications were perceived to be of high quality, concise, and easy to read, several individuals thought they could be more focused/brief, personalized with local examples, and distributed more widely and frequently.

Field demonstration tours were said to be effective because local vivid examples were presented and discussed by both peer and expert sources. It was felt that there should have been more field events at various times and that they should have been more widely publicized.

Media coverage, viewed as very important, was apparently too scattered and infrequent. It was felt that more effort needed to be spent cultivating and maintaining media contacts in various media outlets. Most respondents were unaware of the existence of project PSAs and felt these were not worth the investment it took to produce and distribute them.

The direct mail video employed in the beginning of the project was effective in establishing awareness and interest in the project because it was well targeted, personal, entertaining, and easy to use. It was felt that the video needed to be distributed more widely and shown more frequently, and an instructional counterpart video was needed depicting the technical aspects of implementing forest stewardship plans.

A website could become an important communication tool, especially if it has a chatroom/bulletin board function. Yet several individuals cautioned that they did not feel it would be an appropriate tool in this watershed because the advanced age of the average landowner meant that they might not be technologically inclined.

Outcome Evaluation

Introduction

The project's final outcome evaluation survey was conducted four years after the project began. A comparison of baseline data collected in the beginning of the project and final assessment data identifying changes that took place during the life of the project are presented here. Eight specific objectives posited during the planning phase of the project are addressed. Two additional objectives were developed as the project progressed.

SURVEY METHODS

Baseline survey

As stated earlier, Tax Assessors' maps and mailing lists were used to create a database of all 686 landowners who owned five or more acres of land in the watershed. A mail survey was then conducted at the beginning of the project with this population. Important determinants of stewardship behavior that could guide the development of survey questions were identified in relevant literature. A focus group interview with a small group of landowners was conducted to discuss potential questions and to gauge their feelings and knowledge levels concerning forest stewardship. The baseline Eight Mile River watershed landowner survey questionnaire was then finalized (see Appendix 2 for questionnaire).

The questionnaire was mailed with a cover letter and return envelope to all 686 landowners. A lottery prize of $100 was offered as an incentive for returning the questionnaire. Phone calls were made to landowners shortly after the mailing to encourage participation in the study. One hundred ninety four landowners (28.3%) completed the questionnaire. Additional phone calls were made to 50 nonrespondents after data collection was completed to check for potential response bias. No significant mean differences were discovered between respondents and nonrespondents for 15 demographic, attitudinal and behavioral variables.

Final Evaluation Survey

A mail survey was conducted four years after the project began with many of the same individuals that were surveyed in the beginning. There were additions and deletions to the original landowner database. During the four years of the project, 63 new landowners were added to the database and 74 were omitted, resulting in a population of 675 landowners that were surveyed. The final evaluation survey questionnaire was closely patterned on the baseline questionnaire (see Appendix 3 for questionnaire).

A three-wave mailing of the survey was employed. The questionnaire was initially mailed with a cover letter and return envelope to landowners.

A postcard reminder was mailed two weeks later asking people to comply and alerting them to a forthcoming second mailing of the questionnaire. A second mailing of the questionnaire, cover letter and return envelope was made to people who had not yet responded two weeks after the post card was mailed. Brief reminder phone calls were made just after the second mailing of the questionnaire. One hundred forty landowners (20.7%) completed the questionnaire.

LIMITATIONS

It should be noted that other conservation-oriented communication/ education events that took place during the life of the project, but were not part of the project, may have influenced the change process (e.g., various newspaper articles on the environment, special events by local land trusts). There were few of these and, though we had no way to measure these effects, their influence is perceived to be minor. It should also be noted that respondents who provided baseline data in the beginning of the project, final evaluation data at the end of the project, or both, probably exhibit more interest in forest stewardship than landowners who did not respond. Evaluation results may therefore be best generalized to a group with higher than normal landowner interest in the subject. Evaluation results should be interpreted in this regard.

ANALYSIS

Demographics of survey respondents

The average age of respondents to the pre-project baseline survey and the post-project final evaluation survey was 53.5 (sd=12.4) and 56.8 (sd=13.8), respectively. Respondents to the baseline and final evaluation surveys were 62.3% male/37.7% female and 68.6% male/31.4% female, respectively. Concerning years of education, respondents reported an average of 17.2 (sd=10.6) and 15.7 (sd=4.7), respectively for baseline and final evaluation surveys. On average, respondents to the baseline and final evaluation surveys own 55.5 acres (sd=130.3) and 44.8 acres of land (sd=83.6) and 78.8% and 78.2% reported that they live on this land 10 to 12 months of the year (respectively). It would appear that though respondents to the two surveys are not identically matched in terms of basic demographics, they are very similar. Subsequent analyses will be based on the assumption that valid comparisons can be drawn.

Objective 1: Landowners will increase their familiarity with the Eight Mile River Watershed Project

Respondents to the final evaluation survey were asked if they had heard of the Eight Mile River Watershed Project -- 89.1% indicated they had. They were then asked to indicate their familiarity with the project on a one to seven scale, low to high familiarity. The average response was 3.9 (sd=2.1). It would appear that the project was very successful in creating awareness of its existence and moderately successful in establishing familiarity.

Objective 2: Landowners will increase their knowledge of what is involved in conducting a forest inventory/evaluation and stewardship plan

Respondents to the final evaluation survey were asked to indicate how much they think they know about having their forest resources inventoried and/or evaluated. On a one to seven scale, low to high knowledge, the average response was 3.5 (sd=2.2). They were also asked to indicate how much they know about having a forest stewardship plan developed. On a one to seven scale, low to high knowledge, the average response was 3.3 (sd=2.0). It would appear that the project was somewhat less successful in increasing landowner knowledge of resource evaluation and stewardship planning issues. This slightly low figure could be an indication that landowners perceive stewardship practices to be complex and a reflection of low self-efficacy.

Objective 3: Landowners will seek information about forest stewardship planning.

The following table lists the principal sources of information about forest stewardship made available by the project. The first column indicates what percent of respondents to the final evaluation survey obtained information through these sources in the ten year period prior to the project. The second column indicates what percent obtained information from these sources during the project. The third column indicates the average rating by respondents when they were asked to indicate their intentions (on a one to seven scale, low to high intentions) regarding intended future use of these information sources.

Sources of information	Usage ten years prior to project	Usage during project	Intended future usage
Demonstration tours	14.5%	30.2%	3.8 (sd=2.1)
Brochures	38.0%	65.2%	4.4 (sd=2.1)
Books or manuals	29.6%	42.9%	4.2 (sd=2.2)
Website material	4.3%	9.6%	3.8 (sd=2.3)
Newspaper articles	41.7%	58.2%	4.3 (sd=2.2)
Videos	15.5%	37.1%	3.7 (sd=2.1)
Television ads	9.8%	15.5%	3.8 (sd=5.3)
Television shows	11.3%	20.5%	3.7 (sd=2.2)

It would appear that use of all information sources increased considerably during the life of the project and that respondents are moderately likely to maintain their use of these sources in the future. The most widely used information source during the project was printed material – used by between half and two thirds of respondents. Videos were the next most widely used source – used by slightly more than one third of respondents. Demonstration tours were attended by slightly less than one third of respondents.

Objective 4: Landowners will exhibit positive changes in key attitudes predictive of stewardship planning

When respondents to the final evaluation survey were asked to indicate how important they felt it was for landowners to practice good forest stewardship (on a one to seven scale, low to high importance), the average response was 5.5 (sd=1.7). Because this question was only asked on the post-project final evaluation survey, there is no way to tell if this high rating is due to project activity or if individuals felt this way prior to the project. However, the fact that the figure remains high is a positive legacy of the project.

Several questions were asked on both the pre-project baseline survey and the post-project final evaluation survey concerning key attitudes that predict stewardship planning – issue involvement, perceived threat to oneself, perceived threat to community, self efficacy, collective efficacy, family norms, anticipated personal consequences, and anticipated community consequences. A t-test was employed to test for statistical significance between pre-project baseline and post-project final evaluation scores for all variables used to measure these attitudes. There were three instances of statistical significance at the $p<.05$ level. Interestingly, all three variables were used to measure the attitude labeled "anticipated consequences to community." The following table depicts mean scores for all variables for both the pre-project baseline survey and the post-project final evaluation survey.

Survey question (N ranges from 49 to 59)	Baseline survey	Final evaluation survey
I. Issue involvement (rated on 1 to 7 scale, low to high importance)		
a) How important to you is wildlife on your land.	6.3 (sd=1.0)	6.2 (sd=1.4)
b) How important to you is natural beauty of your land.	6.4 (sd=.91)	6.5 (sd=.97)
c) How important to you is drinking water on your land.	6.6 (sd=1.1)	6.3 (sd=1.6)
d) How important to you are rivers and streams on your land.	6.3 (sd=1.3)	6.3 (sd=1.5)
e) How important to you are trees and plants on your land.	6.3 (sd=1.1)	6.5 (sd=.82)
f) How important to you are each are the soils on your land.	6.1 (sd=1.3)	6.1 (sd=1.2)
g) How important to you is production of forest products on your land.	3.9 (sd=2.4)	3.3 (sd=2.4)
II. Perceived threat to oneself		
a) The natural resources on my property are: Not at risk 1 2 3 4 5 6 7 Very much at risk	2.3 (sd=1.3)	2.4 (sd=1.6)
b) The natural resources on my property are: In danger 1 2 3 4 5 6 7 Very safe	5.1 (sd=1.7)	4.7 (sd=2.2)
c) The natural resources on my property are: Protected from harm 1 2 3 4 5 6 7 Susceptible to harm	3.2 (sd=1.6)	2.8 (sd=1.7)
III. Perceived threat to the community		
a) The natural resources in the watershed are: Not at risk 1 2 3 4 5 6 7 Very much at risk	4.4 (sd=1.5)	4.7 (sd=1.9)

b) The natural resources in the watershed are: In danger 1 2 3 4 5 6 7 Very safe	3.6 (sd=1.5)	3.9 (sd=1.4)
c) The natural resources in the watershed are: Protected from harm 1 2 3 4 5 6 7 Susceptible to harm	4.7 (sd=1.4)	4.5 (sd=1.6)

IV. Self efficacy (rated on 1 to 7 scale, strongly disagree to strongly agree)

a) Developing a stewardship plan for my property sounds like a task beyond my ability.	3.6 (sd=1.6)	3.5 (sd=1.7)
I am confident that I can successfully develop a Stewardship plan.	4.1 (sd=1.7)	4.5 (sd=1.6)

V. Collective efficacy (rated on 1 to 7 scale, strongly disagree to strongly agree)

a) I doubt landowners in the community have the skills necessary to successfully develop a stewardship plan.	3.8 (sd=2.4)	3.4 (sd=2.0)
b) I am confident that landowners in the community can successfully develop stewardship plans.	4.9 (sd=1.5)	4.7 (sd=1.4)

VI. Family norms (rated on 1 to 7 scale, strongly disagree to strongly agree)

a) Developing a stewardship plan for my property is something my family would think we should do.	4.3 (sd=1.7)	4.2 (sd=1.5)
b) Developing a stewardship plan for my property is something my family would think is a waste of time.	3.6 (sd=1.9)	3.6 (sd=1.4)
c) Developing a stewardship plan for my property is something my family would agree is important.	4.5 (sd=1.9)	4.9 (sd=1.4)

VII. Anticipated personal consequences (rated on 1 to 7 scale, strongly disagree to strongly agree)

a) Developing a stewardship plan for my property would take more time than I am willing to spend.	3.9 (sd=1.7)	3.8 (sd=1.6)
b) Developing a stewardship plan for my property would increase my property's value.	3.9 (sd=1.7)	3.8 (sd=1.4)
c) Developing a stewardship plan for my property would require too much money on my part.	4.1 (sd=1.3)	4.1 (sd=1.3)
d) Developing a stewardship plan for my property would help those who will inherit my land.	5.2 sd=1.6)	5.0 (sd=1.6)
e) Developing a stewardship plan for my property would help preserve the beauty of my property.	5.0 (sd=1.7)	5.2 (sd=1.5)
f) Developing a stewardship plan for my property would require too much effort on my part.	3.9 (sd=1.6)	3.9 (sd=1.3)

g) Developing a stewardship plan for my property would improve recreational opportunity on my property.	3.8 (sd=1.7)	4.2 (sd=1.8)
h) Developing a stewardship plan for my property would help increase wildlife on my property.	4.5 (sd=1.8)	4.6 (sd=1.8)

VIII. Anticipated consequences to community (rated on 1 to 7 scale, strongly disagree to strongly agree)

* a) If other landowners in the community developed stewardship plans for their properties it would help keep our ground water safe to drink.	5.3 (sd=1.3)	6.0 (sd=1.2)
b) If other landowners in the community developed stewardship plans for their properties it would interfere with nature across the watershed.	2.8 (sd=1.6)	2.3 (sd=1.3)
c) If other landowners in the community developed stewardship plans for their properties it would harm trees and plants across the watershed.	2.5 (sd=1.4)	2.1 (sd=1.3)
d) If other landowners in the community developed stewardship plans for their properties it would cause wildlife to leave the watershed.	2.3 (sd=1.3)	2.0 (sd=1.4)
e) If other landowners in the community developed stewardship plans for their properties it would lower property values across the watershed.	3.0 (sd=1.6)	2.8 (sd=1.8)
* f) If other landowners in the community developed stewardship plans for their properties it would help preserve the beauty of the watershed.	5.2 (sd=1.5)	6.0 (sd=1.3)
* g) If other landowners in the community developed stewardship plans for their properties it would help make sure that future landowners are able to enjoy the same natural resources we do now.	5.3 (sd=1.4)	5.8 (sd=1.3)

* significant difference between pre-project baseline survey and the post-project final evaluation survey variables at p<.05.

It appears that the project was particularly successful in changing attitudes associated with the impact forest stewardship has on the community. This is an important factor because forest stewardship is inherently about caring for resources that extend beyond individual property boundaries. Successful stewardship of a watershed requires community-wide participation. A greater sense of importance concerning the community consequences of forest stewardship should increase individual participation.

Objective 5: Landowners will obtain expert assistance for stewardship planning

The following table lists the principal sources of professional assistance for stewardship planning promoted by the project. The first column indicates what percent of respondents to the final evaluation survey obtained assistance through these sources in the ten-year period prior to the project. The second column indicates what percent obtained assistance from these sources during the project. The third column indicates the average rating of respondents when they were asked to indicate their intentions (on a one to seven scale, low to high intentions) regarding intended future contact with these professionals.

It would appear that landowners' contact with the University of Connecticut Forest Stewardship program increased by about a third during the project. Contact with State Department of Environmental Protection service foresters increased slightly. Contact with University of Connecticut Cooperative Extension remained about the same. These three sources of assistance will continue to be the most widely used in the future. Contact with consultant foresters and volunteer master stewards appear to have dropped off a little during the project and they are apt to be the least likely contacted in the future. This is a limitation as they could have played a vital role during the project and their future participation is key to continued adoption/diffusion of project objectives.

Sources of assistance to project	Contact ten years prior	Contact during project	Intended future usage
UConn Forest Stewardship Program	5.9%	9.2%	3.3 (sd=2.0)
UConn Cooperative Extension System	18.8%	19.0%	3.6 (sd=2.1)
State DEP service forester	10.7%	13.1%	3.4 (sd=2.0)
Private consultant forester	13.8%	11.4%	2.1 (sd=1.8)
Volunteer master stewards	6.0%	4.8%	2.8 (sd=2.2)

Objective 6: Landowners will assess the condition of their forestland and/or compile a written inventory of their forest resources

In the ten years prior to the project (1985-1994), 29.9% of respondents reported having inventoried and/or evaluated their forest resources. When asked to indicate the extent that they had assessed/evaluated their forest resources during the time period of the project, 57% of respondents said they had not completed an assessment, 28% said they had completed a basic assessment by themselves or with the help of a friend/neighbor, 11% said they had completed an informal inventory with the help of a professional forester, and 4% said that a formal written inventory had been completed by a professional forester. When asked how likely they were to inventory/evaluate their forest resources in the future, the average response was 3.8 (sd=2.1)(on a one to seven scale, not likely to very likely).

It appears that the frequency and overall number of completed resource inventories/evaluations increased during the project and that this pace will continue in a moderate fashion in the future. Forty three percent of respondents report having completed at least some form of assessment during the project, two thirds of which are basic and completed without the help of a professional. Though the project promoted more formal professionally completed resource inventories/evaluations, the importance of teaching landowners to complete their own basic assessment without professional assistance is highlighted. Further support for this can be seen in the following acreage analysis.

In terms of acreage, 3681 acres were inventoried/evaluated in some manner during the project. A total of 1645 acres were inventoried/evaluated by those that said they had completed a basic assessment by themselves or with the help of a friend/neighbor, 1174 acres were inventoried/evaluated by those that said they had completed an informal inventory with the help of a professional forester, and 862 acres were inventoried by those that said that a formal written inventory had been completed by a professional forester.

Objective 7: Landowners will formulate specific stewardship goals

The table below depicts what respondents defined as their primary stewardship goals for their forestland for the next ten years. When asked to rate how well defined these goals were on a one to seven scale (very vague to very well defined), the average response was 4.2 (sd=2.0) indicating a moderate degree of clarity/concreteness. It is clear that many landowners want to keep their land in its natural state and undeveloped and are willing to manage their land principally for the health of trees and the benefit of wildlife.

Stewardship goals	Number of respondents
1. Leave it as is/do nothing/keep natural	49
2. Remove diseased/damaged tress/thin trees/selective cutting/pruning	26
3. Keep open space/keep development out/employ conservation easement	10
4. Enhance wildlife/wildlife habitat	9
5. Protect watershed/good forest stewardship/stewardship planning	8
6. Manage/cut for firewood	4
7. Manage/cut for lumber/timber	4
8. Agriculture (crops/bees/livestock)	4
9. Plant trees/plant material	3
10. Protect water supply/streams	2
11. Develop/maintain meadow	2
12. Develop land/build on land	2
13. Maintain/improve beauty/aesthetics	1
14. Establish/maintain trails	0

Objective 8: Landowners will develop written forest stewardship plans.

In the ten years prior to the project, 7.6% of respondents reported having developed written stewardship plans for their property. Only 1.3% said they had requested cost sharing assistance for these plans. When asked to indicate the extent that they had developed stewardship plans for their properties during the time period of the project, 66% of respondents said they had no specific plans prepared, 26% said they had general plans that were thought out but not recorded, and 8% said they had completed formal written stewardship plans. Approximately 7% said they had requested federal cost sharing assistance for these plans. When asked how likely they were to develop written stewardship plans for their property in the future, the average response was 3.1 (sd=2.1), on a one to seven scale (not likely to very likely). When asked on the same scale how likely they were to request federal cost-sharing assistance for stewardship plans in the future, the average response was 2.6 (sd=1.9) indicating relatively low intentions.

Paralleling the increase in landowner resource inventory/evaluation efforts discussed above, it appears that the frequency and overall number of completed stewardship plans also increased during the project. This pace will continue in a slightly less than moderate fashion in the future. Thirty four percent of respondents report having completed at least some form of stewardship plan during the project, three quarters of these are general plans that are thought out but unrecorded. Again, paralleling previous comments about the need for a less formal approach to landowner resource inventory/evaluation efforts, though the project promoted more formal written stewardship plans, the importance of less formal plans that may reside only in the minds of landowners should be highlighted. Support for this can be seen in the following acreage analysis.

Collectively, landowners who stated they had developed a stewardship plan during the project, written or not, own a total of 3628 acres. Of this, 2407 acres were put under general plans that are thought out but not recorded and 1221 acres were put under formal written stewardship plans.

Objective 9: Landowner will take steps to permanently protect their land

In the 10 years prior to the project, ten respondents reported that they placed a conservation restriction on their land deed and seven reported donating land to a land trust. The table below depicts what respondents said when asked what steps they had taken to permanently protect some or all of their land from future development during the life of the project. It is interesting to note that the frequency of implementing estate conservation measures over the 10 year period before the project is very nearly equal to that achieved during the much shorter (four-year) time frame of the project.

Steps to permanently protect land	Number of respondents
1. Register as open space.	11
2. Not develop/not fragment the land	7
3. Conservation easement/deed restriction	7
4. Sell to state or town/give to state or town	4
5. Nature Conservancy easement	3
6. Donation to local land trust	3

When asked what they intended to do with their land in the future, 72 respondents said they intend to sell it to family/close friends, 48 respondents said they intend to sell it on the open market, 35 said they intend to specify a conservation restriction on some or all of the land, 21 said they intend to give it to family/close friends, and 18 said they intend to donate some or all of the land to a land trust. It would appear that, though the estate conservation planning objectives of the project were never formally developed, the project has had a positive impact on the future intentions of several landowners in this regard.

Objective 10: Landowners will not in engage in practices they might otherwise have engaged in prior to the project

The table below depicts what respondents said when asked what activities they had decided <u>not</u> to do during the four years of the project because of what they learned about forest stewardship. This is an important concept as curbing detrimental land use practices, even if this results in nonactivity, is often times as important as engaging in positive forest stewardship behaviors. It is interesting to note that two of the nine practices mentioned by respondents have to do with estate planning objectives that were never formally developed by the project.

Practices not engaged in	Number of respondents
1. No clear cutting	7
2. Not sell to developer	5
3. Not let forest go unattended	3
4. Not fragment/cut-up land	2
5. Not cut timber without a plan	2
6. Use less chemicals	2
7. Not build next to water	1
8. Not hire logging company	1
9. Not remove snags/dead trees	1

CONCLUSION – OUTCOME EVALUATION

The conclusions presented here will be drawn from results of the Outcome Evaluation discussed above. In addition, conclusions drawn in the project Process Evaluation will be reiterated here when applicable.

1. According to respondents to the Outcome Evaluation survey, the project was very successful in creating awareness of its existence but only moderately successful in establishing familiarity. Approximately half of the project staff and partners that responded to the Process Evaluation survey believe that the project was "marginally" successful in establishing familiarity among watershed forest landowners. Given that project familiarity is crucial to fulfilling subsequent higher-level project objectives (e.g., knowledge, attitude, and behavior change), it is disconcerting that respondents to both surveys felt the project was only moderately successful in establishing familiarity among watershed forest landowners. This may have been caused by lack of project publicity, little activity by volunteer master stewards, and the fact that there were few state and consultant foresters to assist landowner. The publications mailed directly to landowners and the demonstration field tours were considered the most successful channels of information for establishing project familiarity.

2. Not unexpectedly given the above conclusion concerning project familiarity, respondents to the Outcome Evaluation survey feel that the project was slightly less than moderately successful in increasing landowner knowledge of resource evaluation and stewardship planning issues. This slightly low figure could be an indication that landowners perceive stewardship practices to be complex and a reflection of their low self-efficacy. Based on results of the Process Evaluation, the success the project had in increasing knowledge about forest resource inventory and stewardship planning resides mostly in those landowners who attended the demonstration field tours. The type of personal contact that landowners had with professional foresters at these events and subsequently on their own properties is key to teaching about complex tasks.

3. Outcome Evaluation findings show that use of all information sources increased considerably during the life of the project and that respondents are moderately likely to maintain their use of these sources in the future. The most widely used information source during the project was printed material – used by between half and two thirds of respondents. Videos were the next most widely used source – used by about one third of respondents. Demonstration tours were attended by slightly less than one third of respondents.

Findings concerning print material and demonstration tours were confirmed in the Process Evaluation. The mail-in card requesting personal assistance that accompanied one of the mailings was cited as a particularly effective communication tool. Greater publicity for the project would probably have generated more information-seeking behavior on the part of landowners. More personal contact by private consultant foresters and volunteer master stewards would be key follow-up activities to this publicity.

4. Outcome Evaluation results show that the project was particularly successful in changing attitudes associated with the impact forest stewardship has on the community. This is an important factor because forest stewardship is inherently about caring for resources that extend beyond individual property boundaries. Successful stewardship of a watershed requires community-wide participation. A greater sense of importance concerning the community consequences of forest stewardship should increase individual participation.

5. Outcome Evaluation results show that landowners' contact with the University of Connecticut Forest Stewardship program increased by about a third during the project. Contact with State Department of Environmental Protection service foresters increased slightly. Contact with University of Connecticut Cooperative Extension remained about the same. These three sources of assistance will continue to be the most widely used in the future. Contact with private consultant foresters and volunteer master stewards dropped off a little during the project and they are apt to be the least likely contacted in the future. This is an impediment. Process Evaluation results show that the project was successful in helping landowners who requested assistance get the assistance they asked for. Many landowners now know that assistance is available and how to obtain it. Interpersonal contact between landowners and forestry professionals at project events and the referral system linking landowners and professional foresters on landowner properties are key components of the project. Interpersonal contact with private consultant foresters and volunteer master stewards is key to continued adoption/diffusion of project objectives.

6. Outcome Evaluation results show that the frequency and overall number of completed resource inventories/evaluations increased

during the project and that this pace will continue in a moderate fashion in the future. Forty three percent of respondents report having completed at least some form of assessment during the project, two thirds of these are basic and completed without the help of a professional. In terms of acreage, 3681 acres were inventoried/evaluated in some manner during the project. A total of 1645 acres were inventoried/evaluated by those that said they had completed a basic assessment by themselves or with the help of a friend/neighbor, 1174 acres were inventoried/evaluated by those that said they had completed an informal inventory with the help of a professional forester, and 862 acres were inventoried by those that said that a formal written inventory had been completed by a professional forester. Process Evaluation results show that only larger acreage landowners had their resources professionally evaluated. The structured nature of the program is seen as strength, but the project should not focus solely on formal professionally conducted resource inventories. A mechanism for working with underfunded landowners or landowners less motivated to develop formal resource inventories should be developed. Outcome Evaluation results highlight the importance of teaching landowners to complete their own basic assessment without professional assistance.

7. Outcome Evaluation results show that landowners' stewardship goals for the most part are moderately clear/concrete and primarily involve wanting to keep their land in its natural state and undeveloped and they are willing to manage their land principally for the health of trees and the benefit of wildlife. Process Evaluation results show that larger acreage landowners are more inclined to develop formally stated stewardship goals. Discussion during field events and with professional foresters is key to helping landowners develop their goals.

8. Outcome evaluation results show that the frequency and overall number of completed stewardship plans increased during the project. This pace will continue in a slightly less than moderate fashion in the future. Thirty four percent of respondents report having completed at least some form of a stewardship plan during the project; three quarters of these are general plans that are thought out but unrecorded. In terms of acreage, collectively,

landowners who stated they had developed a stewardship plan during the project, written or not, own a total of 3628 acres. Of this, 2407 acres were put under general plans that are thought out but not recorded and 1221 acres were put under formal written stewardship plans. Process Evaluation results confirm that only a few landowners developed formal written stewardship plans and that contact with forestry professionals was the key to this process. It is felt that there are too few professional foresters to adequately assist landowners in developing expensive/resource intensive formal stewardship plans and that developing these plans requires a large commitment from landowners. Again, paralleling previous comments about the need for a less formal approach to landowner resource inventory/evaluation efforts, though the project promoted more formal written stewardship plans, the importance of less formal plans that may reside only in the minds of landowners is highlighted.

9. Outcome evaluation results show that the frequency of implementing estate conservation planning measures over the ten year period before the project is very nearly equal to that achieved during the much shorter (four year) time frame of the project. It appears that, though the estate conservation planning objectives of the project were never formally developed, the project has had a positive impact on the future intentions of several landowners in this regard.

10. Outcome evaluation results show that several landowners did not engage in practices they might otherwise have engaged in prior to the project. This is an important concept, as curbing detrimental land use practices, even if this results in inactivity, is often times as important as engaging in positive forest stewardship behaviors.

Appendix 1

Eight Mile River Watershed Project
Process Evaluation Questionnaire

You have been selected to participate in an interview survey. This interview concerns the role you have played in the forest stewardship component of the Eight Mile River Watershed Project. We are in the process of evaluating the strengths and weaknesses of the project and would appreciate your candid opinions. I have several questions I would like you to respond to, please take your time thinking through your answers.

1. How long have you been involved with the forest stewardship component of Eight Mile River Watershed project?
2. What has been your role in the forest stewardship component of the project?
3. What do you consider to be the goals of the forest stewardship component of the project?

Eight specific objectives for the forest stewardship component of the project have been defined. I will now read these to you one at a time. For each objective, please indicate:

    a) How successful do you think the forest stewardship component of the project has been in achieving the objective?
    b) What do you think have been the strengths of the forest stewardship component of the project in regard to the objective?
    c) What do you think have been the weaknesses of the forest stewardship component of the project in regard to the objective?
    d) What would you advise someone in another watershed to do differently in regard to the objective?

4. Obj1: Landowners will become familiar with the forest stewardship component of the Eight Mile River Watershed Project
    a) How successful do you think the forest stewardship component of the project has been in achieving the objective?
    b) What do you think have been the strengths of the forest stewardship component of the project in regard to the objective?

c) What do you think have been the weaknesses of the forest stewardship component of the project in regard to the objective?

d) What would you advise someone in another watershed to do differently in regard to the objective?

5. Obj2: Landowners will know what is involved in conducting a forest inventory/assessment and stewardship plan
   a) How successful do you think the forest stewardship component of the project has been in achieving the objective?
   b) What do you think have been the strengths of the forest stewardship component of the project in regard to the objective?
   c) What do you think have been the weaknesses of the forest stewardship component of the project in regard to the objective?
   d) What would you advise someone in another watershed to do differently in regard to the objective?

6. Obj3: Landowners will seek information about forest stewardship planning
   a) How successful do you think the forest stewardship component of the project has been in achieving the objective?
   b) What do you think have been the strengths of the forest stewardship component of the project in regard to the objective?
   c) What do you think have been the weaknesses of the forest stewardship component of the project in regard to the objective?
   d) What would you advise someone in another watershed to do differently in regard to the objective?

7. Obj4: Landowners will show positive pre-survey to post-survey changes in key beliefs/attitudes regarding forest stewardship (personal and community consequences, perceived threats, family and community norms, self confidence/ability, perceived motivation /ability of community members)
   a) How successful do you think the forest stewardship component of the project has been in achieving the objective?
   b) What do you think have been the strengths of the forest stewardship component of the project in regard to the objective?
   c) What do you think have been the weaknesses of the forest stewardship component of the project in regard to the objective?

      d) What would you advise someone in another watershed to do differently in regard to the objective?

8. Obj5: Landowners will obtain professional assistance for stewardship planning
      a) How successful do you think the forest stewardship component of the project has been in achieving the objective?
      b) What do you think have been the strengths of the forest stewardship component of the project in regard to the objective?
      c) What do you think have been the weaknesses of the forest stewardship component of the project in regard to the objective?
      d) What would you advise someone in another watershed to do differently in regard to the objective?

9. Obj6: Landowners will assess conditions of forestland and/or compile a written inventory of forest resources
      a) How successful do you think the forest stewardship component of the project has been in achieving the objective?
      b) What do you think have been the strengths of the forest stewardship component of the project in regard to the objective?
      c) What do you think have been the weaknesses of the forest stewardship component of the project in regard to the objective?
      d) What would you advise someone in another watershed to do differently in regard to the objective?

10. Obj7: Landowners will formulate specific stewardship goals
      a) How successful do you think the forest stewardship component of the project has been in achieving the objective?
      b) What do you think have been the strengths of the forest stewardship component of the project in regard to the objective?
      c) What do you think have been the weaknesses of the forest stewardship component of the project in regard to the objective?
      d) What would you advise someone in another watershed to do differently in regard to the objective?

11. Obj8: Landowners will to develop forest stewardship plans
      a) How successful do you think the forest stewardship component of the project has been in achieving the objective?

b) What do you think have been the strengths of the forest stewardship component of the project in regard to the objective?

c) What do you think have been the weaknesses of the forest stewardship component of the project in regard to the objective?

d) What would you advise someone in another watershed to do differently in regard to the objective?

Lastly I would like your opinion about some of the educational methods that were used in the forest stewardship component of the Eight Mile River Watershed Project. I will now read a list of six methods. For each method please comment on:

a) How successful do you think the method has been?

b) What do you think have been the strengths of the method?

c) What do you think have been the weaknesses of the method?

d) What would you advise someone in another watershed to do differently?

12. Publications produced/ distributed
   a) How successful do you think the method has been?
   b) What do you think have been the strengths of the method?
   c) What do you think have been the weaknesses of the method?
   d) What would you advise someone in another watershed to do differently?

13. Field days and workshops held
   a) How successful do you think the method has been?
   b) What do you think have been the strengths of the method?
   c) What do you think have been the weaknesses of the method?
   d) What would you advise someone in another watershed to do differently?

14. Newspaper, radio, TV feature stories/articles placed
   a) How successful do you think the method has been?
   b) What do you think have been the strengths of the method?
   c) What do you think have been the weaknesses of the method?
   d) What would you advise someone in another watershed to do differently?

15. PSAs aired/printed
    a) How successful do you think the method has been?
    b) What do you think have been the strengths of the method?
    c) What do you think have been the weaknesses of the method?
    d) What would you advise someone in another watershed to do differently?

16. Videos produced/distributed
    a) How successful do you think the method has been?
    b) What do you think have been the strengths of the method?
    c) What do you think have been the weaknesses of the method?
    d) What would you advise someone in another watershed to do differently?

17. Use of the website
    a) How successful do you think the method has been?
    b) What do you think have been the strengths of the method?
    c) What do you think have been the weaknesses of the method?
    d) What would you advise someone in another watershed to do differently?

This concludes the interview, please feel free to make any additional comments.

Appendix 2

Eight Mile River Watershed Landowner Baseline Survey

I. The first set of questions ask about some environmental and land management issues. Your answers will help us determine how we should adapt our instructional activities.

We are interested in your first answers. Please do not search for the "correct" answer or change your answers based on the sections that follow. We appreciate your honesty. Please fill in the blank or circle the statement that reflects your current thinking.

1) Landowners need to hire professional forestry consultants to write a stewardship plan.   True   False   Not sure

2) Stewardship plans are generally of short duration (about 1 or 2 years) that spell out what one hopes to get out of the land.   True   False   Not sure

3) Wooly Adelgid damage may well affect soil erosion.   True   False   Not sure

4) The way that private property in the Eight Mile River watershed is managed can help protect endangered species such as Purple Loosestrife and Barberry.   True   False   Not sure

5) The way that private property in the Eight Mile River watershed is managed has little effect on migratory waterfowl along the shore of the Long Island Sound.   True   False   Not sure

6) Please name the agency that you think could provide financial help in developing a stewardship plan? _____.

7) Please name two agencies that you think could provide information about stewardship planning?
a) _____.
b) _____.

8) Please list two potential threats to water quality in the community:
a) _____.
b) _____.

9) What are the three steps to take in creating a stewardship plan?
   a) _____.
   b) _____.
   c) _____.

10) The following activities could be part of a stewardship plan:

a)	Removing wildlife snags	True	False	Not sure
b)	Harvesting firewood	True	False	Not sure
c)	Clearing brush from the forest	True	False	Not sure
d)	Removing vegetative buffers along water courses	True	False	Not sure
e)	Collecting maple sap for syrup	True	False	Not sure

II. The next set of questions ask about your past practices and future intentions concerning stewardship planning. Stewardship plans are written documents that describe the natural resources on your property and your future plans for managing your land. Please circle the number of the response that best reflects your thoughts.

1) For each stewardship activity listed below, please indicate if you have already done it at least once in the past ten years.

		I have already done it (Yes)(No)		Not likely I will					Moderately likely I will		Very likely I will	
a)	Evaluate your forest resources.	1	2	1	2	3	4	5		6	7	
b)	Develop a stewardship plan for your property.	1	2	1	2	3	4	5		6	7	
c)	Attend workshops about forest stewardship.	1	2	1	2	3	4	5		6	7	
d)	Read materials about forest stewardship.	1	2	1	2	3	4	5		6	7	
e)	Participate in community groups involved with stewardship planning in the watershed.	1	2	1	2	3	4	5		6	7	
f)	Read newspaper articles about stewardship	1	2	1	2	3	4	5		6	7	
g)	Watch TV specials about forest stewardship.	1	2	1	2	3	4	5		6	7	
h)	Contact The Nature Conservancy.	1	2	1	2	3	4	5		6	7	
i)	Contact the Cooperative Extension System.	1	2	1	2	3	4	5		6	7	
j)	Request cost sharing assistance for land evaluation and stewardship planning activity.	1	2	1	2	3	4	5		6	7	
k)	Contact volunteer "Master Stewards".	1	2	1	2	3	4	5		6	7	
l)	Listen to radio talk shows about stewardship.	1	2	1	2	3	4	5		6	7	
m)	Contact the Connecticut Department of Environmental Protection Service Forester.	1	2	1	2	3	4	5		6	7	

n)	Hire a professional forestry consultant to assist with stewardship planning activity.	1	2	1	2	3	4	5	6	7
o)	Check out videos from the local library about forest stewardship.	1	2	1	2	3	4	5	6	7
p)	Place conservation restrictions on your land.	1	2	1	2	3	4	5	6	7
q)	Donate land to a land trust.		1	2	1	2	3	4	5	6	7
r)	Enrol your property in a tax incentive program for land conservation (e.g., PL 490).	1	2	1	2	3	4	5	6	7

2) Now go back to the previous question (Section II, question 1, a - r) and please indicate how likely, over the next 10 years, you are to do the activities that are listed.

3) When, if ever, do you intend to develop a stewardship plan.

I never intend to	I have already done it	I intend to in the next next year	I intend to in the next 2 to 5 years	I intend to in the next 6 to 10 years	I intend to after 10 years
1	2	3	4	5	6

III. The next set of questions ask about your feelings about developing a stewardship plan. Please circle the number that best reflects your thoughts.

1) I feel developing a stewardship plan is:

a)	foolish	1	2	3	4	5	6	7	wise
b)	good	1	2	3	4	5	6	7	bad
c)	desirable	1	2	3	4	5	6	7	undesirable
d)	detrimental	1	2	3	4	5	6	7	beneficial
e)	helpful	1	2	3	4	5	6	7	harmful
f)	wrong	1	2	3	4	5	6	7	right
g)	advantageous	1	2	3	4	5	6	7	damaging
h)	practical	1	2	3	4	5	6	7	impractical

2) How important to you are each of the following natural resources on your land?

		not important		moderately important			very important	
a)	Wildlife	1	2	3	4	5	6	7
b)	Natural beauty	1	2	3	4	5	6	7
c)	Drinking water	1	2	3	4	5	6	7
d)	Rivers and streams	1	2	3	4	5	6	7
e)	Trees and plants	1	2	3	4	5	6	7

f)	Soils	1	2		3	4	5		6	7
g)	Production of forest products	1	2		3	4	5		6	7

IV. This set of questions ask about threats to natural resources. Please circle the number that best reflects your thoughts.

1) Indicate the extent of risk facing each of the following natural resources <u>on your property</u>.

		no risk		moderate risk			high risk		not applicable
a)	Wildlife	1	2	3	4	5	6	7	NA
b)	Natural beauty	1	2	3	4	5	6	7	NA
c)	Drinking water	1	2	3	4	5	6	7	NA
d)	Rivers and streams	1	2	3	4	5	6	7	NA
e)	Trees and plants	1	2	3	4	5	6	7	NA
f)	Soils	1	2	3	4	5	6	7	NA
g)	Production of forest products	1	2	3	4	5	6	7	NA

2) The natural resources (wildlife, plants, trees, soil, and water) **on my property** are:

a)	not at risk	1	2	3	4	5	6	7	very much at risk
b)	endangered	1	2	3	4	5	6	7	very safe
c)	protected from harm	1	2	3	4	5	6	7	susceptible to harm
d)	very threatened	1	2	3	4	5	6	7	very secure

3) The natural resources (wildlife, plants, trees, soil, and water) that are found **throughout the entire watershed** are:

a)	not at risk	1	2	3	4	5	6	7	very much at risk
b)	endangered	1	2	3	4	5	6	7	very safe
c)	protected from harm	1	2	3	4	5	6	7	susceptible to harm
d)	very threatened	1	2	3	4	5	6	7	very secure

V. This question concerns your beliefs about you doing a stewardship plan for your property. Please circle the number that best reflects your thoughts.

Developing a stewardship plan for my property.....

		strongly disagree			neutral			strongly agree
a)	is something my family would think we should do.	1	2	3	4	5	6	7
b)	would take more <u>time</u> than I am willing to spend.	1	2	3	4	5	6	7
c)	would increase my <u>property's value</u>.	1	2	3	4	5	6	7

d)	would require too much <u>money</u> on my part.	1	2	3	4	5	6	7
e)	is something my close friends would think is useless.	1	2	3	4	5	6	7
f)	would help make sure that those who <u>inherit</u> my land enjoy the natural resources that I do now.	1	2	3	4	5	6	7
g)	would help <u>preserve the beauty</u> of my property.	1	2	3	4	5	6	7
h)	is something my family would think is a waste of time.	1	2	3	4	5	6	7
i)	would improve chances I could <u>make a little money</u> from forest products.	1	2	3	4	5	6	7
j)	is something my family would agree is important.	1	2	3	4	5	6	7
k)	would cause <u>wildlife</u> to leave my property.	1	2	3	4	5	6	7
l)	is something my close friends would agree I should do.1	2	3	4	5	6	7	5
m)	would help keep my <u>well water</u> safe.	1	2	3	4	5	6	7
n)	would require too much <u>effort</u> on my part.	1	2	3	4	5	6	7
o)	would improve <u>recreational opportunity</u> on my property.	1	2	3	4	5	6	7
p)	would help <u>increase wildlife</u> on my property.	1	2	3	4	5	6	7
q)	would <u>interfere with nature</u> on my property.	1	2	3	4	5	6	7
r)	would harm <u>trees and plants</u> on my property.	1	2	3	4	5	6	7

VI. Now, similar questions, but this time they are about landowners who own more then five acres of land in the Eight Mile River watershed "community". Please circle the number that best reflects your thoughts.

Concerning stewardship planning <u>by community landowners</u>....

		strongly <u>disagree</u>			<u>neutral</u>			strongly <u>agree</u>
a)	most folks would agree it is an important activity.	1	2	3	4	5	6	7
b)	they would be <u>too busy</u> to do this.	1	2	3	4	5	6	7
c)	they wouldn't be willing to make the <u>effort</u>.	1	2	3	4	5	6	7
d)	they would think it requires too much <u>money</u>.	1	2	3	4	5	6	7
e)	most folks would agree it is useless thing to do.	1	2	3	4	5	6	7
f)	they wouldn't <u>understand the need</u>.	1	2	3	4	5	6	7
g)	it would help <u>increase wildlife</u> across the watershed.	1	2	3	4	5	6	7
h)	most folks would think it is a waste of time.	1	2	3	4	5	6	7
i)	it would help keep our <u>ground water safe</u> to drink.	1	2	3	4	5	6	7
j)	it would help <u>increase town revenue</u> from forest products.	1	2	3	4	5	6	7
k)	it would <u>interfere with nature</u> across the watershed.1	2	3	4	5	6	7	7

l)	it would harm <u>trees and plants</u> across the watershed.	1	2	3	4	5	6	7
m)	it would cause <u>wildlife to leave</u> the watershed.	1	2	3	4	5	6	7
n)	most folks would agree it is their responsibility.	1	2	3	4	5	6	7
o)	it would help maintain the quality of <u>recreational opportunities</u> across the watershed.	1	2	3	4	5	6	7
p)	it would <u>lower property values</u> across the watershed.	1	2	3	4	5	6	7
q)	most folks would think it is a positive thing to do.	1	2	3	4	5	6	7
r)	it would help <u>preserve the beauty</u> of the watershed.	1	2	3	4	5	6	7
s)	it would help make sure that <u>future landowners</u> are able to enjoy the same natural resources we do now.	1	2	3	4	5	6	7

VII. This set of questions asks about some additional beliefs concerning stewardship planning. Please circle the number that best reflects your thoughts.

		strongly disagree		neutral			strongly agree	
1)	I am confident that landowners in the community can successfully develop stewardship plans.	1	2	3	4	5	6	7
2)	Having my close friend's agree with how I manage my land means a lot to me.	1	2	3	4	5	6	7
3)	Having fellow community members agree with how I manage my land means a lot to me.	1	2	3	4	5	6	7
4)	When it comes to deciding how to manage my land, I will do what I think most of my friends would do.	1	2	3	4	5	6	7
5)	I doubt landowners in the community have the skills necessary to successfully develop a stewardship plan.	1	2	3	4	5	6	7
6)	Developing a stewardship plan sounds like a task beyond my ability.	1	2	3	4	5	6	7
7)	What other people in the community are doing with their land is a good indicator of what works in the area.	1	2	3	4	5	6	7
8)	I am confident that I can successfully develop a stewardship plan.	1	2	3	4	5	6	7
9)	Currently, I believe landowners in the community can properly develop stewardship plans.	1	2	3	4	5	6	7
10)	Having my family agree with how I manage our property means a lot to me.	1	2	3	4	5	6	7
11)	I plan to manage my land the same way most people in my community do.	1	2	3	4	5	6	7

12) When it comes to deciding how to manage our land,   1   2   3   4   5   6   7
I will go with the consensus of family members.

13) At this point, I'm not sure that landowners in the   1   2   3   4   5   6   7
community have the ability to develop stewardship
plans

14) I doubt that I have the skills necessary to   1   2   3   4   5   6   7
successfully develop a stewardship plan.

VIII. This set of questions asks about you. All of your responses are completely confidential and are for statistical purposes only. They are asked because they help us better understand the context of your responses to earlier questions. Please fill in the blank where indicated or circle/check the response that best reflects your thoughts.

1) Age _____   2)   Gender _____
3) Years of formal education _____
4) What is or was (if you are retired) your occupation: _____
5) The amount of acreage you own _____
6) Is your land in the Eight Mile River watershed your primary residence?   yes -- no
                                                      (please circle)
7) During the course of a year, how many months do you live in the Eight Mile River watershed:

10-12 months	7-9 months	4-6 months	1-3 months	less than 1 month
5	4	3	2	1

8) What do you think you will do with your land in the future? (check all that apply)
_____ sell it on the open market.
_____ sell it to family/close friends.
_____ give it to family/close friends.
_____ donate some or all of the land by donating to a land trust.
_____ specifying a conservation restriction on some or all of the land.

9) Please indicate how credible (knowledgeable and trusting) you think the following sources of information on stewardship planning are:

		Not credible				Very credible		
a)	Cooperative Extension System environmental specialists	1	2	3	4	5	6	7
b)	Connecticut Department of Environmental Protection foresters	1	2	3	4	5	6	7
c)	Conservation Commission, Planning Officers or other town officials	1	2	3	4	5	6	7
d)	Members of local land trusts	1	2	3	4	5	6	7
e)	The Nature Conservancy	1	2	3	4	5	6	7

f) Private foresters   1 2 3 4 5 6 7

g) Volunteer "Master Stewards"   1 2 3 4 5 6 7

h) Neighbors who have attended workshops on   1 2 3 4 5 6 7
    forest stewardship

10) Which newspapers do you read? (please fill in)

a) _____

b) _____

c) _____

11) Please indicate your agreement/disagreement with the following statements: strongly

		strongly disagree					strongly agree	
a)	Mankind was created to rule over the rest of nature.	1	2	3	4	5	6	7
b)	Plants and animals exist to be used by humans.	1	2	3	4	5	6	7
c)	Humans have the right to modify the natural environment to suit their needs.	1	2	3	4	5	6	7
d)	We are approaching the limit of the number of people the earth can support.	1	2	3	4	5	6	7
e)	The balance of nature is delicate and easily upset.	1	2	3	4	5	6	7
f)	Humans must live in harmony with nature to survive.	1	2	3	4	5	6	7
g)	To maintain a healthy environment, we have to develop a steady economy where industrial growth is controlled.	1	2	3	4	5	6	7
h)	The earth is like a spaceship with only limited room and resources.	1	2	3	4	5	6	7
i)	Mankind is severely abusing the environment.	1	2	3	4	5	6	7
j)	When humans interfere with nature, it often produces disastrous consequences.	1	2	3	4	5	6	7
k)	Humans need not adapt to the natural environment because they can remake it to suit their needs.	1	2	3	4	5	6	7
l)	There are limits to growth beyond which our industrialized society cannot expand.	1	2	3	4	5	6	7

Appendix 3

Eight Mile River Watershed Landowner
Final Evaluation Survey

I. The first set of questions concern stewardship of lands in the Eight Mile River Watershed. Your answers will help us determine how the Eight Mile River project should adapt its instructional activities to better suit your needs.

1) Have you heard of the Eight Mile River Watershed Project? yes/no (circle your answer) (if yes, go to question 2; if no, go to question 3)

2) On the following one to seven scale, please indicate how familiar you are with the forest stewardship messages/activities of the Eight Mile River Watershed Project? (circle the number reflecting your response)

Not Familiar   Very Familiar

   1   2   3   4   5   6   7

3) What are your primary stewardship goals for your forestland for the next ten years?

_____

_____

_____

_____

4) On the following one to seven scale, how well defined are these goals? (circle the number reflecting your response)

Very vague   Very well defined

   1   2   3   4   5   6   7

5) To what degree do you know how to go about having your forest resources inventoried and/or evaluated? (circle the number reflecting your response)

No knowledge   High knowledge

   1   2   3   4   5   6   7

6) To what degree do you know how to go about having a forest stewardship plan developed? (circle the number reflecting your response)

No knowledge   High knowledge

  1   2   3   4   5   6   7

7) Please indicate to what extent you have assessed the condition of your forestland and/or compiled a written inventory of your forest resources over the past four years. (circle the category that best describes you situation)

no real assessment completed to date	basic assessment conducted by self or with help from friend/neighbor	informal inventory completed with help from professional forester	formal written inventory completed by professional forester
1	2	3	4

8) Please indicate to what extent you have developed a stewardship plan for your forestland over the past four years. (circle the category that best describes you situation)

a formal written plan has been prepared	general plans have been thought out and discussed but are not recorded	no specific plans have been made to date
1	2	3

9) What steps, if any, have you taken to permanently protect some or all of your land from future development in the past four years?

    _____

    _____

    _____

10) What activities, if any, have you decided NOT to do in the past four years because of what you learned about forest stewardship?

    _____

    _____

    _____

11) Given the ongoing work by professionals in your area to manage state and municipal forests, how important is it that private landowners also practice good stewardship of their forests? (circle the number reflecting your response)

Not important   Very important

  1   2   3   4   5   6   7

II. The next set of questions ask more about your past practices and future intentions concerning the stewardship of your forest. Please circle the number of the response that best reflects your thoughts.

1) For each stewardship activity listed below, please indicate in the proper columns, if you did this between 1985 and 1994 (yes/no), b) you did this between 1995 and 1999 (yes/no), and c) if you intend to do this over the next ten years (on a one to seven scale, not likely to very likely).

		a) I did this between 1985&1994 (Yes)(No)	b) I did this between 1995&1999 (Yes)(No)	c) In the next ten years it is: Not likely I will	Moderately likely I will	Very likely I will
a)	Inventoried and/or evaluate your forest resources.	1 2	1 2	1 2 3	4 5	6 7
b)	Develop a stewardship plan for your property.	1 2	1 2	1 2 3	4 5	6 7
	(for the question above stewardship plans are defined as written documents describing the natural resources on your property and plans for managing your forest).					
c)	Request cost sharing assistance for stewardship activities.	1 2	1 2	1 2 3	4 5	6 7
d)	Attend workshops about forest stewardship	1 2	1 2	1 2 3	4 5	6 7
e)	Attend walking tours of properties that exhibit good forest stewardship.	1 2	1 2	1 2 3	4 5	6 7
f)	Read materials about stewardship.	1 2	1 2	1 2 3	4 5	6 7
	- brochures	1 2	1 2	1 2 3	4 5	6 7
	- books or manuals	1 2	1 2	1 2 3	4 5	6 7
	- website material	1 2	1 2	1 2 3	4 5	6 7
	- newspaper articles/stories	1 2	1 2	1 2 3	4 5	6 7
g)	Participate in community groups involved with stewardship	1 2	1 2	1 2 3	4 5	6 7
h)	Watch videos about stewardship	1 2	1 2	1 2 3	4 5	6 7
i)	Watch television ads about stewardship	1 2	1 2	1 2 3	4 5	6 7
j)	Watch television shows about stewardship	1 2	1 2	1 2 3	4 5	6 7
k)	Contact the Connecticut Forest Stewardship program for assistance	1 2	1 2	1 2 3	4 5	6 7
l)	Contact the UConn Cooperative Extension System for assistance	1 2	1 2	1 2 3	4 5	6 7

m)	Contact the Connecticut Department of Environmental Protection Service Forester for assistance.	1	2	1	2	1	2	3	4	5	6	7
n)	Hire a private professional forester to assist with stewardship activities	1	2	1	2	1	2	3	4	5	6	7
o)	Contact volunteer for assistance (e.g., Coverts Volunteers)	1	2	1	2	1	2	3	4	5	6	7
p)	Contact another conservation organization for assistance. Please list name(s):_____.	1	2	1	2	1	2	3	4	5	6	7
q)	Place conservation restrictions on your land.	1	2	1	2	1	2	3	4	5	6	7
r)	Donate land to a land trust.	1	2	1	2	1	2	3	4	5	6	7

III. This set of questions asks about the natural resources on your property and in the watershed. Please circle the number that best reflects your thoughts.

1) How important to you are each of the following natural resources on your land?

		not important		moderately important		very important	
a)	Wildlife	1	2	3	4	5	6	7
b)	Natural beauty	1	2	3	4	5	6	7
c)	Drinking water	1	2	3	4	5	6	7
d)	Rivers and streams	1	2	3	4	5	6	7
e)	Trees and plants	1	2	3	4	5	6	7
f)	Soils	1	2	3	4	5	6	7
g)	Production of forest products	1	2	3	4	5	6	7

2) The natural resources (wildlife, plants, trees, soil, and water) **on my property** are:

a)	not at risk	1	2	3	4	5	6	7	very much at risk
b)	in danger	1	2	3	4	5	6	7	very safe
c)	protected from harm	1	2	3	4	5	6	7	susceptible to harm

3) The natural resources (wildlife, plants, trees, soil, and water) that are found throughout the Eight Mile River watershed are:

a)	not at risk	1	2	3	4	5	6	7	very much at risk
b)	in danger	1	2	3	4	5	6	7	very safe
c)	protected from harm	1	2	3	4	5	6	7	susceptible to harm

IV. This question concerns your beliefs about you doing a stewardship plan for your property. Please circle the number that best reflects your thoughts.

Developing a stewardship plan for my property.....

		strongly disagree		neutral			strongly agree	
a)	is something my family would think we should do.	1	2	3	4	5	6	7
b)	would take more <u>time</u> than I am willing to spend.	1	2	3	4	5	6	7
c)	would increase my <u>property's value</u>.	1	2	3	4	5	6	7
d)	would require too much <u>money</u> on my part.	1	2	3	4	5	6	7
e)	sounds like a task beyond my ability.	1	2	3	4	5	6	7
f)	would help make sure that those who <u>inherit</u> my land enjoy the natural resources that I do now.	1	2	3	4	5	6	7
g)	would help <u>preserve the beauty</u> of my property.	1	2	3	4	5	6	7
h)	is something my family would think is a waste of time.	1	2	3	4	5	6	7
i)	is something my family would agree is important.	1	2	3	4	5	6	7
j)	would require too much <u>effort</u> on my part.	1	2	3	4	5	6	7
k)	would improve <u>recreational opportunity</u> on my property.	1	2	3	4	5	6	7
l)	would help <u>increase wildlife</u> on my property.	1	2	3	4	5	6	7
m)	I am confident that I can successfully develop a stewardship plan.	1	2	3	4	5	6	7

V. Now, similar questions, but this time they are about landowners who own more than five acres of land in the Eight Mile River watershed "community". Please circle the number that best reflects your thoughts.

If other landowners in the community developed stewardship plans for their properties...

		strongly disagree		neutral			strongly agree	
a)	it would help keep our <u>ground water safe</u> to drink.	1	2	3	4	5	6	7
b)	it would <u>interfere with nature</u> across the watershed.	1	2	3	4	5	6	7
c)	it would harm <u>trees and plants</u> across the watershed.	1	2	3	4	5	6	7
d)	d) it would cause <u>wildlife to leave</u> the watershed.	1	2	3	4	5	6	7
e)	I doubt landowners in the community have the skills necessary to successfully develop a stewardship plan.	1	2	3	4	5	6	7
f)	it would <u>lower property values</u> across the watershed.	1	2	3	4	5	6	7

g) g) it would help <u>preserve the beauty</u> of the   1   2   3   4   5   6   7
watershed.

h) it would help make sure that <u>future landowners</u> are   1   2   3   4   5   6   7
able to enjoy the same natural resources we do now.

i) I am confident that landowners in the community   1   2   3   4   5   6   7
can successfully develop stewardship plans.

VI. This last set of questions asks about you. All of your responses are completely confidential and are for statistical purposes only. They are asked because they help us better understand the context of your responses to earlier questions. Please fill in the blank where indicated or circle/check the response that best reflects your thoughts.

1) Age _____ 2) Gender _____
3) Years of formal education _____
4) Amount of acreage you own in the Eight Mile River Watershed _____
5) How long have you owned this property? _____
6) During the course of a year, how many months do you live in the Eight Mile River watershed?

10-12 months	7-9 months	4-6 months	1-3 months	less than 1 month
5	4	3	2	1

7) What do you think you will do with this land in the future? (check all that apply)
_____ sell it on the open market.
_____ sell it to family/close friends.
_____ give it to family/close friends.
_____ donate some or all of the land to a land trust.
_____ specifying a conservation restriction on some or all of the land.

Chapter 12
Case Studies from New Zealand

The following three previously published articles are reprinted here with permission of the journal editor.

1) Tyson, B., Edgar, N, & Robertson, G. (2012). Facilitating Collaborative Efforts to Redesign Community Managed Water Systems. *Applied Environmental Education and Communication Journal*, Vol 10, No. 4.

2) Robertson, J., Edgar, N, & Tyson, B., (2013). Engaging Dairy Farmers to Improve Water Quality in the Aorere Catchment of New Zealand. *Applied Environmental Education and Communication Journal.* Vol 12, No. 4.

3) Tyson, B,. Unson, C. & Edgar, N. (2017). Predictors of Success for Community-Driven Water Quality Management – Lessons from Three Catchments in New Zealand. Applied *Environmental Education and Communication Journal.* Vol.16. No. 3.

The first article provides a case study describing the design, implementation and evaluation of a project that followed a dialogic/ participatory and nonformal education approach to developing systems for the future management of a limited communal water supply. Particular attention is paid to the role of stakeholders and strategic partners. The case study illustrates many of the social influence strategies and survey research methods discussed in this text.

The second article provides a case study describing the design, implementation and evaluation of a project that followed a dialogic/participatory and nonformal education approach to improving the quality of communal water resources threatened by an intensifying agriculture industry. Particular attention is paid to efforts at developing a truly community-led initiative. The case study illustrates many of the social influence strategies and survey research methods discussed in this text.

The third article provides a case study based on findings from three different catchment projects addressing threats to water quality caused by an intensifying agriculture industry. This case study identifies the primary predictors of effective community engagement in managing communal water resources. These factors can help determine the type of attention that needs to be paid to campaign social influence strategies and assist with campaign evaluation efforts. The identification of these factors augments the theoretical discussion included in Chapter 4 of this text.

Case Study 1

Facilitating Collaborative Efforts to Redesign Community Managed Water Systems

Abstract

The Upper Taieri River catchment is an arid area in the Otago region of the South Island of New Zealand faced with intensifying agriculture production. This article describes an assessment of the education/communication processes of a water resource management project and the effects on farmer beliefs/attitudes and targeted outcomes. Lessons learned from this project guided future activities in the catchment and may have had wider significance in developing community-determined allocation and management regimes in other areas faced with water shortage and water quality issues.

Introduction

Freshwater ecosystems are intrinsically connected to the health, livelihood and culture of New Zealand. The country's lakes and rivers have influenced patterns of settlement, supported economic development, and helped to shape the national identity (Ministry for the Environment, 2005). However, more intensive agriculture and the difficulties of managing intensive land use and water abstraction are adversely affecting these water bodies. The increasing intensification of farming in New Zealand is leading to increased productivity and profitability. However, there is a growing awareness that the nation must face some difficult decisions related to the economic benefits of intensifying land use versus the adverse impacts on water resources (Edgar, 2009). The government recognizes the value in identifying successful partnerships and collaborative initiatives at the catchment scale as a way of building momentum for transferring the successful elements of these initiatives to various areas of the country. The Upper Taieri Water Resource Management Project has been identified as a successful community-led initiative for managing water.

The Upper Taieri Water Resource Management Project, funded by the Ministry of Agriculture and Forestry in New Zealand and implemented by

New Zealand Landcare Trust, has been working with farmers since 2007 to help them help themselves redesign their catchment's water management system. The project works with a multi-stakeholder community-led group comprised of irrigators, local government officials, and representatives from conservation, energy and recreation interests. The Upper Taieri River catchment is a rural area in the Otago region of the South Island of New Zealand. The area is one the driest parts of the country, receiving as little as 350mm rainfall per year. In the past, farmers focused mainly on dryland sheep and beef production. These were marginal ventures for the most part and because of this, some communities in the area suffered from out-migration and lost the ability to support some basic services. Recent changes to more intensive agriculture production involving irrigated pasture and dairy production has made farming more economically viable. However, more intensive agriculture has negatively affected water quality conditions in the past and based on average flows between 1998 and 2007, the river is estimated to be "over allocated" (i.e., if all water users extracted the maximum allowed by their permits the river would be dry). In addition, historical water-use rights based on mining privileges that date back to the late 1880s are set to expire in 2021.

It is in this context that the Upper Taieri Water Resource Management Project helped farmers and stakeholder groups plan for future management of their water resources in a way that will be economically and environmentally sustainable. These plans will include:

- Development of a group rather than individual approach to catchment and subcatchment water management.
- Improvements in stakeholder relationships so they can reach consensus on water allocations thus avoiding lengthy legal battles.
- Rules for water allocation and management through a permitting system that honors historical priority right access to water in dry times (which affect farm values).
- Rules for legally recognizing informal agreements between landowners and for transferring water rights between farms.
- Mechanisms for developing group storage infrastructure, metering and reporting systems.
- Development of a system for safeguarding water quality and instituting water rationing/ sharing measures under low flow conditions.

This article will describe an assessment of the education/ communication processes used by the project and the effects the project has had on farmer beliefs/attitudes and targeted outcomes. Lessons learned from this project guided future activities in the catchment and may have had wider significance in developing community-determined allocation and management regimes in other areas faced with water shortage and water quality issues.

Research Methods

Project progress was assessed between December 2010 and February 2011. As part of this evaluation, two surveys were conducted by mail -- one survey for 118 famers in the area and another survey for 19 members of the project management group. Farmers were those included in the project's mailing list that was based on waterusers with consents approved and registered by the Otago Regional Council. The management group was comprised of members representing various governmental and nongovernmental agencies (e.g., Fish and Game Department, Department of Conservation, Otago Regional Council, the (hydro) power industry) and farmers from the five key subcatchments. Standard survey methods were used to conduct the assessments (Tyson, 2009). Survey recipients were first contacted by postcard alerting them to the upcoming surveys. An initial survey was then sent out with a return postage envelope. Respondents were tracked so that nonrespondents could be identified and contacted by email or phone to remind them to participate. Finally, a second copy of the surveys was mailed to nonrespondents. Fifty nine (50%) of the farmers and 18 (95%) of the management group members responded prior to the cut-off date. Baseline data used for comparison purposes for the farmer survey were collected in December 2007 (Robertson and Robertson, 2008). Seventy-six farmers were surveyed by mail and phone at that time; 31 (41%) responded.

Farmer Survey

DEMOGRAPHICS

Respondents for both the 2007 and 2010 surveys evidenced a similar pattern in terms of farm location, size, and residency. Respondents on average have lived in the area a significant amount of time (more than 36 years) and have farmed significant amounts of land (over 1400 acres) for over a quarter century. On average, they irrigate about 12% of that land.

Education/Communication Activities

Three separate questions assessed respondents' views about the education/ communication activities of the project and their preferences for receiving information. The first question asked respondents to rate the *successfulness* of 10 specific education/communication activities of the project. The three most successful activities, all rated well above "moderately successful" on a 1 to 5 scale, were efforts of the project management group to facilitate communication (mean = 4.04), field days hosted by farmers on local issues (mean = 3.96), and newsletters (mean = 3.93). Still considered successful, but slightly less so, were field days for external audiences to show case project issues (mean = 3.67), subcatchment level meetings on localized issues (mean = 3.64), and the national/regional workshop that was held in March, 2010 (mean = 3.53). One-on-one technical support, media releases, practical information on legal planning methods, and practical information on water storage were rated in a more neutral fashion (mean = 3.49 to 3.22).

The second question asked respondents to rate the *usefulness* of 10 specific education/ communication activities of the project. The three most useful activities, all rated well above moderately useful (on a 1 to 3 scale), were farmer field days (mean = 2.59), newsletters (mean = 2.57), and discussion with other farmers (mean = 2.57). Still considered useful, but slightly less so, were one-on-one and group discussion with management group members (mean = 2.41 and 2.34, respectively), field days (mean = 2.38), one-on-one discussions with technical specialists (mean = 2.35), and printed materials (mean = 2.33). The usefulness of the national/regional workshop that was held in March 2010 and use of the internet were rated in a more neutral fashion (mean = 2.08 and 2.07 respectively).

The third question asked respondents to list up to four ways that they prefer to receive information from the project. Newsletters was the most commonly cited channel preference (mentioned by 27.7% of respondents). Surprisingly, given its low usefulness rating, internet was listed as the second most preferred channel (mentioned by 15.8% of respondents). Field days and one-on-one conversation were also preferred channels (mentioned by 11.9% and 10.9% of respondents respectively).

Hence, farm tours/visits/field days and newsletters should be considered the two most important channels. These have been considered successful and useful in the past and are highly preferred by respondents. Any event that includes one-on-one discussion with other farmers, technical specialists and management group members should also be considered an important channel for similar reasons. Internet, though considered neutral in terms of past usefulness, is considered to be a preferred channel and should probably be used more strategically in the future. Group discussion with management group members, field days with technical specialists and printed materials, though considered useful in the past, were not mentioned as preferred channels. Nevertheless, the project should not disregard their potential importance. Lastly, the national/regional workshop that was held in March 2010 (see: Newman & Robertson, 2010), though considered successful in the past, only received a neutral usefulness rating with respondents and was not listed as a preferred channel. In the future, the project might want to reconsider embarking on such a resource-intensive undertaking if impact on the local farming community is the objective. If the primary objective is to gather experts together to share lessons learned, then the undertaking may be worth the expense.

BELIEFS/ATTITUDES

Respondents to both the 2007 and 2010 surveys essentially agreed on how much water they will receive after 2021 (when mining rights expire). Approximately three quarters agree they will receive the same amount. Only 16% of 2010 respondents believe they will receive less. This may be somewhat optimistic. It is concern over limited water availability that will help motivate water-users to plan for future allocations. Unrealistic levels of optimism can work against these motivations.

Respondents in 2010 are also a bit more optimistic about water quality conditions compared with 2007 respondents. More respondents in 2007 felt conditions were less healthy (48% vs. 21%, 2007 vs. 2010, respectively). A larger percentage of 2010 respondents believe that conditions had changed little in the past 10 years (21% vs. 39% in 2007 vs. 2010, respectively). This may be a result of the project's efforts to highlight how farmers are motivated to address water quality problems. Farmers may now be more optimistic because they now know the issue is being addressed. Yet, many 2010 respondents remain unsure about water quality conditions (14% vs. 26% in 2007 vs. 2010, respectively). Concern about water quality should help motivate water-users to take measures to improve/safeguard conditions. Excessive optimism or uncertainty can work against these motivations.

Nearly all respondents (>90%) in both 2007 and 2010 agreed or strongly agreed on the following issues:

- It is important for farmers to be leaders in developing future water management systems.
- The company/scheme structure increases the viability of future group storage systems.
- It is important for water users to form ongoing relationships with the wider community/stakeholders.
- Schemes/Companies are an effective way to manage water for whole community good.

In addition, more than two thirds of respondents in both 2007 and 2010 agreed on the following issues:

- It is important to have minimum flows to protect waterways.
- Schemes/companies hold more power than individual water rights.
- I am currently worried about future water allocation and management in the Upper Taieri.
- Knowing how much water is being taken (through metering) will prove that the Taieri is only 'over-allocated" on paper and not in reality.

Respondents agree that they must provide their own leadership, engage the broader community, and that schemes/companies that represent the interest of a collective of farmers are the way to go. They are worried about future water allocations (despite the fact that 75% believe they will receive the same amount of water in 2021) and realize the importance of monitoring flow levels. This level of agreement bodes well for future community/project efforts.

It is noteworthy that there were sizeable changes from 2007 to 2010 for two issues. The most dramatic increase pertained to the following issue: *There are currently good working relationships between water users and other interested groups/agencies in the Upper Taieri.* In 2007 only 50% of respondents agreed or strongly agreed with this issue; in 2010 the figure rose to 90.2%. The project has obviously been very successful in getting stakeholders together to discuss issues openly. One of the New Zealand Landcare Trust's greatest strengths is the ability to unify the interests of individuals and organizations that might otherwise have conflicting views.

A sizeable increase was also evidenced with the following issue: *External stakeholders perceive Upper Taieri users as environmentally responsible.* In 2007 only 50% of respondents agreed or strongly agreed with this issue; in 2010 the figure rose to 80.7%. The project has obviously been successful in instilling a sense of optimism that was not present in 2007. Project efforts to engage a wide array of stakeholders in a transparent fashion is reducing farmers' perceptions that the public views them as being environmentally irresponsible.

Management Group Survey

EDUCATION/COMMUNICATION ACTIVITIES

Two separate questions assessed respondents' views about the perceived success and usefulness of various education/communication activities of the project. The three most *successful* activities, all considered highly successful with mean scores of 4.44 (on a 1 to 5 scale) were efforts of the project management group to facilitate communication, field days hosted by policy makers, industry, etc, to showcase the project, and field days hosted by farmers in subcatchments on local issues. Four other activities were rated well above the scale value of 3.0 meaning they too were considered very successful. These include efforts of the Upper Taieri Water subcatchment water-user groups to facilitate communication (mean = 4.28), newsletters (mean = 4.28), the national/regional workshop that was held in March 2010 (mean = 4.17), and subcatchment meetings on specific local issues (mean = 4.00). Media releases, one-on-one famer support, and practical information on water storage were rated in a more neutral fashion (mean scores between 3.53 and 3.27).

The three most *useful* activities, all rated close to "very useful" (a 3 on a 1 to 3 scale), included discussion with other farmers (mean = 2.81), field days with farmers (mean = 2.76), and newsletters (mean = 2.71). Based on the previous findings, it is noteworthy that these three activities were also considered very successful. One-on-one discussion with management group members and one-on-one discussion with technical specialists were also rated highly useful (mean = 2.69 and 2.64, respectively). Field days with technical specialist, group discussion with management group members, printed material, and internet were rated about halfway between partly and highly useful (mean scores between 2.56 and 2.38). It is interesting to note that workshops for regional/national audiences, which would include the workshop that was held in March 2010 that was rated as being more than fairly successful, received the lowest usefulness score (mean = 2.13, albeit still above the scale midpoint meaning partly useful).

Hence, in terms of communication channels to be used in the future, management group members think that their efforts and the efforts of subcatchments groups to facilitate communication with farmers, field days with farmers, and newsletters should be considered the most important channels. These have been considered successful and useful in the past and are highly preferred by respondents. One-on-one discussion with management group members and technical specialists are also considered useful channels, albeit only partially successful with the project. Two topics may need to be addressed more fully in the future: a) legal/planning methods for water resource management and b) water storage/infrastructure. Workshops for national/regional audiences, though considered successful in the past, only received a neutral usefulness rating with respondents. This is a similar finding to that of the farmers. As was stated for the farmers, if the objective of such an event is to assist local farmers, than embarking on such a resource-intensive undertaking might not be worth it; but if the objective is to share information and learn from others outside the catchment than it may be worth the effort.

PROJECT OUTCOMES

Respondents agree that five of the project outcomes originally proposed by the project were met to more than a moderate degree (mean scores between 4.34 and 4.08 on a 1 to 5 scale). These five outcomes together paint an optimistic picture. Respondents believe the project has helped the community develop effective leaders and achieve greater cohesion amongst stakeholders so they can better maintain historical priority rights and strategize to protect long-term community values concerning water. They believe that the process that led to these outcomes can serve as a model for regional/national application. Five other outcomes received scores slightly below the scale value of 4.0 but high enough above the scale midpoint to be considered noteworthy accomplishments (mean scores between 3.83 and 3.69). These five outcomes reflect the fact that respondents believe the project has helped farmers develop an innovative framework for managing water resources that through supply agreements, group infrastructure (storage), metering, and reporting, will help mitigate negative effects of their water use on environmental conditions. The two outcomes that received the lowest scores (albeit still above the scale midpoint) concerned a means of legally recognizing 'gentlemen's agreements' on water use (mean = 3.45) and a structure to react progressively under low flow conditions (mean = 3.19). It should be noted that future work with farmers in the catchment should continue to address all the outcomes listed because these factors can progress or regress depending on the attention they are paid. The lower the agreement score perhaps, the greater the need for additional attention.

Conclusion

The ability to take the successful lessons learned from this Upper Taieri catchment initiative and apply them both regionally and nationally is a key priority for New Zealand, The government has been supporting the Land and Water Forum - a collaborative governance process aimed at reforming the country's management of freshwater resources. The Forum has identified the importance of early engagement by local government with both the community and resource users as a way of building effective collaborative partnerships for catchment management. The Forum has identified a number of exemplars of good practice in community-led partnerships for water management. The Upper Taieri Water Resource Management Project has been recognized for its achievements in developing improved working relationships between stakeholders for addressing catchment-wide water quantity management (Land and Water Forum, 2010).

Project assessment findings show that farmers agree that they must provide their own leadership, engage the broader community, and that schemes/companies that represent the interest of a collective of farmers are the way to go. They are worried about future water allocations and realize the importance of monitoring flow levels to help with this. In 2007 only 50% of farmers thought there were good working relationships between water users and other interested groups/agencies in the Upper Taieri; in 2010 the figure rose to 90.2%. In 2007 only 50% of farmers thought that external stakeholders perceive Upper Taieri users as environmentally responsible; in 2010 the figure rose to 80.7%.

Findings also show that members of the management group believe the project has helped the community develop effective leaders and achieve greater cohesion amongst stakeholders so they can better maintain historical priority rights and strategize to protect long term community values concerning water. They also believe (albeit to a slightly lesser extent) that the project has helped farmers develop an innovative framework for managing water resources that through supply agreements, group infrastructure (storage), metering, and reporting, will help mitigate negative effects of their water use on environmental conditions. They believe that the process that led to these outcomes can serve as a model for regional/national application.

Farm tours/visits/field days and newsletters were the two most important education/ communication activities of the project that led to the advances discussed above. Local meetings and discussion with other farmers are also important channels. Internet, though considered neutral in terms of past usefulness, is considered to be a preferred channel by farmers and should probably be used more strategically in the future. Discussion with management group members and technical specialists, though considered useful in the past by both farmers and management group respondents were not mentioned as preferred channels by farmers. Workshops for national/regional audiences, though considered successful in the past, only received a neutral usefulness rating.

One of the New Zealand Landcare Trust's greatest strengths is the ability to unify the interests of individuals and organizations that might otherwise have conflicting views. The project has been very successful in this regard. Present levels of agreement bode well for future community/ project efforts. The project has helped instill a sense of optimism with farmers that was not present in 2007.

It should be noted that future work with farmers in the catchment needs to maintain the momentum that has been established. Productive changes in farmers' beliefs and attitudes and the outcomes of these changes can progress or regress depending on the attention they are paid. It is concern over limited water availability and water quality that will help motivate water-users to plan for future allocations. Excessive optimism or uncertainty can work against these motivations. Four topics will need to be addressed more fully in the future: a) legal/planning methods for water resource management, b) development of water storage/infrastructure, c) a means of legally recognising 'gentlemen's agreements' on water use, and d) development of a mechanism that will allow farmers to react progressively under low flow conditions. Finally, in the future, the decision to launch events aimed at a national audience rather than a local audience will need to weigh the importance of providing local impacts versus the need to share information and learn from others outside the catchment.

Case Study 2

Engaging Dairy Farmers to Improve Water Quality in the Aorere Catchment of New Zealand

Abstract

In 2006, dairy farmers in the Aorere Catchment of New Zealand began to investigate allegations that they had a pollution problem affecting the viability of the community's shellfish industry. From 2007 to 2010, the New Zealand Landcare Trust's Aorere Catchment Project helped farmers engage in actions to improve conditions in their waterways. The degree of community involvement that was achieved during the project served as a major indicator of success. The actions farmers took to protect waterways and improvements in the health of these waterways were also used to assess the efficacy of the project. This article describes the catchment and the project in detail, methods used to evaluate outcomes of the project, and evaluation results. Conclusions contrasting the situation in 2007 and 2010 show that great strides were made in terms of community involvement and application of best management practices, and there is evidence that this has resulted in improved water quality and safer conditions for shellfish harvesting.

The Context

Agriculture physically dominates New Zealand's geography with over half the land area classified as farmland (Statistics New Zealand, 2009). A further third of the country is conservation land, leaving only a small area for all remaining land uses. Not only is farming physically dominant but it is also a major sector of the New Zealand economy, particularly in the export sector and in employment. Overall, the primary sector accounts for 7.1% of GDP and contributes over 50% of New Zealand's total export earnings (The Treasury, 2010).

The dairy sector in particular is fundamental to the country's economic performance, contributing approximately 25% of total merchandise export earnings ($NZ10 billion in 2008-09) (International Dairy Federation, 2010). While New Zealand produces only 2% of total world production at around 16 billion liters per annum, unlike most other countries, around 95% of its dairy produce is exported (International Dairy Federation, 2010). A rising demand from developing countries in recent years has seen a rise in dairy prices to their highest ever level (The Treasury, 2010).

A rise in the world price for dairy can often create economic incentives to expand and intensify dairy production. This has been observed in the past few decades in New Zealand where the milk solids pay out received by dairy farmers between 1990 and 2008 increased by 83%. The dairy cow population increased by 67% and the national stocking rate (cows per hectare) increased by 18% (DairyNZ, 2010). The international competitiveness of the New Zealand dairy industry is built on low cost ryegrass/clover-based systems and a favourable temperate climate that enables cows to graze pastures year round (Monaghan, 2008). While this grazed pasture farming system is very efficient at producing milk, it has also been identified as a significant source of nutrient (nitrogen and phosphorus) and fecal bacteria contamination (Monaghan, 2008) which are the causes of water quality degradation in many regions (Hamill & McBride, 2003; Vant, 2001).

There has been increasing attention in recent years both nationally and internationally regarding how expansion and intensification of the dairy industry has affected water quality (Dominion Post, 2010; Kissun, 2008). A recent Environment Waikato report states that a deterioration of water quality in the last decade has resulted in over 75% of waterways tested in the region being unsafe even for livestock to drink (Environment Waikato, 2008). A 2010 report on lake water quality in New Zealand (Verburg et al., 2010) suggests 32% of New Zealand's monitored lakes are likely to have poor or very poor water quality, and the lakes with the poorest water quality tend to be surrounded by grazing lands. Thus, reducing pollution from dairy farms remains a significant challenge in improving and protecting New Zealand's waterways. In response to these concerns, a variety of mitigation measures available to farmers to reduce environmental emissions have been developed. These environmental best management practices (BMPs) are promoted and enforced by local and regional governments guided by the principles of the national Resource Management Act (RMA).

The Setting

The Aorere River Catchment is located in Golden Bay at the top of the South Island of New Zealand. The Aorere River begins with its headwaters in Kahurangi National Park and flows for 40 kilometres before draining into the Ruataniwha Estuary. The estuary covers 1610 ha and is listed as nationally significant. Dairying is the most common farming type in the catchment with approximately 11,000-13,500 cows being grazed (Robertson & Stephens, 2007). According to the 2007 Aorere Dairy Farming Survey, dairy farming households in the Aorere are generally small, averaging three family members and there are relatively few residents in their 20s and 30s, while older (40 – 65yrs) and younger (5 – 19 yrs) residents are well represented (Peters, Robertson & Fitzgerald, 2007). Average time spent living in the district is 42 years and dairy farming on the home property averages 24 years. A profile of farm businesses reveals that 58% are owner-operators living on the property (Peters, Robertson & Fitzgerald, 2007).

Many of the farms are located on flood plains so management of effluent and riparian areas is especially important. In 2004-6 the catchment was depicted as a high level polluter in media articles and at community meetings. In particular, microbial contamination from dairy pollution was said to reduce the local shellfish industry's harvesting windows from 70% to as low as 30% per year. The situation was unique in that the reduced harvest time for the shellfish farmers offered a 'canary in the coalmine' indicator of environmental problems. This situation was also different from other farming situations in that the primary pollutant was fecal bacteria run-off rather than nutrient run-off.

The Aorere Catchment Project

In 2006 the farming community began to investigate allegations that there was a pollution problem and, with funding from the Ministry of Agriculture and Forestry, the New Zealand Landcare Trust (a nonprofit organization specializing in environmental mediation within the agriculture sector) was brought in to help facilitate discussions among stakeholders. From 2007 to 2010, the Aorere Catchment Project (ACP) implemented a number of key initiatives including: interviews with farmers, an initial assessment of nutrient and pathogen impacts, presentations to farmers, field days allowing peer-to-peer interaction, and assistance with developing tailored farm plans based on accepted BMPs.

The project strategy was based on Participatory Theory, which asserts that to establish BMPs one must actively involve the farming community at all stages of the process (Brechin et al., 2002; da Silva, 2004; Haller et al., 2008; Wilshusen et al., 2002). Local community participation is demonstrated by numerous studies to be a crucial component of natural resource management (Adams & Hulme, 2001; Carpenter, 1998; Horwich & Lyon, 2007; Ostrom, 1990; Spiteri & Nepal, 2006; Tai, 2007; Thakadu, 2005). The project was guided by the following principles: empowering farmers as leaders, keeping technical experts on tap - not on top, and utilizing local knowledge and peer mentoring.

An evaluation of the project conducted in 2010 showed that the project was successful in engaging farmers in actions to improve water quality. The farmers are investing in BMPs and this has resulted in improved water quality, which in turn has enhanced harvesting opportunities for the local shellfish industry. Evaluation results identified several elements necessary for engaging farmers in successful participatory community-based action for improving water quality. Evaluation methods and results pertaining to these elements are discussed below.

Project Evaluation

Between May and June 2007, 30 of the 34 farm households in the catchment were surveyed by one of four New Zealand Landcare Trust staff to determine farm characteristics and farmers' goals, issues and information gaps. The questionnaires were administered in face-to-face semi-structured interviews. Interviews took between 30 minutes and 150 minutes depending on the level of detail provided and the number of household members present. In February 2010, the same 30 farm households in the catchment were again surveyed by one of three New Zealand Landcare Trust staff. The questionnaires were administered in face-to-face structured interviews. These interviews took between 20 minutes and two hours. Answers to open-ended questions were audio recorded and later analysed for key themes. The surveys assessed the following factors:

ATTITUDES ABOUT FARMING AND WATER QUALITY IN THE AORERE CATCHMENT

Respondents in 2010 were asked to respond to several statements using a 1 to 5 Likert scale ranging from strongly disagree to strongly agree. Farmers indicated that they disagreed with the following statements:

- *The Aorere dairying community no longer needed to invest in environmental BMPs as water quality issues are now fixed* (90% disagree or strongly disagree).
- *The cost of on-farm works to improve water quality would exceed the benefit* (63% disagree or strongly disagree).

Farmers generally agreed with the following statements:

- *The relationship with local shellfish farmers has improved over the past three years* (100% agree or strongly agree).
- *The New Zealand Landcare Trust has been useful in building relationships and sharing information in a non-threatening way* (97% agree or strongly agree).
- *Shellfish harvesting closures may continue to occur from time to time but will not be serious enough to cause permanent closures* (96% agree or strongly agree).
- *Local dairy farmers have a clear idea what practices they could implement on their farms to protect water quality* (93% agree or strongly agree).
- *The Aorere dairy farming community deserve positive publicity for environmental enhancement work* (93% agree or strongly agree)
- *A mutual understanding of issues has developed between the Aorere dairy community and the Tasman District Council over the past three years* (93% agree or strongly agree).
- *The ACP continues to have an important role in bringing the Aorere dairying community together* (87% agree or strongly agree).
- *The ACP has been important for building a sense of community between Aorere dairy farmers* (87% agreed or strongly agreed).
- *Cow manure can carry micro-organisms that can cause illness in humans* (80% agree or strongly agree).

Opinions were mixed regarding the following statement:

- *The Aorere waterways still have nutrient and/or bacterial runoff problems* (60% agree, 23% disagree or strongly disagree, 17% were neutral).

Only a few of the above statements were present in the 2007 survey. Of these, noteworthy differences were noted for two:

- *Local dairy farmers have an idea what practices they could implement on their farms to protect water quality* (56% agreed or strongly agreed in 2007 versus 93% in 2010).
- *The cost of on-farm works to improve water quality would exceed the benefits* (38% in 2007 disagreed or strongly disagreed versus 63% in 2010).

Overall these results are positive and indicate a) a strengthening of the Aorere dairy community, b) the development of understanding and trust between dairy farmers, the local shellfish industry and Tasman District Council, c) a strong sense of pride within the community and d) a clear understanding of what farmers can do to improve water quality.

Best Management Practises

Farmers were asked to list up to five environmental BMPs that they had implemented on their farms and to express their degree of confidence in the ability of these BMPs to improve local water quality. In addition, they were asked to state their motivations for implementing these BMPs. Findings clearly demonstrate increased implementation of BMPs from 2007 to 2010.

- Efforts to improve effluent management practices increased from 87% to 100% of respondents.
- Efforts to install fences to stop stock entering waterways increased from 83% to 100% of respondents.
- Efforts to plant riparian buffers increased from 33% to 57% of respondents.
- Efforts to install bridges/culverts increased from 67% to 83% of respondents.

According to 2010 survey respondents, the three most important motivations for farmers to implement best management practices were a) pride in the beauty and quality of local waterways (97% rated this important or very important), b) a desire to see local shellfish farmers able to maintain viable businesses (86% rated this important or very important), and c) a desire to have healthier local waterways (84% rated this important or very important).

Enabling safe recreation in the Aorere River, regulatory requirements, a desire to maintain a good community reputation, needing to live up to positive publicity, negative media attention on dairy pollution issues, and improvements in stock health were considered more moderate motivations. When compared with motivations assessed in the 2007 survey, most notable is the increase in 2010 regarding the desire to see local shellfish farmers maintain viable businesses. Those who rated this issue as important or very important increased from 41% to 97%.

PROJECT EDUCATION/COMMUNICATION INTERVENTIONS

Respondents were asked to rate the usefulness of several project education/ communication interventions. One-on-one discussions with an advisor were regarded as very useful by 75% of farmers both in 2007 and in 2010. Discussions with neighbours and fellow farmers were considered more useful than they were in 2007; with 70% finding them very useful in 2010, compared with 53% previously. Local field days were regarded as very useful by only 40% of farmers in 2010. This rose to 66% when the field days included independent specialists. Printed information sheets were regarded as very useful by 43% of farmers. This was a decrease from 2007 when 66% of farmers considered them very useful. The internet was rated relatively poor in both 2007 and 2010 with only 23% considering this method very useful.

PROJECT EFFECTIVENESS

Farmers were asked whether they thought the Aorere Catchment Project had been useful and why. All respondents reported that the project had been useful and provided the following reasons:

- "Cleaning up farms and the valley has long term benefits to the catchment"
- "Makes us into a group; increases peer pressure to get more to tow the line"
- "Increased awareness, helps people discuss what they are going to do"
- "Gives us a bit of direction, motivation, more than just being left up to council enforcement; made farmers be more proactive"
- "If project had not happened, mussel industry would have taken farmers to court; so we avoided legal action and increased environmental performance"
- "Helped farmers to be proactive; council has been easier to deal with because of this open group and farmers are more willing to share information"

Discussion

The main objective of the Aorere Catchment Project was to facilitate community involvement so that farmers would be more apt to engage in actions to improve their waterways. As stated in the beginning of this article, the following three characteristics served as indicators of project success: 1) community involvement, 2) the actions farmers have taken to improve and protect waterways, and 3) the health of the waterways.

COMMUNITY INVOLVEMENT

As theory on participatory decision making and integrated catchment management suggests, local community participation is a crucial component of successful community-based natural resource management (e.g., Adams & Hulme 2001; Carpenter 1998; Horwich & Lyon 2007; Kothari 2006; Ostrom 1990; Spiteri & Nepal 2006; Tai 2007; Thakadu 2005; Tyson 2005). Aorere dairy farmers all indicated that they considered the project to be useful. The overarching theme supporting this contention is that farmers were engaged in the project. Farmers noted that the project helped give the power to the farmers, allowed them to become proactive in environmental issues, brought the community together and united towards a common goal, and put farmers in a position to come up with their own solutions. Several key factors helped engage farmers in this manner. These include community led initiatives, issue identification, understanding the community, experts on tap - not on top, effective communication, constant feedback, and inherent community values.

Community led initiatives

A fundamental concept underlying any community-based natural resource management project is to involve the landowner community from the very beginning. This project was gifted in that it was actually initiated by the members of the dairy farming community who then approached NZLT for facilitation assistance. Theory suggests that one way to engage the community is to form a community advisory board involving interested stakeholders from a variety of concerns who then collect data on a target audience, determine the perceived benefits and barriers of promoting a specific behaviour, and implement a campaign based on this information, (McKenzie-Mohr & Smith 1999). In contrast, the Aorere Catchment Project followed a more localised approach by forming a project management team open to all 34 dairy farmers in the catchment and facilitated by NZ Landcare Trust staff. All farmers were invited to attend all project management meetings. Research results show that nearly 70% of farmers attended at least one management meeting. The management group played a similar role as a community advisory board. However, non-farmer stakeholders (e.g., technical experts) were not directly involved in the management group but were only brought in for consultation as needed.

Issue identification

In line with social marketing principles, Edgar, Nimo & Ross (2005) point out that there must be some recognition within the farming community that a problem exists and farmers must have a good grasp of the issue (Dresser 2008). In this project, farmers were able to eventually understand how poor water quality was affecting shellfish farmers. An independent water quality specialist hired by the farmers confirmed excessive fecal bacteria during low to medium river flows. It was thought that this came primarily from intensive dairy operations. Most water quality issues related to intensive farming are nutrient issues, which are difficult to identify and quantify the losses. In this particular situation, the issue was bacterial contamination that was more easily traced. Economic losses faced by shellfish farmers could also be clearly quantified, something farmers could empathise with.

Understanding the community

Understanding the background, history and challenges of farmers is crucial to gaining the respect and goodwill of the farming community (Edgar, Nimo & Ross 2005). Accordingly, the project conducted interviews with 30 of the 34 dairy farms within the catchment at the beginning of the project in an effort to better understand them. The information gathered allowed project coordinators to tailor project activities to farmers' needs and identify barriers to action and plans to remedy these.

Experts on tap – not on top

An expert scientist specialising in the management of fecal bacteria was initially tapped to help farmers help themselves develop a number of BMPs. Afterwards, the implementation of these BMPs was facilitated by a series of community problem solving field days that were hosted on local farms and utilized farmer expertise while tapping outside expert advice as needed.

Communication

Fairly frequent meetings, workshops and field-days were venues for sharing questions and answers among farmers during the project. A project newsletter also helped keep everyone informed. As other studies have shown (Dresser 2008; Edgar, Nimo & Ross 2005), regular communication between project coordinators, experts and the community are necessary to build trust and understanding. Results of the 2010 survey indicated that one-on-one discussions with project staff was regarded as the most useful way of receiving information, followed by discussions with fellow farmers, and field days involving independent technical specialists. The perceived value of the internet was rated poorly.

Feedback

According to the pro-environmental change model developed by Kollmuss & Agyeman (2002), insufficient feedback concerning participants' actions is a major barrier to pro-environmental behaviour. The project therefore provided frequent feedback in the form of water quality updates to depict the progress that was being made. In addition, improvements that farmers made were celebrated in several ways including a field day celebrating the winning of a national environmental award, a dairy/shellfish farmers' joint luncheon, and a boat tour with local shellfish farmers.

Community Values

Arguably the most important element leading to success of the project was the underlying values that community members harboured. According to 2010 survey results, the two most important influencing factors for farmers in implementing BMPs were '*a desire to have healthier local waterways*' and '*a pride in the beauty and qualities of local waterways*'. Without these underlying values the project may well have been less successful.

ACTIONS TAKEN TO IMPROVE AND PROTECT WATERWAYS

There were large improvements to effluent systems, riparian fencing, riparian plantings, and stock crossings (bridges and culverts) between 2007 and 2010. These were BMPs specifically designed by farmers and experts to reduce bacterial contamination. Research results show that the desire to have healthier waterways is the most influential factor for Aorere farmers in their decision to implement BMPs on their farms. Results also show positive changes between 2007 and 2010 in the belief that '*individual farm changes will improve Aorere water quality*' and strong disagreement that '*costs for water quality improvement will exceed the benefits*'. This change in perception is most likely linked to farmers' awareness of water quality improvements and their understanding of how their farm management practices have contributed to this. In addition, comparisons between the 2007 and 2010 research results show that farmers' confidence in promoted BMPs has grown significantly. For example, confidence in bridging or culverting stock crossings as a measure to improve water quality increased dramatically from 16% to 100% over the survey period.

THE HEALTH OF THE WATERWAYS

Water monitoring results indicate that there may have been a reduction in disease-causing organisms in the catchment since project inception. However results were not statistically significant due to the relatively short monitoring period. The monitoring regime is not ideal because measurements are taken quarterly. A more frequent monthly monitoring regime would give the opportunity to sample at various flows and provide superior data. Yet, since 2007 there has been a reduction in closures of local aquaculture farms and wild-catch areas due to high fecal contamination and an increase in average harvest days from 50% to 71%.

Farmers' perceptions of the health of waterways did not vary dramatically between 2007 and 2010. This is likely due to farmers already perceiving the waterways as being healthy in 2007. The 2007 survey was undertaken before an independent assessment convinced farmers there were problems with water quality. Farmer optimism about water quality in 2010 is no doubt based on what they see as the progress that has been made addressing this issue since 2007.

Conclusion

The underlying participatory philosophy that served as the foundation of the Aorere Catchment Project has been vital to its success. The project's 'farmers as leaders' model allowed dairy farmers in the Aorere catchment to take ownership of their own environmental performance and move the issue of environmental performance into mainstream thinking and action. However, the exact duplication of the Aorere Catchment Project model would no doubt have limited application elsewhere because catchment communities are unique, issues vary, the underlying causes and effects are different, and some indicators of success pertinent to the Aorere project may be difficult to control in other settings. The first two indicators of farmer engagement, 1) the health of the waterways and 2) actions farmers have taken to improve and protect waterways are specific to the Aorere Catchment; but the third, community involvement, is not. This has universal relevance. The seven factors related to community involvement that were discussed above (i.e., community led initiatives, issue identification, understanding the community, experts on tap (not on top), wide communication, effective feedback, and inherent community values) may help guide implementation of other environmental conservation projects that wish to follow a more sustainable community-led approach.

Case Study 3

Predictors of Success for Community-Driven Water Quality Management: Lessons from Three Catchments in New Zealand

Abstract

Three community engagement projects on the south island of New Zealand are enacting education and communication initiatives to improve the uptake of best management practices on farms regarding nutrient management for improving water quality. Understanding the enablers and barriers to effective community-based catchment management is fundamental to planning, implementing and evaluating these initiatives. This article investigates some key predictors of success or determinants of effective community engagement. Six factors were identified: access to science, training and information, confidence in regulatory policies, leadership, farm planning and monitoring, trust in the public, and concern for water quality.

Introduction

In New Zealand, the intensification of agriculture, in particular pastoral farming, has had significant adverse effects on freshwater ecosystems (Drummond, 2006; Land and Water Forum 2010; Tyson, Edgar & Robertson, 2011). Much of this degradation of water resources has resulted from the complexities of managing non-point source agricultural water pollution (Edgar, 2009; Anastasiadis, et al, 2014). One of the key responses to these water quality issues has been increased resourcing for, and application of, catchment management initiatives across the country (Edgar, 2007; Duncan, 2013). The devolution of natural resource management decision-making to local government, combined with significant efforts to engage communities through education/communication initiatives addressing water resource management, has led to a resurgence in community-driven approaches to catchment management (Curtis, et al, 2014; Lees, et al., 2012).

Considerable attention is now being focused on methods to enhance the participation of communities in solving water quality issues. One of the most significant challenges is developing effective methods to engage farmers and landowners who are directly responsible for managing land and water resources both at the farm and catchment scale (Tyson, et al. 2011). The New Zealand Landcare Trust (NZLT) is an independent nongovernmental organization that promotes sustainable land management through community involvement (Lees, et al. 2012). The NZLT focuses on working with farmers and landowners at the catchment scale through education and communication initiatives to encourage economically and environmentally sustainable farming practices that result in both profitable farms and improved water quality. This organization won the inaugural Morgan Foundation NZ River Prize for their support of farmers improving water quality in the Aorere River catchment, Tasman District, New Zealand (International River Foundation, 2015).

The NZLT Trust has recognized that one of the most significant challenges to improving catchment management is to identify the determinants of effective community engagement where all relevant stakeholders participate productively in developing policies and managing water resources in a sustainable fashion (Lees, et al. 2012). Reviews and case studies of some of the Trust'ss most successful catchment management projects, including the Aorere and Taieri River initiatives, have helped to identify critical success factors. Understanding the enablers and barriers to effective community-based catchment management is fundamental to planning, implementing and monitoring catchment management education and communication initiatives. This article aims to build further understanding of the key predictors of success for community-driven water quality management by examining lessons from the NZLT's implementation of three new catchment management initiatives on the south island of New Zealand.

The Setting

In 2014 three community-driven water quality management projects were launched by the NZLT: the Kakanui Community Catchment Project, the North Canterbury Sustainable Farming Systems Project, and the Upper Buller Enhancement Group Project. The settings for the three projects were three separate catchments on the south island of New Zealand. The aim of these projects was to enact education and communication initiatives to improve the uptake and implementation of best management practices on farms, particularly in relation to nutrient management for improving water quality. Table 1 (below) describes the characteristics of these farming communities.

Table 1: Farming Characteristics by Catchment

Farming Characteristics	Catchments	N	Mean	Std. Deviation
Number of Years Farming	Upper Buller	23	40.5	41.2
	Kakanui	29	53.8	39.8
	North Canterbury	37	61.3	45.0
	Total (all three catchments)	89	53.5	42.7
Farm Size (Hectares)	Upper Buller	23	596.0	737.5
	Kakanui	29	568.9	498.7
	North Canterbury	37	1178.2	1068.4
	Total (all three catchments)	89	829.3	877.4
Irrigated Land (Hectares)	Upper Buller	23	42.6	60.6
	Kakanui	29	140.5	238.4
	North Canterbury	23	121.4	89.6
	Total (all three catchments)	75	104.6	163.6
Sheep (%)	Upper Buller	9	19.8	20.1
	Kakanui	18	44.3	31.0
	North Canterbury	33	60.1	15.0
	Total (all three catchments)	60	49.3	25.7
Beef (%)	Upper Buller	14	28.7	26.6
	Kakanui	14	33.5	23.3
	North Canterbury	33	22.2	12.5
	Total (all three catchments)	61	26.3	19.4
Deer (%)	Upper Buller	5	27.6	30.8
	Kakanui	5	18.0	29.3
	North Canterbury	8	19.0	7.4
	Total (all three catchments)	18	21.1	21.6

Dairy (%)	Upper Buller	16	84.4	23.0
	Kakanui	16	62.7	40.4
	North Canterbury	20	25.7	19.7
	Total (all three catchments)	52	55.1	37.5
Crops (%)	Upper Buller	2	5.0	0.0
	Kakanui	9	32.6	35.0
	North Canterbury	14	15.6	20.6
	Total (all three catchments)	25	20.9	27.0

As shown in Table 1, on average, respondents' families had been working their farm for 53.5 years. The average farm size was 829.3 hectares. On average, farms in North Canterbury were significantly larger than either Upper Buller and Kakanui farms (Welch F $(2,86)$ = 5.53, p = .00). However, North Canterbury, on average, had significantly more irrigated farm land than Upper Buller (Welch F$(2, 44.41)$ = 7.3, p = .002). In terms of agricultural land use, on average, 49.3% of farm land was devoted to sheep and 55.1% to dairy. Significant differences in land use were found across the three watersheds. North Canterbury had significantly larger proportion of land devoted to sheep compared to Upper Buller (Welch F$(2, 18.22)$ = 16.1, p < .001) and had significantly smaller proportion devoted to dairy compared to both Upper Buller and Kakanui (Welch F$(2, 28.6)$ = 32.97, p < .001).

Research Methods

Three surveys were completed in the three catchments between April and July, 2014 (see Tyson 2014a-c). The surveys were launched to collect information needed to design effective community-driven water quality management projects in these catchments. Thirty-one farmers were successfully surveyed in the Kakanui catchment, 37 in the North Canterbury catchment, and 23 in the Upper Buller catchment, for a total of 89 farmers. Survey data was collected from farmers in face-to-face interviews with project staff. The combined sample of 89 represents a near census of farmers in these catchments (i.e., a greater than 90% response rate was obtained in each catchment).

One section of the surveys asked about enabling and challenging issues affecting community-led water resource management. The identification of these issues drew from key literature on the determinants of successful community management groups. One primary source (Newman & Robertson, 2010) and two secondary sources (Agrawal, 2002; Tyson, 2009) were tapped. The primary source was a report based on results of a national workshop conducted by the Upper Taieri Water Resource Management Project in March 2010 (Newman & Robertson, 2010). Workshop participants represented 14 diverse community-led water resource management projects operating across New Zealand (including farmers and project staff), five regional authorities, and seven governmental or nongovernmental agencies. A list of "enablers and challenges" to successful community-led water resource management was generated collaboratively by participants at the workshop. The two secondary sources are credible efforts to reconcile available theoretical literature on a) determinants of successful common property resource management groups (Agrawal, 2002) and b) determinants of behavior change in an environmental context (Tyson, 2009). Agrawal's work focuses on the behaviors of individuals working to cooperatively manage communal resources. Tyson's work focuses on environmental social marketing in which behavior change is the ultimate objective. From these three sources a list of 31 issues were intuitively categorized into the 10 topics listed below (for detailed information on these issues see Tyson, Edgar & Robertson, 2011).

Collaboration	Trust
Education/Communication	Training
Science/Information	Water quality
Water quantity/allocation	Regulations, monitoring, enforcement
Infrastructure/Technology	Government policies

For the Kakanui, North Canterbury and Upper Buller surveys, the 31 issues were captured in 35 statements or questions (items). Respondents replied to 29 of these items using a one to five scale (strongly disagree/negative to strongly agree/positive) and six of these items using a one to three scale (poor/negative to good/positive). In an effort to go beyond the intuitive clustering of these items into categories and provide some statistical validity to our efforts at identifying the determinants of effective communities managing water resources, we conducted a factor analysis and inter-reliability tests using the 35 items. The scree plot of the initial analysis showed six viable factors. However, one factor fell just a bit short of the ideal Cronbach alpha (.70). The factors and the items associated with these factors along with their Cronbach alphas are presented below:

Factor 1: Access to Science, Training and Information (Cronbach alpha = .76)

Item 1: farmers in the catchment believe that they have good access to the science they need to make good decisions about nutrient and water management.

Item 2: farmers in the catchment believe that information they need to make good decisions about nutrient and water management is shared and available.

Item 3: farmers in the catchment believe they have sufficient access to the training they need to reduce nutrient loading and improve water quality.

Item 4 – farmers in the catchment believe that scientific research that has been complied to help guide nutrient and water management policies is accurate and fair.

Item 5 – farmers in the catchment believe they have sufficient access to training that will help them develop ways to govern their efforts to manage water resources.

Factor 2: Confidence in Regulatory Policies (Cronbach alpha = .74)

Item 1: farmers in the catchment believe that methods for monitoring nutrient loading and water quality being developed by regional authorities will be fair.

Item 2: farmers in the catchment believe that regional polices to regulate water quality are fair.

Item 3: farmers in the catchment believe that penalties imposed by District Council for breaking rules will be fair.

Item 4: farmers in the catchment believe that penalties imposed by District Council will be effective in preserving water quality.

Factor 3: Leadership (Cronbach alpha = .86)

Item 1: farmers in the catchment believe they have effective leaders in their community that can help them develop, implement and maintain farming systems that are economically and ecologically sustainable.

Item 2: farmers in the catchment believe they have skilled champions and coordinators in their community that represent various age groups so that farming systems that are economically and ecologically sustainable can be maintained across several generations.

Factor 4: Farm Planning and Monitoring (Cronbach alpha = .71)

Item 1: to what degree have you developed plans for your farm that identify areas of environmental concern?
Item 2: how well thought out are these plans?

Factor 5: Trust in the Public (Cronbach alpha = .76)

Item 1: farmers in the catchment believe that the general public understands their perspective on nutrient and water resource management.
Item 2: farmers in the catchment believe that public perceptions of their efforts to develop nutrient and water resource management plans are fair and accurate.

Factor 6: Concern for Water Quality (Cronbach alpha = .66)

Item 1: how good do you think water quality was in the waterways of the catchment ten years ago?
Item 2: how good do you think water quality was in the waterways of the catchment is at present?

Results and Recommendations

Survey findings pertaining to these factors and their associated items help identify the type of attention that the projects might devote to their education and communication efforts. Findings also help set a benchmark for subsequent project evaluation. Given that these issues are determinants of effective communities managing water resources, it would be hoped that significant improvements in how these factors and associated items are rated would be detected at the end of the projects.

Table 2 shows the means of the factors by watershed. As can be seen from the table, in general, ratings for the two factors a) Access to Science, Training and Information and b) Confidence in Regulatory Policies are at about the scale midpoint meaning there is both a foundation to build on and room for improvement in all three catchments. Ratings for the two factors a) Leadership and b) Farm Planning and Monitoring are above the scale midpoint meaning a more solid foundation exists upon which the project can build and improve. The factor, Trust in the Public, was rated well below the scale midpoint in all three catchments meaning that farmers are feeling a bit victimized by public opinion about the environmental conditions on their farms. Communication efforts by the project aimed at improving public perceptions of farmers' efforts to maintain environmentally sustainable operations could help cultivate a better climate for motivating farmers.

One-way Anova was conducted to determine whether there were significant differences across the three watersheds pertaining to the six factors. No significant differences were detected with regard to factors pertaining to Leadership, Farm Planning and Monitoring, and Trust in the Public. However, North Canterbury had significantly lower mean scores compared to Upper Buller with regard to Access to Science, Training and Information (F $(2,83)$ = 3.39, p = .04) and Confidence in Regulatory Policies (F $(2,86)$ = 4.07, p = .01). In other words, respondents in North Canterbury believe they have less access to science, training and information and were less confident in the efficacy of regulatory policies than respondents in Upper Buller. In addition, the three watersheds significantly differed in their assessment of water quality in the past and in the present (Welch F$(3,44)$ = 44, p < .004). Post-hoc tests showed that Kakanui respondents assessed their water quality as significantly less healthy than the two other watershed respondents and Upper Buller respondents assessed their water quality as significantly less healthy than North Canterbury respondents.

Table 2: Means and Standard Deviations of the Factors by Watershed

Factors	Watersheds	N	Mean	Std. Deviation
1. Access to Science, Training and Information (assessed on a 1 to 5 scale, negative to positive)	Upper Buller	23	3.42	.59
	Kakanui	28	3.17	.68
	North Canterbury	35	2.97	.66
	Total (all three catchments)	86	3.15	.67

2. Confidence in Regulatory Policies (assessed on a 1 to 5 scale, negative to positive)	Upper Buller	23	3.26	.46
	Kakanui	29	3.07	.69
	North Canterbury	37	2.75	.69
	Total (all three catchments)	89	2.99	.67
3. Leadership (assessed on a 1 to 5 scale, negative to positive)	Upper Buller	23	3.37	.84
	Kakanui	29	3.81	.87
	North Canterbury	37	3.54	.88
	Total (all three catchments)	89	3.58	.88
4. Farm Planning and Monitoring (assessed on a 1 to 3 scale, negative to positive)	Upper Buller	23	2.33	.61
	Kakanui	29	2.26	.71
	North Canterbury	36	2.18	.45
	Total (all three catchments)	88	2.24	.59
5. Trust in the Public (assessed on a 1 to 5 scale, negative to positive)	Upper Buller	23	1.85	.63
	Kakanui	29	1.97	.64
	North Canterbury	37	1.80	.75
	Total (all three catchments)	89	1.87	.68
6. Water Quality (assessed on a 1 to 3 scale, negative to positive)	Upper Buller	21	2.62	.57
	Kakanui	29	1.97	.72
	North Canterbury	36	2.99	.08
	Total (all three catchments)	86	2.55	.67

Conclusion

Agriculture is an important component of the New Zealand economy and with the conversion of more land to agricultural practices, and the intensification of agriculture, there have been concomitant impacts on the country's water resources (Foote, Joy & Death, 2015). Integrated catchment management, with a focus on a combination of both regulation and voluntary measures aimed at land user adoption of best management practices has been promoted by government, industry and communities as an effective way of improving the sustainable management of water (Edgar, 2007; Edgar, 2009). Due to its complexity, there are a range of challenges to achieving the effective implementation of catchment management practice on the ground. The NZLT has worked with a number of government, agribusiness and community organizations to identify the key success factors, or predictors, of catchment management. Identifying these predictors of success for community-driven water quality management can help with planning education and communication catchment management initiatives, monitoring their implementation, prioritizing resources, identifying where further support is required, and in evaluating whether such initiatives have achieved their aims and objectives (Lees, et al., 2012).

One recent example of a NZLT education/communication intervention is a catchment management guide and a series of catchment management education masterclasses focused on training land and water management professionals on how to undertake community-based catchment management (Lees, et al., 2012). The NZLT was contracted by the New Zealand Ministry for the Environment to develop this. The catchment management guide identified nine key tasks necessary for successful initiatives. Three of these tasks are: developing community leadership by supporting farmers willing to play a coordinating role with stakeholders, developing a common knowledge platform, and using science and technical expertise to assess potential interventions. These key tasks were identified from reviews of successful catchment management initiatives that have been implemented broadly across New Zealand (Feeney, Allen, Lees & Drury, 2010) as well as successful projects undertaken by the NZLT.

It is important to note the similarities between these key catchment management tasks and three of the key predictors that have been identified in the Kakanui, North Canterbury and Upper Buller catchment surveys. In particular, a) Access to Science, Training and Information; b) Leadership, and c) Farm Planning and Monitoring. These three predictors were all rated at or above the scale midpoint in the three surveys indicating that a foundation of knowledge, science and leadership exists upon which the catchment projects can build.

The catchment guide also identified seven key tasks for encouraging the degree of community ownership required to implement successful catchment management initiatives. These tasks address the need for: 1) Community Champions; 2) Strong Environmental Bottom Lines; 3) Independent Facilitation; 4) Technical Support; 5) Adequate Time; 6) Communication Plans; and 7) Resourcing. These tasks highlight the importance of community champions to support community-driven leadership of catchment management initiatives (i.e., support farmers willing to play a coordinating role with stakeholders in the community). They also identify the importance of quality science and information to establish environmental bottoms lines by which the community can assess biophysical improvements in catchment management following ecosystem restoration work or other management interventions. These tasks also identify the importance of technical support and knowledge so as to achieve a level playing field concerning access of information. Everybody needs to understand the current situation, the need for change and the form this change should take and why (Lees, et al., 2012).

These key tasks, community champions (community leadership), strong environmental bottom lines, and technical support are again reflected in the outcomes of the Kakanui, North Canterbury and Upper Buller catchment surveys. In particular, higher item ratings indicate that respondents believe 1) they have good access to the science they need to make good decisions about nutrient and water management, 2) that methods for monitoring nutrient levels and water quality being developed by regulatory authorities will be effective in preserving water quality, and 3) they have effective leaders in their community that can help them develop, implement and maintain farming systems that are economically and environmentally sustainable.

The factor, Trust in the Public, was rated well below the scale midpoint in all three catchments implying that farmers do not consider the public to fully understand their perspective on nutrient and water resource management nor that public perceptions of their efforts to develop nutrient and water resource plans are fair and accurate. This stems from the current contentious public debate regarding farming impacts on New Zealand's water resources. Because of the considerable amount of public criticism about farming that has been generated in recent years (for example, Fish and Game New Zealand's "Dirty Dairying" campaign), many farmers feel threatened by negative public sentiment regarding their stewardship of environmental resources (Foote et al., 2015). To counter negative public opinion, farmers in these three catchments need to develop communication strategies to promote the efforts they undertake to sustainably manage land and water resources. More positive public opinion should help bolster farmers' motivations to continue these efforts. Negative public opinion causes defensiveness and erodes their motivation. An example of a NZLT education/communication intervention to address this are the engagement opportunities between farmers and the wider catchment community that are facilitated by the project. These activities aim to improve understanding of the challenges involved with balancing the economics of farming with the need to preserve and restore water quality in local waterways. If the non-farming public are provided with education opportunities to see firsthand the efforts being made by farmers to farm sustainably, there is potential for this factor (trust in the public) to improve over time.

The challenge with all three of these catchment projects will be to build on the current ratings of all the factors involved in predicting successful community-driven water management where possible. Clearly there are strong foundations for potential success with all three projects given the current survey ratings for leadership, farming planning and monitoring, access to science, training and information, and confidence in regulatory policies for managing water quality. There is also an opportunity to use concern for poor water quality to motivate further adoption by farmers of sustainable farm management practices. Greater trust by the broader communities in each of these catchments can be built by showcasing these efforts by famers.

References

Chapter 1

Archie, M., Mann L., & Smith, W. (1993). *Environmental Social Marketing and Environmental Education.* Academy for Educational Development, Washington, D.C.

Baron, D., Siegel, R. & Wertheimer, L. (1996). *Economy and Emissions.* National Public Radio. Washington, D.C.

Creighton, M. (2005). *State of Fear.* Harper Collins.

Creighton, M. (2003) Remarks to the Commonwealth Club. September 15.

Focht, W. (1995). A proposed model of environmental communication ethics. *National Association of Professional Environmental Communicators Quarterly,* Spring issue, 8-9.

Little, A. G. (2005). The Misleaders. *Rolling Stone,* 987, 83 (November).

Thorson, R.M. (2005). The Fearful Practice of Treating Global Warming as Fiction. Hartford Courant Editorial. January 14.

Chapter 2

Archie, M., Mann L., & Smith, W. (1993). *Environmental Social Marketing and Environmental Education*. Academy for Educational Development, Washington, D.C.

Association of Public and Land-grant Universities (2011). *Land-grant Heritage*. [ONLINE] Available at: http://www.aplu.org/page.aspx?pid=1565. [Last Accessed October 23, 2012].].

Focht, W. (1995). A proposed model of environmental communication ethics. *National Association of Professional Environmental Communicators Quarterly*, Spring issue, 8-9.

Connecticut Forest & Park Association, (n.d.). Project Learning Tree CT Educator Workshops. Retrieved July 18, 2012, from http://www.ctwoodlands.org/PLT

Ct.gov. (n.d.)#1. *DEP: Connecticut Project Learning Tree*. Retrieved October 05, 2012, from http://www.ct.gov/dep/cwp/view.asp?a=2691&q=472510&dep Nav_GID=1627

Ct.gov. (n.d.)#2. *Deep: About Us*. Retrieved October 05, 2012, from http://www.ct.gov/deep/cwp/view.asp?a=4114&Q=482278

Ctwoodlands.org. (n.d.). *About Us | Connecticut Forest & Park Association*. Retrieved October 05, 2012, from http://www.ctwoodlands.org/about

Kleis, J., Lang, L., Mietus, J.R. & Tiapula, F.T.S. (1973). Toward a contextual definition of non formal education. Non-formal education discussion papers, East Lansing, MI: Michigan State University.

Mateleska, M. (2012,). Interviewed by B.W.Washington, Mystic aquarium, Connecticut

Monroe, M., Day, B., & Grieser, M. (2000). *Environmental Education & Communication for a Sustainable World Handbook for International Practioners*. Washington, DC: Academy for Education Development.

Monroe, M., Andrews, E., & Biedenweg, K. (2007). A Framework for Environmental Education Strategies. *Applied Environmental Education and Communication*, *1*, 13. Retrieved July 18, 2012, from http://envacapstone.wiki.usfca.edu/file/v

USDA (2011). *Extension*. [ONLINE] Available at: http://www.csrees.usda.gov/qlinks/extension.html.

Chapter 3

Andreasen, A. R. (1995) *Marketing Social Change*. Josset-BassSanFrancisco

Archie, M., Mann L., & Smith, W. (1993). *Environmental Social Marketing and Environmental Education*. Academy for Educational Development, Washington, D.C.

Cialdini, R.B. (2001). *Influence: Science and Practice*. Needham Heights, MA: Allyn & Bacon.

Focht, W. (1995). A proposed model of environmental communication ethics. *National Association of Professional Environmental Communicators Quarterly*, Spring issue, 8-9.

McKenzie-Mohr, D. & Smith, W. (1999). *Fostering Sustainable Behavior*. New Society Publishers, British Columbia.

Ostrom, E. (1990). *Governing the Commons - The Evolution of Institutions for Collective Action*. Cambridge University Press: New York.

Thelen, H. A. (1949). Group dynamics in instruction: principles of least group Size. *School Review*, 57, 139-48.

Tyson, C. B. (2003). *Strategic Environmental Communication: Communicating Strategies for Influencing Environmental Behaviors*. Xanedu Publishers.

Chapter 4

Ajzen, I. & Fishbein, M. (1980). *Understanding attitudes and predicting social behavior.* Prentice Hall: New Jersey.

Ajzen, I. & Madden, T. J. (1986). Prediction of goal-directed behavior: attitudes, intentions, and perceived behavioral control. *Journal of Experimental Social Psychology,* 22, 453-474.

Andreasen, A. R. & Tyson, C. B. (1994). Applying social marketing to ecological problems through consumer research. In J. A. Cote & S. M. Leong (Eds.), *Asia Pacific Advances in Consumer Research:* Vol.1. Utah:Association for Consumer Research.

Bandura, A. (1982). Self-efficacy mechanism in human agency. *American Psychologist,* 37(2), 122-147.

Bandura, A. (1980). Gauging the relationship between self-efficacy judgement and action. *Cognitive Therapy and Research,* 4(2), 263-268.

Bandura, A. (1978). The self system in reciprocal determinism. *American Psychologist,* April, 344-358.

Bandura, A. (1977). Self-efficacy: Toward a unifying theory of behavioral change. *Psychological Review,* 84(2), 191-215.

Becker, M. H. & Maiman, L.A. (1975). Sociobehavioral determinants of compliance with health and medical care recommendations. *Medical Care,* 13, 10-24.

Bettinghaus, Erwin P. and Cody, Michael J. (1994). *Persuasive Communication* (5th Edition). Fort Worth: Harcourt Brace College Publishers.

Bloomquist, W. & Ostrom, E. (1985). Institutional capacity and the resolution of a commons dilemma. *Policy Studies Review,* 5, 383-393.

Bott, S., Cantrill, J. G., & Myers, O. E. 2003. Place and the promise of conservation psychology.

Human Ecology Review, 10, 100-112.

Brewer, M. B. & Kramer, R. M. (1986). Choice behavior in social dilemmas: effects of social identity, group size, and decision framing. *Journal of Personality and Social Psychology,* 50(3), 543-549.

Bohlen, J.M. (1955). *How a farm people accept new ideas.* Iowa State College, Ames.

Cantrill, J. G., & Senecah, S. L. 2001. Using the "sense of self-in-place" construct in the context of environmental policy-making and landscape planning. *Environmental Science & Policy, 4,* 185-204.

Cialdini, R. B., Reno, R. R., & Kallgren, C. A. (1990). A focus theory of normative conduct: recycling the concept of norms to reduce littering in public places. *Journal of Personality and Social Psychology,* 58(6), 1015-1026.

Cross, K. P. (1981). *Adults as learners.* San Francisco: Jossey-Bass Classics.

Fishbein, M. & Ajzen, I. (1975). *Belief, Attitude, Intention and Behavior: An Introduction to Theory and Research.* Reading, Mass.: Addison-Wesley.

Geller, E. S. (1992). Solving environmental problems: A behavior change perspective. In S. Staub & P. Green (Eds.), *Psychology and Social Responsibility: Facing Global Challenges.* New York: New York University Press.

Hamilton, M., Hunter J., & Burgoon, M. (1990). An empirical investigation of an axiomatic model of the effect of language intensity on attitude change. *Journal of Language and Social Psychology,* 9, 235-255.

Hamilton, M. & Stewart, B. (1993). Extending an information processing model of language intensity effects. *Communication Quarterly,* 41, 231-246.

Hamilton, M. & Thompson, W. (1994). Testing an information processing model of message intensity effects. *World Communication*, 23, 1-14.

Hines, J. M., Hungerford, H. R., & Tomera, A. N. (1986/87). Analysis and synthesis of research on responsible environmental behavior: A meta-analysis. *The Journal of Environmental Education*, 18(2), 1-8.

Kramer, R. M. & Brewer, M. B. (1984). Effects of group identity on resource use in a simulated commons dilemma. *Journal of Personality and Social Psychology*, 46(5), 1044-1057.

Janz, N. K. & Becker, M. H. (1984). The health belief model: a decade later. *Health Education Quarterly*, 11(1), 1-47.

Lamble, R. D. (1984). Diffusion and adoption of innovations. In D. J. Blackburn (Ed.), *Extension Handbook*, University of Guelph, Ontario.

Lynn, M. & Oldenquist, A. (1986). Egoistic and nonegoistic motives in social dilemmas. *American Psychologist*, 41(5), 529-534.

Ostrom, E. (1990). *Governing the Commons – The Evolution of Institutions for Collective Action*. Cambridge University Press: New York.

Pryor, B. T. (1990). Predicting and explaining intentions to participate in continuing education: An application of the theory of reasoned action. *Adult Education Quarterly*, 40(3), 146-157.

Reno, R. R., Cialdini, R. B., & Kallgren, C. A. (1993). The transitional influence of social norms. *Journal of Personality and Social Psychology*, 64, 1, 104-112.

Rogan, R., O'Connor, M., Horwitz, P. (2005). Nowhere to hide: Awareness and perceptions of environmental influence on relationships with place. *Journal of Environmental Psychology*, 25: 147-158.

Rogers, E. M. (1995). *Diffuison of Innovations* (fourth edition). New York: The Free Press.

Rogers, E. M. (1983). *Diffuison of Innovations* (third edition). New York: The Free Press.

Rogers, E. M. & Shoemaker, F. (1971). *Communication of innovation. A cross-cultural approach* (second edition). New York: The Free Press.

Rosenstock, I. M. (1974). The health belief model and preventative health behavior. *Health Education Monographs, 2,* 354-386.

Sia, A. P., Hungerford, H. R., & Tomera, A. N. (1985/86). Selected predictors of environmental behavior: an analysis. *The Journal of Environmental Education,* 17(2), 31-40.

Sivek, D, J. & Hungerford, H. (1989/90). Predictors of responsible behavior in members of three Wisconsin conservation organizations. *Journal of Environmental Education,* 21(2.

Snyder, L. B. & Broderick, S. H. (1992). Communicating with Woodland Landowners. *Journal of Forestry* (March)

Tough, A. (1979). Choosing to learn. In G. M. Healy and W. L. Ziegler (eds.), *The Learning Stance: Essays in Celebration of Human Learning.* Washington, D.C.:National Institute of Education.

Turner, T. & Turner, S. 2006. Place, Sense of Place and Presence. *Presence: Tele-operators and Virtual Environments, 15: 204-217.*

Tuan, Yi-Fu. *Topophilia: A Study of Environmental Perception, Attitudes, and Values.*

Englewood Cliffs, NJ: Prentice-Hall, 1974.

Tuan, Yi-Fu. *Space & Place: The Perspective of Experience.* Minneapolis, MN: University of Minnesota Press, 1977.

Tyson, C. B. (1995). *The effects of individual versus community messages on conservation behavior.* University of Connecticut doctoral dissertation.

Vining, J. & Ebreo, A. (1990). What makes a recycler? A comparison of recyclers and nonrecyclers. *Environment and Behavior*, 22(1),55-73

Wiener, J. L. & Doescher, T. A. (1994). *Cooperation and expectations of cooperation.* Paper presented at Marketing and Public Policy Conference, Washington, D.C.

Witte, K., Stokols, D., Ituarte, P., & Schneider, M. (1993). Testing the health belief model in a field study to promote bicycle safety helmets. *Communication Research*, 20(4), 564-585.

Chapter 5

Appleton, A. (2002). How New York City used an ecosystems services strategy carried out through an urban-rural partnership to preserve the pristine quality of its drinking water and save billions of dollars. *Forest Trends.* Tokyo, Japan

Bettinghaus, Erwin P. and Cody, Michael J. (1994). *Persuasive Communication* (5th Edition). Fort Worth: Harcourt Brace College Publishers.

Bowles, Samuel (2008). Policies Designed for Self-Interested Citizens May Undermine the Moral Sentiments. *Science.* V.320. June.

Dawes, R. (1980). Social dilemmas. *Annual Review of Psychology,* 31, 69-93.

Focht, W. (1995). A proposed model of environmental communication ethics. *National Association of Professional Environmental Communicators Quarterly,* Spring issue, 8-9.

Kaufman, L. (2011, Nov. 27). Partnership Preserves Livelihoods and Fish Stock. *New York Times.* Retrieved July 28, 2012 from http://www.nytimes.com/2011/11/28/science/earth/nature-conservancy-partners-with-california-fishermen.html?pagewanted=all.

McKenzie-Mohr, D. & Smith, W. (1999). *Fostering Sustainable Behavior.* New Society Publishers, British Columbia.

Morgan, R. (2008, Sept. 8). Beyond Carbon: Scientists Worry About Nitrogen's Effects. *New York Times*. Retrieved June 18, 2012 from http://www.nytimes.com/2008/09/02/science/02nitr.html?_r=1.

New Zealand Ministry for the Environment (2007). *Environment New Zealand (ME 848)*. Retrieved on June 18, 2012 from www.mfe.govt.nz.

Ostrom, E. (1990). *Governing the commons – the evolution of institutions for collective action.* Cambridge University Press: New York.

Stillman, J. (2008, Feb. 5). What is Carbon Credit? CBSNews. Retrieved Aug. 21, 2012 from http://www.cbsnews.com/8301-505125_162-51187036/what-is-carbon-credit/

The Economist (2005a). *Rescuing Environmentalism.* April 23, 2005.

The Economist (2005b). *Environmental Economist,* Are you being served? April 23, 2005.

The Environmental News Service (2002, Aug. 27). *Conservancy, Paper Company Protect Maine Woods.* Retrieved on June 12, 2012 from http://www.ens-newswire.com/ens/aug2002/2002-08-27-07.html

The Nature Conservancy. (2011, Sept. 15). *Groundbreaking Fishing Agreement Enters Uncharted Territory – Keeps California Ports in Business.* Retrieved on June 12, 2012 from http://www.nature.org/ourinitiatives/regions/northamerica/unitedstates/california/newsroom/groundbreaking-california-fishing-agreement-enters-uncharted-territory-1.xml.

The Nature Conservancy. (2002). *Kathadin Forest Project.* Retrieved on June 12, 2012 from http://www.nature.org/ourinitiatives/regions/northamerica/unitedstates/maine/placesweprotect/katahdin-forest-project.xml

USDA Forest Service. (2006, Dec.). *Protecting Jobs and Forests – The Katahdin Forest Project in Maine.*

Wiener, J. L. & Doescher, T. A. (1991). A framework for promoting cooperation. *Journal of Marketing*, 55, 38-47.

Chapter 6

Ascroft, J. & Agunga, R. (1994). Diffusion Theory and participatory decision-making. In S.A White (Ed), *Participatory Communication*. Thousand Oaks:Sage Publications.

COCE (Conference on Communication and the Environment) listserv (1997).

Cox, R. (2012). *Environmental Communication and the Public Sphere*. Thousand Oaks: Sage Publications.

Cox, R. (2006). *Environmental Communication and the Public Sphere*. Thousand Oaks: Sage Publications.

Daniels, S.E. and G.B. Walker. 2001. *Working through environmental Conflict: The Collaboration Learning Approach*. Westport, CT: Praeger.

Depoe, S. & Delicath, J.(2004). Introduction. In S. Depoe, J. Delicath & M-F. Elsenbeer (Eds.), *Communication and Public Participation in Environmental Decision Making* (pp1-10) Albany: SUNY Press.

EPA website. *Brownfields and Land Revitalization*. [ONLINE] Available at: http://www.epa.gov/brownfields/basic_info.htm. [Last Accessed September 9 2012].

Faust, A. (2012, July 06). Interview by K.G. LaBarre [Personal Interview].

Focht, W. (1995). A proposed model of environmental communication ethics. *National Association of Professional Environmental Communicators Quarterly*, Spring issue, 8-9.

Harrison, Bruce (1992). *Environmental Communication and Public Relations Handbook, 2nd Edition*. Government Institutes, Inc., Rockville, MD.

Kelly, M. R. (2012, July 20). Interview by K.G. LaBarre [Personal Interview].

Moyer, B. (2005). A Question for Journalists: How do We Cover Penguins and Politics of Denial? *Common Dreams Newscenter.* (www.commondreams.org) October 1.

National Research Council (2008). *Public Participation in Environmental Assessment and Decision Making.* National Academies Press.

Rahim, Syed A. (1994). Participatory development communication as a dialogic process. In S.A White (Ed). *Participatory Communication.* Thousand Oaks, CA:Sage Publications

Rogers, E. M. (1983). *Diffuison of Innovations* (third edition). New York: The Free Press.

Senecah, S.L. (2004). The trinity of voice: The role of practical theory in planning and evaluating the effectiveness of environmental participatory processes. *Communication and Public Participation in Environmental Decision Making, 13-33.* Albany, NY: State University of New York Press.

Schusler, T.M., Decker, D.J. and Pfeffer, M.J. (2003). Social learning for collaborative natural resource management. *Society and Natural Resources, 15:309–326.* Taylor and Francis Group.

Shannon, Claude E. & Weaver, W. (1969). *The mathematical theory of communication.* Urbana, Illinios: The University of Illinois Press.

Walker, G.B., Daniels, S.E. and Emborg, J. 2006. *Tackling the Tangle of Environmental Conflict: Complexity, Controversy and Collaborative Learning.* Paper presented at the World Congress on Communication for Development, Rome Italy, October 2006.

Walker, G., S. Senecah, and S. Daniels. 2006. From the forest to the river: citizens' views of stakeholder engagement," *Human Ecology Review* 13(2):193-202.

Walker, G. (2004). The roadless area initiative as national policy: is public participation an oxymoron? In S. Depoe, J. Delicath & M-F. Elsenbeer (Eds.), *Communication and Public Participation in Environmental Decision Making* (pp 124) Albany: SUNY Press.

White, A. T.(1982). Why community participation? a discussion of the arguments. *Assignment Children,* pp 59-60. Geneva: UNICEF.

White, Shirley A. (1994). The concept of participation: Transforming rhetoric into reality. In S.A White (Ed), *Participatory Communication.* Thousand Oaks:Sage Publications.

Chapter 7

Adams, J. (1958). *Interviewing procedures: A Manual for Survey Interviewers.* The University of North Carolina Press.

Creighton, J. (1999). *A Strategic Communication Campaign for the Mattabesset River Watershed.* Masters degree thesis. University of New Haven, December, 1999.

Dillman, D., Smyth, J. & Christian, L. (2009). Internet, Mail, and Mixed-Mode Surveys: The Tailored Design Method, New York: Wiley.

Tyson, B. (1998). *Northeast Neighborhood Pocket Park Research Project.* Research report for Urban and Community Forestry Program, University of Connecticut Cooperative Extension System.

Chapter 8

Coffman, Julia. (2002). *Public Communication Campaign Evaluation.* Communications Consortium Media Center, Harvard Family Research Project. Cambridge, MA.

Connell, P. James, Anne C. Kubisch, Lisbeth B. Schorr, and Carol H.Weiss, *New Approaches to Evaluating Communities Initiatives: Concepts, Methods, and Contexts*, Washington, DC: The Aspen Institute, 1995.

Hornick, Robert. (2007). *Evaluating Communication Campaigns.* Robert Wood Johnson Foundation. Princeton, NJ (W.K.) Kellogg Foundation (2010). *Evaluation Handbook.* Battle Creek, MI. (https://www.wkkf. org/resource.../w-k-kellogg-foundation-evaluation-handbook)

Nielson, Joyce M. (1990). Introduction in J. Nielson (ed.), *Feminist Research Methods,* Boulder: Westview Press.

Patton, Michael Quinn, *Practical Evaluation,* Newbury Park, CA: Sage Publications, 1982.

Stacks, Don. (2011). *Primer of Public Relations Research.* The Guilford Press

Chapter 9

Broom, G. M. and Dozier, D. M. (1990). *Using Research in Public Relations.* Prentice Hall, Englewood Cliffs, NJ.

Dillman, D., Smyth, J. & Christian, L. (2009). Internet, Mail, and Mixed-Mode Surveys: The Tailored Design Method, New York: Wiley.

(W.K.) Kellogg Foundation (2010). *Evaluation Handbook.* Battle Creek, MI. (https://www.wkkf.org/resource.../w-k-kellogg-foundation-evaluation -handbook)

Tyson, B., Faust, A., Marin, P. (2002). *A Rural Application of the Sustainable Brownfields Redevelopment Process.* Proceedings of Brownfields 2002 Conference, Charlotte, NC (Nov.).

Watson, T. and Noble, P. (2005). *Evaluating Public Relations.* London, U.K.: Kogan Page Publishers.

Chapter 10

Beebe, S. A. and Masterson, J. T. (1994). *Communicating in Small Groups.* 4th Ed. HarperCollins, New York, NY

Bolling, D. M. (1994). *How to Save a River, A Handbook for Citizen Action.* Island Press, Washington, D.C.

Creighton, J. (2002). Establishing the Mattabesset River Association. Sidebar essay in B. Tyson, Chapter 4 of *Strategic Communication For Influencing Environmental Behaviors.*

Harrison, Bruce (1992). *Environmental Communication and Public Relations Handbook, 2nd Edition.* Government Institutes, Inc., Rockville, MD.

Chapter 11

Ajzen, I. & Fishbein, M. (1980). *Understanding Attitudes and Predicting Social Behavior.* Prentice Hall: New Jersey.

Andreasen, A. R. & Tyson, C. B. (1994). Applying social marketing to ecological problems through consumer research. In J. A. Cote & S. M. Leong (Eds.), *Asia Pacific Advances in Consumer Research: Vol.1.* Utah:Association for Consumer Research.

Bandura, A. (1982). Self-efficacy mechanism in human agency. *American Psychologist, 37*(2), 122-147.

Focht, W. (1995). A proposed model of environmental communication ethics. *National Association of Professional Environmental Communicators Quarterly,* Spring issue, 8-9.

Ostrom, E. (1990). *Governing the Commons – The Evolution of Institutions for Collective Action.* Cambridge University Press: New York.

Rogers, E. M. (1995). *Diffusion of Innovation.* New York: Free press.

Tyson, B., Worthley, T. & Danley, K. (2004). Layering natural resource and human resource data for planning watershed conservation campaigns. *Society and Natural Resources.* Vol.17 No.2 (February).

Tyson, C. B. (1999). 1) The Eight Mile River Watershed Resource Planning and Outreach Project – A Model for the Connecticut River

Ecosystem, 2) The Eight Mile River Watershed Resource Planning and Outreach Project Process Evaluation Report, and 3) The Eight Mile River Watershed Resource Planning and Outreach Project Outcome Evaluation Report. Research reports for the University of Connecticut Cooperative Extension System Forestry Program.

Tyson, C.B., Broderick, S. H., & Snyder, L. B. (1998). A Social marketing approach to landowner education in Connecticut. *Journal of Forestry*; Vol. 96, No.2, (February).

Tyson, C. B., Hamilton, M. A., & Snyder, L. B. (1996). *The effects of individual and community messages on conservation behavior.* Paper presented at the annual meeting of the International Communication Association, Chicago, IL.

Witte, K., Stokols, D., Ituarte, P., & Schneider, M. (1993). Testing the health belief model in a field study to promote bicycle safety helmets. *Communication Research*, 20(4), 564-85.

Chapter 12

Case Study 1: References listed below stem from: Tyson, B., Edgar, N, & Robertson, G. (2012). Facilitating Collaborative Efforts to Redesign Community Managed Water Systems. *Applied Environmental Education and Communication Journal*, Vol 10, No. 4.

Edgar, N. B. (2009) Icon Lakes in New Zealand: Managing the tension between land development and water resource protection. *Society and Natural Resources*, 22, 1-11.

Land and Water Forum (2010). *Report of the Land and Water Forum: A Fresh Start for Fresh Water.* Available at: www.landandwater.org.nz

Ministry for the Environment. (2005). *Reflections: A summary of your views on the sustainable water programme of action.* Wellington, New Zealand. Ministry for the Environment.

Newman. N. & Robertson, G. (2010). *Community-Led Water Resource Management – a report on a national workshop*. Hamilton, NZ: New Zealand Landcare Trust.

Robertson, G. & Robertson, J. (2008). *Upper Taieri Water Management – a report prepared for the Upper Taieri Water Resource Management Group*. Hamilton, NZ: New Zealand Landcare Trust.

Tyson, B. (2009). Research Strategies. Chapter 4 in *Social Marketing Environmental Issues*. B.Tyson (author). Indiana: I-Universe Publishers.

Case Study 2: References listed below stem from: Robertson, J., Edgar, N, & Tyson, B., (2013). Engaging Dairy Farmers to Improve Water Quality in the Aorere Catchment of New Zealand. *Applied Environmental Education and Communication Journal*. Vol 12, No. 4.

Adams, W.M, & Hulme, D. (2001). If community conservation is the answer in Africa, what is the question?, *Oryx*, vol. 35, no. 3, pp. 193-200.

Brechin, S.R., Wilshusen, P.R., Fortwangler, CL & West, PC (2002). Beyond the square wheel: Toward a more comprehensive understanding of biodiversity conservation as social and political process, *Society & Natural Resources*, vol. 15, no. 1, p. 41.

Carpenter, J.F. (1998). Internally motivated Development Projects: A Potential Tool for Biodiversity Conservation Outside of Protected Areas, *Ambio*, vol. 27, no. 3, pp. 211-6. da Silva, PP (2004). From common property to co-management: lessons from Brazil's first maritime extractive reserve. *Marine Policy*, vol. 28, no. 5.

DairyNZ (2010). *NZ Dairy Statistics 2009-2010*, viewed 22 Dec 2010, <www.dairynz.co.nz/dairystatistics>.

Dominion Post (2010). *A nation swimming in a dilemma*, viewed 23 Nov 2010, <http://www.stuff.co.nz/dominion-post/opinion/editorials/4370417/Editorial-A-nation-swimming-in-a-dilemma>.

Dresser, M. (2008). *Social Marketing and Behaviour Change: Working with Landowners Towards Sustainable Land Management*, New Zealand Landcare Trust, Rotorua.

Edgar, N., Nimo. K. & Ross, D/ (2005). *Science and Communities Working Together for Sustainable Land Management.*

Environment Waikato (2008). *The condition of rural water and soil in the Waikato Region; risks and opportunities*, viewed 3 July 2011, <http://www.waikatoregion.govt.nz/Environmental-information/Land-and-soil/The-condition-of-rural-water-and-soil-in-the-Waikato-region---risks-and-opportunities/>.

Fonterra, Ministry for the Environment, Ministry of Agriculture and Forestry & Local Government NZ (2008). *The Dairying Clean Streams Accord: SNAPSHOT OF PROGRESS – 2006/2007.*

Haller, T., Gavin, M., Meroka, P., Alca, J & Alvarez, A. (2008). Who Gains From Community Conservation? Intended and Unintended Costs and Benefits of Participative Approaches in Peru and Tanzania. *The Journal of Environment & Development*, vol. 17, no. 2, pp. 118-44.

Hamill, K.D. & McBride, G.B. (2003), River water quality trends and increased dairying in Southland, New Zealand. *New Zealand Journal of Marine and Freshwater Research*, vol. 37, pp. 323–32.

Horwich, R.H. & Lyon, J. (2007), Community conservation: practitioners' answer to critics. *Oryx*, vol. 41, no. 3, pp. 376-85.

International Dairy Federation World Dairy Summit (2010). *NZ Dairy Statistics*, viewed 4 July 2011, <http://www.wds2010.com/dairystats.html.>.

Kissun, S. (2008). *Dirty Dairying must stop*, viewed 23 Nov 2010, <http://www.ruralnews.co.nz/Default.asp?task=article&subtask=show&item=16121&pageno=1>.

Kollmuss, A. & Agyeman, J. (2002). Mind the Gap: why do people act environmentally and what are the barriers to pro-environmental behavior?. *Environmental Education Research*, vol. 8, pp. 239-60.

LIC (2008). *2006/2007 Dairy industry statistics*, viewed June 2011, <http://www.lic.co.nz/lic 20062007 Dairy Stats.cfm/>.

McKenzie-Mohr, D. & Smith, W. (1999). *Fostering Sustainable Behaviour: An Introduction to Community-Based Social Marketing*, New Society Publishers

Monaghan, R.M. deKlein, C.A.M. & Muirhead, R.W. (2008). Prioritisation of farm scale remediation efforts for reducing losses of nutrients and fecal indicator organisms to waterways: A case study of New Zealand dairy farming. *Journal of Environmental Management*, vol. 87, no. 4, pp. 609-22.

Ostrom, E. (1990). *Governing the Commons: The evolution of institutions for Collective Action.*, Cambridge University Press, Cambridge.

Peters, M., Robertson, G. & Fitzgerald, G. (2007), *Aorere Catchment: Farmers Survey*, Hamilton.

Robertson, B. & Stephens, L. (2007). *Aorere Sustainable Farming Project: Preliminary Assessment of Coastal Issues.*

Spiteri, A. & Nepal, S.K. (2006). Incentive-based conservation programs in developing countries: A review of some key issues and suggestions for improvements. *Environmental Management*, vol. 37, pp. 1-14.

Statistics New Zealand (2009). *New Zealand in Profile:2011*, viewed July 2011, <http://www.stats.govt.nz/browse for stats.snapshots-of-nz/nz-in-profile-2011/agricultural-production.aspx>.

Tai, H.S. (2007). Development through conservation: An institutional analysis of indigenous community-based conservation in Taiwan. *World Development*, vol. 35, no. 7, pp. 186-1203.

Thakadu, O.T. (2005). Success factors in community based natural resources management in northern Botswana: Lessons from practice. *Natural Resources Forum*, vol. 29, no. 3, pp. 199-212.

The Treasury (2010). *New Zealand Economic and Financial Overview 2010*, Wellington.

Vant, W.N. (2001). New challenges for the management of plant nutrients and pathogens in the Waikato River, New Zealand. *Water Science and Technology*, vol. 43, no. 5, pp. 137–44.

Verburg, P., Hamill, K., Unwin, M. & Abell, J. (2010). *Lake water quality in New Zealand 2010: Status and trends.*, Ministry for the Environment, Hamilton.

Wilshusen, P.R., Brechin, S.R., Fortwangler, C.L. & West, P.C. (2002). Reinventing a square wheel: Critique of a resurgent "Protection Paradigm" in international biodiversity conservation. *Society & Natural Resources*, vol. 15, no. 1, pp. 17-40.

Case Study 3: References listed below stem from: Tyson, B,. Unson, C. & Edgar, N. (2017). Predictors of Success for Community-Driven Water Quality Management – Lessons from Three Catchments in New Zealand. *Applied Environmental Education and Communication Journal.* Vol.16. No. 3.

Agrawal, A. (2002). Common resources and institutional sustainability. Chapter 2 in *The Drama of the Commons*, Committee on the Human Dimensions of Global Change, National Research Council. Washington DC: National Academy Press: Washington DC.

Anastasiadis, S., Kerr, S., Nauleau, M., Cox, T. & Rutherford, K. (2014) Does complex hydrology require complex water quality policy? *Australian Journal of Agriculture and Resource Economics.* 1. 130-145.

Curtis, A., Ross, H., Marshall, G., Baldwin, C., Cavaye, J., Freeman, C., Carr, A. & Syme, G. (2014). The great experiment with devolved NRM governance: Lessons from community engagement in Australia and New Zealand since the 19080s. *Australian Journal of Environmental Management*. 21. 175-199.

Drummond, L. (2006). Managing the environmental effects of agriculture under the Resource Management Act: Non-Point source discharges. *New Zealand Journal of Environmental Law*. 10. 255-293.

Duncan, R. (2013). Converting community knowledge into catchment nutrient limits: A constructivist analysis of a New Zealand collaborative approach to water management. *Nature & Culture*. 8. 205-225.

Edgar, N. (2007). Success factors for community-based river management in New Zealand. *Journal of the Australian Water Association*. 34. 84-92.

Edgar, N. (2009). Icon lakes in New Zealand: Managing the tension between land development and water resource protection. *Society and Natural Resources*. 22. 1-11.

Feeney, C., Allen, W., Lees, A. & Drury, M. (2010). Integrated Catchment Management: A Review of Literature and Practices. A Report Prepared for the Ministry for the Environment by Clare Feeney Environmental Communication Ltd. Wellington, New Zealand. Ministry for the Environment.

Foote, K., Joy, M. & Death, R. (2015). New Zealand dairy farming: Milking our environment for all its worth. *Environmental Management*. 56. 709-720.

International River Foundation. (2015). Aorere River Wins 2015 New Zealand Riverprize. retrievedatwww.riverfoundation.org.au/riverprize_new_zealand.php.

Land and Water Forum. (2010). Report of the Land and Water Forum: A Fresh Start for Freshwater. Retrievedatwww.landandwater.org.nz.

Lees, A., Robertson, G., Garvan, N., Barnett, J. & Edgar, N. (2012). Community-owned rural catchment management: A guide for partners. Hamilton, NZ: New Zealand Landcare Trust.

Newman. N. & Robertson, G. (2010). *Community-Led Water Resource Management – Report on a National Workshop*. Hamilton, NZ: New Zealand Landcare Trust.

Tyson, B. (2014a). *Report of the Kakanui Community Catchment Project Resident and Farmer Surveys*. Formative research for Kakanui Community Catchment Project for New Zealand Landcare Trust.

Tyson, B. (2014b). *Upper Buller Enhancement Group Farmer Survey Report*. Formative research for Upper Buller Enhancement Group Project for New Zealand Landcare Trust.

Tyson, B. (2014c). *North Canterbury Farmers Survey Report*. Formative research for North Canterbury Sustainable Farming Systems Project for New Zealand Landcare Trust.

Tyson, B., Edgar, N, & Robertson, G. (2012). Enablers and challenges to community-led water resource management in the Upper Taieri catchment of Otago, New Zealand. Chapter 11 in In *Advances in Environmental Research*, Volume 23. Nova Science Publishers, Inc.

Tyson, B., Edgar, N. & Robertson, G. (2011). Facilitating collaborative efforts to redesign community managed water systems. *Applied Environmental Education and Communication*. 10. 211-218.

Tyson, B. (2009). Theory Driven Environmental Communication. Chapter 3 in *Social Marketing Environmental Issues*. B.Tyson (author). Indiana: I-Universe Publishers

INDEX

A

Accountability 99, 100

Adopter groups 18, 33

Adoption 18, 19, 33, 34, 35, 36, 37, 46, 137, 138, 142, 181, 186, 243, 247, 252

Agriculture 10, 11, 49, 57, 182, 209, 210, 211, 221, 223, 234, 243, 263, 266

Anticipated consequences 25, 26, 30, 177, 179

Archival research methods 68, 109

B

Behavioral-based persuasion 19, 28, 137, 139, 152, 153, 170, 173, 250

Behavior change v, xiv, xv, 1, 4, 11, 15, 17, 22, 24, 25, 34, 43, 102, 116, 132, 136, 148, 153, 170, 185, 238, 251

Behavior intentions 25, 27, 29, 30, 31, 34

Best Management Practices 45, 221, 223, 227, 234, 237, 243

Brownfields Redevelopment Process 59, 110, 260

C

Campaign planning 16, 23, 31, 32, 65, 66, 68, 73, 79, 106, 113

Cap and Trade 48, 49, 50, 51

Case Study xv, 7, 11, 29, 58, 59, 68, 109, 132, 208, 209, 210, 221, 234, 235, 261, 262, 264, 265

Cognitive Dissonance Theory 38

Collaborative Learning 61, 63, 64, 258

Commitment 5, 6, 18, 19, 22, 51, 64, 75, 120, 121, 155, 156, 163, 172, 188

Communication channels 11, 16, 20, 30, 32, 35, 65, 71, 72, 106, 121, 133, 134, 136, 138, 140, 144, 146, 155, 156, 163, 170, 171, 217

Community cohesiveness 25, 26, 28

Community efficacy 25, 26, 28

Community interaction 25, 28, 30, 137, 141, 157

Consensus 2, 4, 5, 15, 27, 41, 51, 52, 54, 56, 57, 61, 62, 64, 117, 118, 127, 133, 200, 211

Consistency 18